Pelican Books
To Him Who Hath

D1477874

Frank Field taught in the London Colleges of Further
Education in Southwark and Hammersmith before joining
the Child Poverty Action Group in 1969. In 1966 he
contested the Buckinghamshire South constituency seat for
the Labour Party and was a councillor in Hounslow for four
years. He edited *Twentieth Century State Education*, *Black
Britons*, *Low Pay*, *Education and the Urban Crisis* and
Are Low Wages Inevitable? and is the author of
Unequal Britain. Since 1974 he has also been Director of the
Low Pay Unit.

Molly Meacher studied Economics at York University,
where she graduated with an Honours Degree. During the
last five years she has organized a national campaign for
the Child Poverty Action Group on the tax credit issue,
and prepared the group's evidence for the select committee.
She has also written *Rate Rebates*, a study of the
effectiveness of the means tests. Molly Meacher now works
for the Mental Health Foundation and is married to
Michael Meacher. They have four children.

Chris Pond studied Economics at the University of Sussex
and worked in the Department of Economics at Birkbeck
College, London, before taking up his present post as
Research Officer at the Low Pay Unit. He has written a
number of articles for various newspapers and journals on
the problem of poverty and low wages and on the effects of
inflation and taxation. He has also contributed to *Inflation
and Low Incomes*, *Trade Unions and Taxation* and *Are Low
Wages Inevitable?*

Frank Field,
Molly Meacher and
Chris Pond

To Him Who Hath
A Study of Poverty and Taxation

Penguin Books

Penguin Books Ltd, Harmondsworth,
Middlesex, England
Penguin Books, 625 Madison Avenue,
New York, New York 10022, U.S.A.
Penguin Books Australia Ltd, Ringwood,
Victoria, Australia
Penguin Books Canada Ltd, 2801 John Street,
Markham, Ontario, Canada L3R 1B4
Penguin Books (N.Z.) Ltd, 182–190 Wairau Road,
Auckland 10, New Zealand

First published 1977

Made and printed in Great Britain by
Richard Clay (The Chaucer Press) Ltd, Bungay, Suffolk
Set in Monotype Times

Contents

Preface

There is never a more dangerous person than one who believes himself to be unbiased. When we came together to write this book on the changing burden of taxation we shared a bundle of prejudices no doubt equal to any of our readers'. We believed that far from taxation crippling richer sections of the community, increasingly the tax burden was falling on its poorer members. We also believed that, irrespective of the level of income, there had been a shift in taxation from single people and childless couples onto those with children. In gathering together the material for this book our views have been challenged. But far from overturning our beliefs we found that the information gathered showed we had underestimated the changing burden of taxation during the last thirty years. In order that readers will be able to challenge our argument point by point as it develops we have carefully footnoted our sources. At other times we have had to do the original digging ourselves as there were no studies relevant to our analysis.

Our discussion begins with an outline of the principles which, it is widely believed, underlie our system of income tax. In the following two chapters we look at the extent to which the belief that income tax should be progressive and that the poor should be exempt has been undermined during the last thirty years. In Chapter 4 we examine the main measures which constitute to-day's welfare state and, more importantly, who pays for these benefits. The next two chapters describe first the structure of in-direct taxation and then its effect on the distribution of income. As we then begin to bring together all this evidence on the overall effect of the tax system, we look (in Chapter 8) at the extent of both tax and social-security abuse. Chapter 9 takes an overall view of the effect that taxation and welfare benefits have on the distribution of income. Our intention is that the material in these first nine chapters should bring about a much more rational debate on the nature of our tax system and the possibilities for reform. And, so that this debate can be seen in an international context, Chapter 10 compares our levels of taxation and family benefits with those of our European partners. This prepares the ground for our final chapter, in which we outline a major reform of Britain's system of direct taxation.

In working on this book we have been helped by a number of people. Some of our ideas were first discussed with Lesley Day, Steve Hannah and Michael Meacher. Alan Bean, Chris Trinder and Steve Winyard commented on parts of the draft. We should like to thank the following MPs: Richard Wainwright, Lynda Chalker, Bruce George, Neil Kinnock, Ralph Howell, Michael Meacher and Ann Taylor, although some of these Members will not necessarily subscribe to the interpretation we have placed on the material they have obtained from Parliamentary Questions. Likewise a great deal of help was given by the information officers at all the EEC's London embassies in preparing the international chapter. We are also grateful to Clare Dennehy, Fiona Eakins, Amy Hall and Jill Sullivan, who prepared the manuscript for publication.

October 1976

Frank Field
Molly Meacher
Chris Pond

1 Spreading the Tax Net

In this chapter we look at the introduction and development of income tax, explaining both the growth and present structure of our tax system as well as the changing ideas which politicians and the public have brought to bear on how best to achieve a fair system of taxation. This will involve us in a discussion on how the meaning of 'fair' as applied to the tax system has changed over time. In doing so we will look at the move to levy a higher rate of tax on unearned income (called differentiation in the early stages of the debate) as well as the introduction of a progressive tax base whereby a supertax was levied on higher incomes (billed as the issue of graduation throughout the debate).

The Beginning of Income Tax

In December 1798 Pitt brought before the House of Commons a bill introducing income tax in order to help pay for the war against the French, and a rate of 2 shillings in the £ was levied on all income in excess of £200 per annum. This measure became effective on 1 January 1799. Between £60 and £200 there was a graduated rate starting at 2d in the £, and the income of those earning below £60 a year was exempt from the new tax. From the outset a number of concessions were allowed against the tax. For example, Pitt accepted that it was important to take family responsibilities into account in determining tax liability. Deductions were also permitted for interest on debts, amounts payable to certain relatives, annuities and life assurance. Repairs could also be set against the value of property in arriving at assessable income tax.

From the very first, one cardinal principle of English taxation has been that the poor should be exempt from its effects. As we will see from Chapter 5, early excise duties exempted 'cottagers and paupers'. Likewise with income tax. Those with incomes of less than £60 were exempt. Sometimes the reasons for excluding the poor had a strong utilitarian flavour. For example, Gladstone went on record as saying: 'There was a certain point on the progress down the scale of direct taxation beyond which it is not advisable to pass. The sums to be levied, for instance, might be so small that they would not pay the cost of collection, or if they were collected, the vexation attending it would be such that it would not be expedient to attempt it.'[1] (Now, of course, much of the expense is passed onto the employer by Pay As You Earn (PAYE) procedures.) At about the same time Charles Babbage noted: 'It is also hopeless to attempt to collect it [income tax] from those whose entire income just enables them to subsist.' These same views were dressed up in more humanitarian clothes a hundred years later by the Royal Commission on the Taxation of Profits and Income. The Commission's view was that: 'There should be no income tax levied upon any income which is insufficient to provide its owner with what he requires for subsistence.' By subsistence the Commission meant 'an income large enough to equip and sustain a healthy and efficient citizen'.

Pitt secured the power to levy income tax for only a limited period. In 1803 Addington, who had succeeded Pitt after the latter resigned over the Catholic Emancipation issue, not only sought a continuation of the power to tax income, but for the first time divided the tax into five schedules, the main structure of which still exists. These were Schedule A, which was a tax on land and buildings, Schedule B, on farming profits, Schedule C, on recipients of public annuities, Schedule D, which was divided into six groups and brought into taxation a range of profit and interest, and finally Schedule E, which levied a charge on income from offices and employment of profit and annuities and pensions. Addington's budget was also important for a second innovation. It allowed for the deduction of tax at source for income arising from interest, dividends or rent, and for income arising from employment by the Crown. As we will see it was not until the Second World War that this embryo PAYE system was spread to the vast bulk of taxpayers.

The imposition of income tax was made necessary to finance the French wars. The victory at Waterloo made the levying of the tax unnecessary, and in 1818 it was abolished, twenty-two years elapsing before it was reintroduced by Peel. Again it was not intended that the tax should be permanent. Peel put forward two reasons for its reintroduction. It was necessary as a means of 'remedying this growing evil' of the government's deficit. It was also required in order to meet the loss of revenue resulting from his free-trade plan, under which the duty on the overwhelming majority of raw materials was not to exceed 5 per cent, that on partially manufactured articles 12 per cent and that on completed manufactured articles 20 per cent.

In 1848 Lord John Russell proposed to continue income tax for a further five years, and when this period expired in 1853 Gladstone sought the permission of the Commons to levy income tax for a further seven years. The rate of 7d in the £ for the first two years was to be reduced to 3d in the £ for the final three years, the extinction of the tax coming in 1860, but Disraeli commented prophetically at the time that income tax was established 'most probably forever'. During the seven years from 1853 to 1860 government expenditure rose from £56 million to £70 million and, as there was no other acceptable way of raising the revenue arising from income tax, the 1860 budget sought powers to continue levying the tax. The rate was set at 7d in the £ on incomes between £100 and £120 a year and 10d for incomes above £120. Three years later the budget abolished the reduced rate, so setting the stage for one of the main arguments concerning income-tax structure. Should the tax be graduated or not?

Graduation

From the very first, powerful voices were raised against levying higher rates of tax against the richer members of the community. In the early years of the nineteenth century Lord Henry Petty declared: 'Of all the dangerous doctrines that could possibly be held out in a legislative assembly, there was not one that could possibly be more mischievous in its tendency than that of equalizing all ranks of society by reducing the higher orders to a level with those of a different class, and depriving them of every comfort which they had a right to expect from their exalted situations.'[2] On another occasion he was moved to say that higher taxes on the rich 'would be a complete subversion of all the principles of justice by which the property of all men should be equally protected by the law'. In the early 1850s even Gladstone recalled that 'the most dangerous of propositions that could be made in a country like this would be an attempt, upon abstract principles, to devise a graduated tax on incomes, arriving at an adjustment of different rates of assessment according to the means of the taxpayer'. At a later date he went on to remark that the principle of a graduated income tax 'tended to communism'.

But the strict Gladstone orthodoxy was not without challenge. The idea of a graduated tax had always been part of the discussion of radicals and chartists. However, as Sabine notes in one of the standard works on this subject, mention of a graduated tax in Parliamentary proceedings was rare until the last twenty-five years of the nineteenth century. A curtain-raiser came in 1877 when Morgan Lloyd and Chadwick made special pleas for a form of graduated income tax. But the big push towards opening up the whole subject came in Joseph Chamberlain's Radical programme. In this he wrote: 'Taxation ought to involve equality of sacrifice and I do not see how this result is to be obtained except by some form of graduated taxation – that is, taxation which is proportionate to the superfluities of the taxpayer. When I am told that this is a new-fangled and a revolutionary doctrine, I wonder if my critics have read elementary books on the subject, because if they had, they must have seen that a graduated tax is not a novelty in this country.' Chamberlain could have quoted in support Adam Smith, one of the high priests of *laissez faire*. Writing in 1776 Smith suggested: 'It is not unreasonable that the rich should contribute to public expense not only in proportion of their revenue, but in something more than that proportion.'[3]

Chamberlain's view was reinforced by Sidney Buxton, whom Sabine classifies as the best fiscal historian of his day. But the most important advocate of a graduated income tax was Sir William Harcourt, who was twice Chancellor of the Exchequer. Speaking in the House in 1890 on the idea that the rate of tax should be smaller for those with low incomes he said: 'I believe it a sound principle of finance.'

The decisive move towards the establishment of progressive tax came with the setting-up of a Select Committee on Income Tax in 1906 chaired by Sir Charles Dilke. The Committee reported that it was possible to have a system of graduated income tax by introducing some form of supertax – an additional tax on high incomes. The Select Committee also commented favourably on the question of differentiating between earned and unearned income. This was the other topic which constantly recurred in discussions on income tax during the nineteenth century.

Almost from the very start of the debate some sections of the community were critical that no difference was made in the amount of tax levied on earned and unearned income. Hobhouse spoke of the 'glaring inequality' of taxing 'a man who had £1,000 a year arising from capital and the man who gained the same sum by a profession or by business'. During the 1848 budget debate Bright tried to secure some measure of differentiation. Using what might now be regarded as rather quaint language he argued: 'if the Income Tax be continued, it is expedient to mend the Act and not to impose the same charge on incomes coming from professional and precarious sources or those derived from realized property.'

The questions of differentiation and of graduation, which remained as grumbling appendices during much of the latter part of the nineteenth century, burst soon after the election of a Liberal government in 1906. When in May 1906 Sir Charles Dilke was elected chairman of the House of Commons Select Committee on Income Tax, its terms of reference were 'to inquire into and report upon the practicability of graduating the Income Tax and of differentiating . . . between permanent and precarious incomes'. Only nineteen weeks elapsed after the Committee reported before action occurred. In his 1907 budget Asquith differentiated between earned and unearned income. Earned income not exceeding £2,000 was to be charged income tax at 9d in the £. The rate for unearned income was 1 shilling in the £. In 1909 Lloyd George brought in a supertax of 6d in the £ on all incomes over £5,000, 'upon the amount by which incomes exceed £3,000'. This budget also brought about two other major changes. The rate of 9d in the £ on earned income up to £2,000 remained, but a form of graduated income tax was also introduced for those below the surtax level. A rate of 1 shilling in the £ was levied on income between £2,000 and £3,000 a year and an additional 2d in the £ on incomes above £3,000. The second major innovation of the budget was the reintroduction of a child tax allowance. Taxpayers were allowed to claim £10 against tax for every child under sixteen years. In order that this proposal might benefit those of modest means the allowance was limited to taxpayers whose income did not exceed £500 a year.

Just before the outbreak of the First World War total government expenditure was £184 million a year. By 1916 it had risen ten-fold – to £1,825 million, necessitating a massive increase in the rates of income tax.[4] In order to spread this load fairly, and weight the increase towards those with least responsibilities, the government began developing what today we call the system of personal allowances. In his 1917 budget Bonar Law allowed taxpayers with incomes of up to £700 to claim a child allowance for each child which, since 1915, had stood at £25 per child. In his 1918 budget an allowance of £25 was allowed for a taxpayer's wife – the beginnings of the married man's allowance. The same sum was allowed for widowers with related housekeepers and for those taxpayers with dependent relatives. Also in the 1918 budget the tax allowance for children was extended to those on incomes from £800 to £1,000 and with three or more children.

The 1920 budget is of crucial importance to the theme of this book. In his second budget statement Austin Chamberlain brought about a major change in the burden of taxation. Implementing the substantial reforms proposed by the Royal Commission on Income Tax (1920), the Chancellor raised all personal allowances and awarded them with no limitation as to the income of the taxpayer. In other words the tax system changed from one which had a tax exemption limit – one which ensures that people below a certain level of income are not required to pay tax – to a fully fledged system of personal allowances which, while guaranteeing a tax floor, thereby benefiting the poor, gave the same concessions to all taxpayers, irrespective of their income. The advantages of returning to a tax exemption limit are discussed fully in the concluding chapter. The same budget also saw the introduction of a relief on earned income of one tenth, with a maximum of £200. In the 1925 budget earned income relief was increased to one sixth, with an equivalent relief given to pensioners with investment incomes not exceeding £500 a year.

PAYE

One of the most important changes in the administration of income tax since it was introduced by Pitt occurred during the Second World War with the introduction of the Pay As You Earn system – PAYE. We have already seen that almost from the word go certain emoluments from the Crown were taxed at source. This scheme, which the civil service had always operated for deducting tax from salaries, was extended to those in the employment of the Royal Household in 1854. Attempts a decade later to persuade the Lancashire and Yorkshire Railway Company to deduct tax at source failed in the courts. The High Court determined that the Board of Inland Revenue was not justified in requiring a company to deduct tax 'from such of their servants as are engaged at weekly wages'. A further attempt to introduce a form of PAYE was made during the First World War. The net of taxation had so spread that large numbers of wage-earners were now regularly paying income tax. In 1915 Arthur Henderson, Labour's grand old 'uncle', argued for collection of income tax through employers. However this scheme did not get off the ground, and quarterly tax returns were to remain the means of collecting income tax from the vast majority of wage-earners and salary-earners until the breakthrough to a fully fledged PAYE during the Second World War.

Discussion did not return in earnest to this issue until 1940, when the budget gave the go-ahead for a prototype PAYE scheme. This allowed the Board of Inland Revenue to determine assessments and collect income tax chargeable under Schedule E from employers. The difficulty had always been that for working people there was (and indeed is) no certainty that one week's

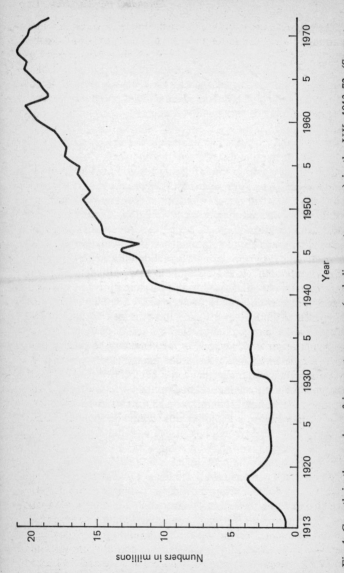

Fig. 1. Growth in the number of income-tax payers (excluding surtax payers) in the UK, 1913–72. (Source: Report of Her Majesty's Commissioners for the Inland Revenue)

earnings would be the same as the next. Possibilities of overtime, sickness, holidays, bonuses and so on all affect the weekly remuneration of the majority of the working population, and it was not until 1943 that the problems associated with building a cumulative tax system were overcome. In his budget speech in April 1943, the Chancellor indicated that he was concerned about a point which had not previously received public attention. When the war ended and hours of work declined, millions of employees would have the greatest difficulty under the existing deduction scheme paying out of reduced wages the tax relating to a previous period of high earnings. Figure 1 shows that a massive increase (over 300 per cent) in the numbers paying income tax occurred during the war years, from 3·8 million in 1938–9 to 13·5 million six years later. He went on to say that he was therefore giving further consideration to a tax scheme based on current earnings. The scheme was in fact announced in a White Paper in September 1943[5] and PAYE began to operate in April 1944.

The essence of the system is that at the first week of the year the employee gets $\frac{1}{52}$ of his personal allowances for the year set against his first week's pay. At the end of the second week he will have benefited from $\frac{2}{52}$ of his allowances against the total of his first two weeks' pay, and so on until the end of the year. In this way the total tax deducted up to any given date is kept in line with the total pay to date. As wages rise or fall so too does a worker's tax burden. Although it was originally envisaged that only weekly wage-earners would be brought within the scope of the scheme, in fact everyone who was assessable under Schedule E became taxable on a PAYE basis, either weekly or monthly.

Conclusion

In 1816 160,223 persons paid income tax. By 1945 the total had grown to 13,500,000. During this time governments began to rely more and more on the revenue from income tax and, as we have seen, as more and more people were required to pay it, the idea that the tax should be progressive gained common acceptance. The arguments wielded by Gladstone and others capitulated to those of Dilke and the reforming budgets of Asquith and Lloyd

George. The need to levy a higher tax on unearned income was also conceded. Likewise there was concern not only that the poor should be exempt from tax but that a taxpayer's responsibilities should be taken into account irrespective of his level of income, and it became accepted that the tax burden of a man with a family should be less than that of a man with the same income but without such commitments. We now turn our discussion to examine the extent to which these principles have been undermined in tax developments since the Second World War.

References

1. These quotations and much of the material for this chapter are based on B. E. V. SABINE, *A History of Income Tax*, Allen & Unwin, 1966.
2. LAURENCE H. SELTZER, *The Personal Exemptions in the Income Tax*, National Bureau of Economic Research, Washington, 1968.
3. *The Wealth of Nations*, Book V, Chapter 2, Part 2.
4. Board of Inland Revenue Reports.
5. *A New System of Taxation on Weekly Wage Earners*, Cmnd 6469, HMSO, 1943.

2 The Shifting Burden of Direct Taxation

In the previous chapter we saw that the number of taxpayers began to rise slowly during the thirties. But it was when the Pay As You Earn system was introduced in 1944 that the foundations were laid for a massive increase in the scope of wage taxation. In its turn, this extension of the tax system brought with it a shift in the incidence of the direct tax burden. In this chapter we consider how the British system of income tax has changed since the war, and the way in which the increased burden of direct taxation has been shared between different groups in the community.

Direct taxes include all those which are assumed (at least for administrative purposes) to be paid by the person or company on which they are levied. This category therefore includes income tax and surtax, employee national-insurance contributions, taxes on capital and those on companies. In this chapter we shall deal only with the first and last of these taxes. In terms of revenue, capital taxation remains insignificant and has a greater bearing on the distribution of wealth than on the spread of incomes with which we are mainly concerned in this book. National-insurance contributions and their growing importance as a form of direct taxation are considered in our fourth chapter. Here we will concentrate on the taxation of personal incomes and on that of companies.

Company Taxation

The relative importance of company taxation has declined considerably in recent years. An OECD study of fiscal policy in seven countries noted that, in Britain, revenue as a percentage of GNP remained almost static (at about 30 per cent) throughout the period 1955 to 1965. This however disguised the changes that were taking place in the contribution of different groups to the total. Direct taxes on households (including social-security contributions) increased from just over 10 per cent of GNP to 15 per cent. At the same time, the authors noted 'a large decline of corporate taxes from 5·1 per cent to 1·9 per cent of GNP, corporate tax revenues declining absolutely'. The proportion of total tax receipts raised from companies fell from 21 per cent to 11 per cent, a decline which was balanced by an increase in the proportion contributed by individuals from 30 per cent to 40 per cent.[1]

The trend away from the taxation of company incomes and towards those of wage-earners and salary-earners has continued over the past ten years. Since 1966, total revenue from direct taxes has increased from £5 billion to over £20 billion. But while the taxes paid by companies accounted for almost one quarter of total direct tax revenue in 1966 (the year in which corporation tax was introduced), the contribution of companies had fallen to one eighth by 1976. Income-tax payers were called upon to make up the difference: their contribution to total tax revenue had increased from 65 per cent of the total in 1966 to over 80 per cent ten years later.

This steady decline in the contribution of the company sector to total revenue was partly the result of falling company incomes. But most of the change was due to government policies designed in part to offset this situation of deteriorating profits. Between 1948 and 1958, and again between 1965 and 1973, a dual system of profits tax operated whereby profits distributed to shareholders as dividends attracted a higher rate of tax than those retained by the company for productive reinvestment. The 1965 corporation tax, for instance, was payable on the profits earned by a company, while shareholders had income tax deducted from their dividends. The response to this 'discrimination' was that companies tended to retain an increasing proportion of their profits over the years, resulting in a subsequent drop in tax revenue.[2] A further reduction in the liability of companies came about with the reduction in the income tax charged on profits after the abolition of the differential system in 1958; by the increasing generosity of initial and investment allowances in the early sixties; and by the subsequent introduction of investment grants and depreciation allowances under the 1964–70 Labour government.[3] Finally, during the late sixties, the tax liabilities of companies began to undergo an upturn owing to the fact that their assessed profits included stock appreciation. With the acceleration of inflation, this meant that companies were having to pay tax on the increase in the value of their stocks during the accounting period despite the fact that these stocks had to be replaced at higher prices. This trend was offset by reductions in the rate of corporation tax from 45 per cent in 1968–9 to 40 per cent in 1972–3. A further attempt was made to halt the increasing tax liability of companies in the November 1974 and April 1976 budgets by limiting the maximum increase in the value of stocks on which tax was payable to a specified proportion of trading profits.[4]

This situation casts important light on the debate surrounding the 'profitability crisis' thought by some to have blighted British industry since the 1950s. Perhaps the best-known contribution to this debate is that of Andrew Glyn and Bob Sutclffe, who

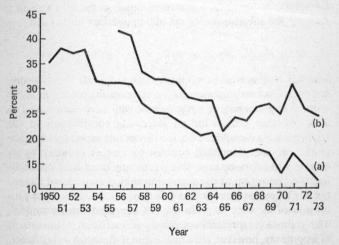

Fig. 2. Effective tax rates on companies, 1950–73. (a) Ratio of effective tax to gross trading profits; (b) ratio of effective tax to gross trading profits less capital consumption less stock appreciation. (Source: M. A. King, 'The United Kingdom Profits Crisis: Myth or Reality?', *Economic Journal*, March 1975)

have argued that both the share of profits in the national income and the rate of profit (per unit of capital employed) have fallen dramatically in the past quarter of a century.[5] This downward trend has, however, been offset by the continual reduction in the rate of tax charged to companies. Indeed, one recent analysis by M. A. King suggests that 'while there has been a long-run decline in the share of pre-tax conventional gross profits, this has coincided with changes in taxes and investment incentives which have left the share of conventional gross profits after tax virtually unchanged'. The fall in the rate of profits tax which has brought this situation about is reflected in Figure 2.

The effective rate of tax on companies (defined as the ratio of effective tax to conventional gross profits) has more than halved, from 37 per cent in 1950–53 to 14 per cent in 1970–73. If an allowance is made for capital depreciation and for the increased value of stocks due to inflation, then the effective tax rate would be higher, but its decline over the years no less remarkable. With the allowances made for stock appreciation in the 1974 and 1976 budgets, the effective rate of tax will have fallen further still.[6]

Increasing Burden of Income Tax

The fall in the amount of taxes collected from the company sector was not accompanied by a corresponding reduction in the revenue requirements of governments, who have been forced to look to other groups for an increasing contribution to the Exchequer. As a consequence, the favourable experience of companies provides a marked contrast to that of ordinary wage-earners and salary-earners. While company taxes have been falling, the proportion of the population subject to personal income tax has increased year by year (see Figure 1, p. 16) and the proportion of incomes taken in tax has increased equally rapidly. This transition represents not merely an extension of the system of income tax, however, but a fundamental change in its incidence. We therefore turn to consider the way in which the distribution of the personal income-tax burden has changed.

The distribution of the tax burden between wage-earners and salary-earners reflects to a great extent the political preferences of the government in power at the time, as does the distribution between firms and individuals. As one might expect, the tax burden changes according to a political cycle. Conservative governments are generally averse to high levels of taxation and tend in particular to relax the amount of tax payable by high-income groups. The Labour Party, when in power, tends to raise the tax liability of the rich. Both parties succumb to the temptation of reducing everyone's tax bill if an election is imminent.

The shape of this political cycle was well illustrated in the Transport and General Workers' Union evidence to the Royal Commission on the Distribution of Income and Wealth which analysed the shifts in the tax burden over the past twenty years. This showed that, under the 1951–64 Conservative administration, the tax burden of all those earning less than twice average earnings increased while those earning above that level enjoyed a substantial reduction in their tax contributions. The succeeding Labour government allowed everyone's tax bill to increase, but ensured that high-income groups paid back some of the concessions granted to them over the previous period, thus raising their tax burden more than most.

When the Tories regained power in 1970, they set about restoring the situation they had left six years earlier. Again, those earning more than twice the average were relieved of some of their tax liabilities. Because the need for tax revenue does not fall, even under Conservative governments, the contribution of the low-income groups was allowed to rise further to compensate for the revenue spent in tax concessions to the rich. Needless to say, the Labour government who took office in 1974 began once again to demand a bigger contribution towards public funds from the wealthy. But they substantially increased the tax burden of the poor as well.[7]

As long as the demands for public revenue continue to grow, tax concessions to one group can be paid for only by an increase in the taxation of other groups. It is therefore important to look not only at the burden on individual taxpayers at different levels of income, but to examine the contribution of a number of income groups towards total income-tax revenue. The first detailed analysis of this kind was carried out by R. J. Nicholson, who examined the distribution of personal incomes over the period 1949–63. He found that, until about 1957, the distribution of incomes in Britain was becoming more equal, but that after that date there was no further significant shift in the amount of income (before tax) going from rich to poor – a conclusion which remains valid today. Looking at the distribution of incomes *after tax*, he reached a surprising conclusion: 'Tax changes underline the ending of the movement towards equality, since their effect is to improve the relative position of the top income groups – a somewhat striking result, conflicting with what might have been expected from a tax system in which rates are steeply progressive.'[8]

Nicholson went on to examine the changes in the contributions of different income groups to total income tax and surtax revenue. Over the period 1949–57, the proportion of total tax collected from the top 5 per cent of income-earners fell from nearly 70 per cent of the total to just over 54 per cent. The explanation for this was simple: the redistribution of before-tax income which had taken place over those years meant that the top income groups actually received a smaller proportion of total income. Since they had less of the income, they paid less of the tax – a factor described as 'loss of taxable capacity'.

Nicholson noted that the tax burden of the rich, relative to that of other taxpaying groups, continued to fall as time went on. Between 1957 and 1963 the contribution of the top 5 per cent fell again, from 54 per cent of the total to 47 per cent. But this time an explanation could not be found in the drop in the proportion of income received by the rich, since the trend towards greater equality had been halted in 1957. He concluded that 'although the burden of direct taxation has shifted over the whole period 1949 to 1963 the explanation of the shift has changed. Before 1957 it was due to loss of taxable capacity in the highest income groups; since then it has been due to changes in tax rates.'[9]

In the years that followed this trend persisted. Updating Nicholson's analysis, Walsh found that over the period 1963–7 the tax burden of the rich had once again lessened despite the fact that their pre-tax income had not fallen significantly. The contribution of the top 1 per cent of taxpayers fell from 28·6 per cent of the total in 1964 to 23·4 per cent in 1967. The top 5 per cent, who had paid 70 per cent of the total income tax in 1949, paid 47 per cent in 1964 and only 40 per cent in 1967.[10] The table below gives us some idea of how the tax burden has shifted over the most recent years for which figures are available, 1967–8 to 1971–2.

TABLE 1. Percentage of total income tax and surtax raised from specified groups of income recipients

Group	1967–8	1968–9	1969–70	1970–71	1971–2
top 1%	20·5	19·5	18	16	15
top 10%	47·5	45	47	41	39·5
top 40%	78	77·5	80	75	73·5
bottom 30%	5·5	5·5	6	7	7
bottom 10%	0·6	0·5	0·7	0·8	0·9
all incomes	100	100	100	100	100

SOURCE: *Hansard*, 20 February 1975, Vol. 886, Cols. 475–6.

Over that five years alone, the contribution of the richest 1 per cent of taxpayers fell again, from over 20 per cent of the total to 15 per cent. The proportion raised from the top 10 per cent also fell, from nearly 48 per cent of the total to less than 40 per cent. Again, this cannot satisfactorily be explained as a reduction in the amount of before-tax income going to the richest groups. The Royal Commission on the Distribution of Income and Wealth found, for instance, that 'while there has been a decline since 1959 in the share of the top 5 per cent of the income distribution, especially in the top 1 per cent, there has been little change in the rest of the distribution'.[11] The contribution of the richest taxpayers has therefore been eased over the years, but the revenue still had to be raised in increasing amounts. Who made up the difference? Turning again to the table, we will not find the loss in revenue made up by any group in the top 40 per cent – who all enjoyed a substantial reduction in their tax burden. We have to look to the lower end of the income distribution to see who helped reduce the tax bill of the rich. Most wage-earners find themselves amongst the lower 60 per cent of the taxpaying population (a population which we should remember now includes the poor), and it is here that the lost revenue was apparently recouped. This

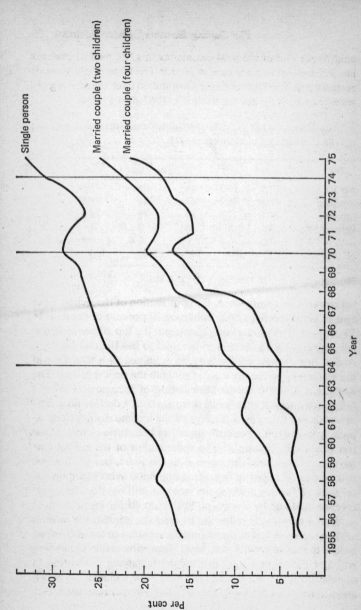

Fig. 3. Income tax and national-insurance contributions of average earners as a proportion of gross income, 1955–75

group paid 22 per cent of total income tax and surtax in 1967 but 26½ per cent in 1971. The poorest 30 per cent paid 7 per cent of total income taxes in 1971, compared with 5½ per cent in 1967.

As far as the rich are concerned, therefore, the tax changes of Conservative and Labour governments tend to be self-cancelling. Each administration undoes what its predecessor has done. But for the mass of wage-earners who earn less than twice the average income, government policies show some consistency: both parties increase the tax burden of those at the bottom. The net effect of these political swings and roundabouts, as we can see from Table 1, has been to raise the tax liabilities of ordinary work-people, while lessening those of high-income groups.

To put the effects of this shift in the tax burden into perspective, let us leave for the moment the effect on the rich, and focus on the way in which taxation has affected the average manual worker over the past twenty years. This is illustrated in Figure 3, which shows the proportion of gross income taken in tax and national-insurance contributions for single people and for families, assuming that they receive the average wage. The vertical lines separate periods of Labour and Conservative governments.

The single person on the average wage paid one third of his income in tax and national-insurance contributions in 1975, compared with less than 16 per cent in 1955. The typical two-child family now pays a quarter of his income in direct taxes, against 3·3 per cent twenty years ago. Even the family on the average wage having four children to support pays over one fifth of its income to the Inland Revenue, compared with 2·5 per cent in 1955.

One thing stands out sharply from the graph. The political cycle which we noted with respect to the rich applies equally to working people. While there has been a steep increase in the proportion of earnings taken in tax by governments of both persuasions, it seems that the trend accelerated in the period of Labour government from 1964 to 1970, and again after 1974. This is not surprising. Labour governments do not have the same aversion to high levels of income tax as their Tory counterparts, largely because they are committed to a high level of social expenditure. But the increase in taxation over the past twenty years has not been progressive in its effects, even under Labour administrations. In the first place it has not been matched by an equivalent increase in the 'social wage'. As the OECD noted, increased taxes on households were not offset by increased 'transfer payments' between social groups.[12] Secondly, the raising of increased tax revenue has been far from egalitarian. As we have seen, the burden has borne most heavily on those at the lower end of the wage and salary scale. Amongst wage-earners as a whole, the increased revenue has been taken from the wage-packets of those least able to afford it – the low paid and those with families.

As we saw in the previous chapter, the 'ability to pay' is a principle which, in theory at least, is at the heart of the British system of income-tax allowances. Hence the demands on family income of bringing up children are acknowledged by the allocation of child tax allowances which effectively reduce the amount of tax paid. Similarly, those with low incomes are (again in theory) called upon to contribute less to public funds than other households. The increase in taxation since the war has been characterized by the erosion of both these principles. Turning again to the graph, we see that the tax burden has increased much more dramatically for families with children than for single people – a trend illustrated in the graph by the convergence of the three lines. The proportion of income paid in tax by the single person on the average wage has more than doubled over the past twenty years (from 16 to 33 per cent), but that of a family with two or even four children has been subject to an eight-fold increase. So the proportionate contribution of a two-child family has increased from one fifth the size of the single-person contribution in 1955 to three quarters its size in 1975.

The second betrayal of principle inherent in the post-war increase in wage-taxation relates to the amount of tax paid by low-income groups. Over the same twenty-year period, the tax payable by a single person on a low wage (defined as two thirds the average) has trebled as a proportion of gross income. That paid by an average wage-earner has doubled, while the high-paid wage-earner (one and a half times the average) has seen an increase of slightly over one half in the proportion of income paid in tax. If the

British system of income tax was not greatly progressive twenty years ago, as we know from the Royal Comission who reported at that time, it is even less so today.

As we have seen, the increased demands for public revenue have led to a massive increase in the level of direct taxation since the war. The burden of this increased taxation has not been spread equally between different social groups, but has been concentrated on the recipients of earned income – ordinary wage-earners and salary-earners. Amongst those dependent on earned income, we have also seen that the top-income groups have enjoyed a reduction in their tax contributions at the expense of those at the lower end. Finally, amongst the mass of ordinary wage-earners who have borne the brunt of the increased taxation, the low-paid and those with families have been called upon to contribute a disproportionate share.

It remains for us to try and explain how this situation has come about. Why has the overall burden of wage-taxation increased so dramatically in the last twenty years, and why have families and low wage-earners received more than their fair share of the increase? Any attempt to unravel the changes that have taken place in post-war taxation inevitably comes up against the problem that many of the effective changes were not necessarily intended by policy-makers. The tax system with which we are faced today (and which will be described in Chapter 3) is not the result of long-term planning or of a consistent development of aims. Rather, it is the result of years of piecemeal reform intended to meet short-term ends, and this is worsened by the fact that each political party wants the tax system to achieve different ends. This was true even when the Royal Commission examined the system of income tax twenty years ago: 'Our tax system has not been developed in obedience to [such] general principles; and to the extent that they do receive recognition in the tax code, it is more the result of ad hoc considerations or of administrative necessities than of any systematic application of a basic conception.'[13]

Nevertheless, we can identify two categories of changes which have taken place in the tax system since the war. The first are the result of changes in the structure of tax rates and allowances deliberately implemented by policy-makers. The second category embraces those changes that have taken place through the inaction of policy-makers – often at times when action was vitally necessary to preserve the equity of the tax system. We will consider this second category first.

Inflation and the Tax Burden

Chancellors don't like raising tax rates. It's unpopular and is believed to lose their party votes. For many years after the war, rates of income tax were therefore reduced substantially to bring them down from the high level which was considered unacceptable in times of peace. More recently, tax allowances have been increased year by year as an apparent way of reducing taxation. But, as we have seen, the tax burden of most working people has continued to rise relentlessly. A second paradox was that outlined by John Pardoe, MP, opening a Parliamentary debate on reform of personal taxation: 'Over the past ten years, Chancellors have claimed to have taken 8 million people out of the tax yet there are now $2\frac{1}{2}$ million more taxpayers than there were ten years ago and the working population has not increased.'[14] If tax rates have been reduced and allowances raised, how has this increase in the number of people, each paying an increased proportion of their income in tax, come about? The answer is simple: inflation.

To understand the connection between inflation and the level of the tax burden, we need to look more closely at the workings of the British tax system – only briefly, since we consider the mechanics in some detail in Chapter 3. Each individual or household is allocated a certain amount of his income which is tax-free, through a system of tax allowances embodied in a tax code. The aim, as we noted earlier, is to discriminate between taxpayers with differing commitments. A single man, for example, will be allowed to earn £735 a year (in 1976–7) before paying tax. A family with two children (assuming that the wife stays at home) will be allowed a much higher income before becoming liable to tax (at present £1,633 a year). The level of income beyond which a household's income will be liable to tax – determined by the value of the allowances which they are entitled to claim – is known as the 'tax threshold'.

We now bring inflation into the picture. Chancellors normally raise tax allowances at each budget (especially in the recent inflationary past) and claim credit for having reduced everyone's tax burden. However, they rarely raise the allowances sufficiently to maintain their real value against inflation. The tax threshold therefore falls in real terms (though it is increased in money terms) and families begin to pay tax on a level of income which is effectively lower in real terms than the year before. If wage-earners manage to increase their pay, either through winning a wage rise or through working overtime and shifts, by just enough to offset the rise in the cost of living their real income remains constant. They will find, however, that an increasing proportion of that income is going in tax. The reason for this is that a progressively smaller proportion of the family's income is allowable as tax free.

The tax threshold has fallen steadily over the past few years, though not at an even pace. The situation was noticed by Paish some twenty years ago, but the rate of inflation at that time was not dramatic and the tax threshold sank only slowly.[15] With the rapid acceleration of inflation to the 20 and 25 per cent rates of the 1970s the problem has correspondingly worsened. Since 1972, the tax threshold has fallen by £4·00 a week for a married couple with one child; by £4·21 for a two-child family and by £4·53 for a family with four children. This shows only the 'high points' of the tax threshold, as they stand after tax allowances have been raised at each budget, but of course the threshold falls much more steeply throughout the months following a budget. By the April 1976 budget for example, families with two children were paying tax on a real income effectively £4·23 a week lower than the year before.

If wage-earners raise their income in line with rising prices, to maintain it at a constant level in real terms, they are pushed further and further into the tax system. For those at the bottom, a rise in money income may mean that the family is pushed into tax for the first time. Indeed, the tax threshold has fallen so low in recent years that even those families officially defined as poor are subject to income tax – an absurd situation which we examine

TABLE 2. Tax threshold as percentage of average earnings

Year	Single person	Married couple	Married couple with 2 children under 11	Married couple with 4 children (2 not over 11, 2 between 11 and 16)
	per cent	per cent	per cent	per cent
1949–50	39·4	62·8	103·2	143·7
1950–51	37·3	59·6	98·0	136·3
1951–2	33·8	56·9	92·5	138·0
1952–3	35·3	60·3	107·3	154·3
1953–4	33·3	56·9	101·2	145·5
1954–5	30·9	52·7	93·8	134·8
1955–6	32·9	55·2	99·5	143·8
1956–7	31·0	51·9	93·4	134·9
1957–8	29·4	49·1	88·4	137·5
1958–9	28·9	48·3	86·8	134·9
1959–60	27·4	45·7	82·2	127·8
1960–61	25·5	42·6	76·0	119·0
1961–2	25·6	41·6	73·8	114·0
1962–3	24·7	40·2	71·4	110·3
1963–4	32·8	50·5	84·5	125·8
1964–5	30·4	46·7	78·1	116·3
1965–6	27·8	43·0	71·9	107·3
1966–7	26·8	41·5	69·4	103·5
1967–8	25·5	39·4	66·0	98·4
1968–9	23·7	36·6	57·4	79·8
1969–70	25·4	37·4	56·1	75·6
1970–71	28·6	41·0	57·6	74·8
1971–2	26·0	37·2	58·6	80·7
1972–3	31·8	41·4	59·9	78·9
1973–4	28·0	36·4	52·4	68·8
1974–5	24·7	34·2	57·1	68·8
1975–6	21·8	30·8	44·6	59·0
1976–7	21·2	31·3	47·1	63·3

NOTES:
1. Average earnings have been taken as the annual equivalent of average weekly earnings of full-time male manual workers aged 21 and over in manufacturing and certain other industries at October of each year. 1976–7 estimated by the authors at £66·72.
2. The tax threshold used takes account where appropriate of the effect of earned income relief and of the family allowance deduction 'clawback'. For years up to and including 1964–5 account has also been taken of the relief given for national-insurance contributions.
SOURCE: *Hansard*, 19 May 1976, Vol. 911, Col. 567.

in some detail in the following chapter. But wage-earners do not always raise their incomes exactly in line with rising prices. During some periods, wages move well ahead of prices, while at other times earnings are held down by pay restraint policies and the cost of living overtakes families' living standards. So it is important to consider the fall in the tax threshold in relation to the rise in average earnings. Table 2 shows how the value of the threshold has fared against the average wage for different types of family.

In 1956 a single person, if he was earning the average wage, would have been allowed just under a third of his income free of tax. Twenty years later, just one fifth of his income is untaxable. Married couples without children have been subject to the same kind of changes. About half their income would have been disregarded for tax purposes in 1956, compared with less than a third in 1976. The tax threshold for families with children has fallen much more dramatically. The relative fall in tax threshold for different types of family explains to a large extent the shift in the tax burden which we noted earlier. For instance, we saw from Figure 3 that the proportion of income tax paid had increased much more rapidly for families than for single people. Table 2 explains why.

Turning again to that table, it can be seen that a two-child family paid no tax twenty years ago until their income was almost equal to the average wage. By the mid-sixties, this type of family would have paid tax on any income which was more than three quarters the average wage. The mid-seventies has seen a drop in the tax threshold to less than half the average.

The path of the tax threshold for a two-child family has been relentlessly downward, with the exception of the tax years 1963–4, 1969–70 and 1972–3. The last of these years saw the famous reflationary budget of the Conservative government. We share the cynicism of other authors in suggesting that the substantial raising of the tax threshold in 1963 and 1969 – years which preceded a general election – may not have been totally coincidental.[16] If take-home pay determines political sympathies, then the fact that both these elections saw a change of government despite temporary displays of generosity on the part of the outgoing administration suggests that the memory of the electorate is not as short as politicians apparently believe.

Looking, however, at the way in which the tax threshold has been allowed to fall for households without children, a different picture emerges. The trend is still downwards, but it is much more erratic. In fact the benevolence of Mr Barber in 1972 raised the value of the single person's threshold above the level at which it had stood in 1956. In the case of the two-child family, even this generosity was insufficient to restore the tax threshold to two thirds of its 1956 level. In each case, the 1972 budget marked a high point which preceded rapid decline: the single person's threshold fell from 30 per cent to 20 per cent of average earnings; the married couple's from 40 to 30 per cent; the two-child family's from nearly 60 per cent to just over 45. All this in the space of four years.

Inflation therefore has the effect that revenue will keep flowing into the Treasury coffers at an increasing rate even if tax rates are left unchanged, merely through the effects of wage-earners trying to maintain their living standards against inflation, or their relative position in the earnings league. This phenomenon, known technically as 'fiscal drag', acts as a built-in regulator of consumer demand, since an increasing proportion of wages will be absorbed as tax as incomes rise and as some taxpayers are pushed into higher tax brackets. Our earlier distinction between 'automatic' and 'deliberate' causes of the increased tax burden may therefore be an artificial one. Chancellors could ensure that the 'automatic' effects were avoided merely by 'indexing' the value of allowances. There are reasons why they do not do this. In the first place, the present arrangements allow Chancellors a flourish of apparent generosity by giving back part (but normally only part) of the extra revenue which has flowed in throughout the year by raising the nominal value of allowances. In addition to the popularity attached to tax 'concessions' (real or imagined) of this sort, governments can trade a reduction in the normal tax bill in exchange for some of the many concessions which they may wish to coax from different sections of the population at budget time. The most recent example is the 1976 agreement for wage restraint with the trade-union movement granted in exchange for an 'increase' in tax allowances.[17]

A second advantage to be gained from allowing inflation to raise revenue is that governments would otherwise have to increase *rates* of tax by a considerable amount to make up the cost of maintaining the value of public expenditures, and this would not be popular. Even though the taxpaying public as a whole would not be paying more in tax to the government, such moves would be seen as an overt attempt to raise the burden of taxation. Finally, the administrative expense of raising revenue through fiscal drag is negligible, since tax rates and nominal allowances remain unchanged.

There are, however, costs involved in raising revenue in this way – costs which are not borne by the Treasury but by those least able to afford them. Inflation is indiscriminate, biting deeply into the standard of living of the low-paid and families with children. As Joel Barnett, Chief Secretary to the Treasury, pointed out in a candid interview: 'when we refrain from increasing the personal allowances in line with inflation, we are taking more in taxation in that way. We've said so straightforwardly; what we are doing in that way is redistributing the tax burden, and we accept this.'[18]

The full redistributive effects of inflation through the tax system are difficult to disentangle. On the one hand, it can have the effect of making the tax system more progressive by narrowing (in real terms) the bands of income at which different tax rates apply. With the simplification of the tax-rate structure in recent years (which we consider in some detail below), this affects only a very small proportion of taxpayers who pay at the higher rates. As far as the mass of taxpayers who pay at the same standard rate (currently 35 per cent) are concerned, inflation can act in three ways on their tax burden. For all taxpayers, inflation raises the average rate of tax by reducing the amount of income which is allowable as tax-free and 'in general, the effect is stronger the lower the level of income or the greater are the nominal values of allowances which are claimed against tax'.[19] The effect is to hit hardest the low-paid and those claiming allowances for children. But the increase in the average tax rate diminishes as we move up the income scale (providing that the marginal rate of tax remains constant) so that within the standard-rate group of taxpayers the impact of inflation is regressive, bearing most heavily on those at

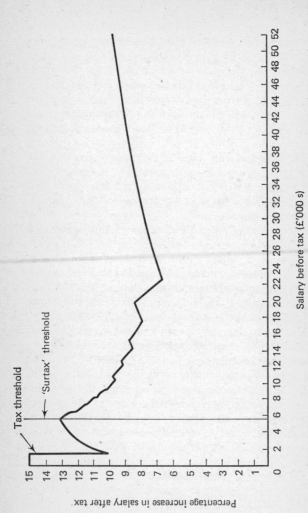

Fig. 4. Percentage increase in net salary resulting from a 15 per cent increase in gross salary for a married man with two children under 11 and deductions allowed against taxable income of 5 per cent of gross salary, 1975–6. (Source: Royal Commission on the Distribution of Income and Wealth, Report No. 3, *Higher Incomes from Employment*, Cmnd 6383, HMSO, January 1976)

the lower end. For those at the top of the standard-rate band, inflation can have the additional effect of making the top slice of income liable to tax at a higher rate. At the bottom, it can mean entry into the tax system for the first time. The jump in marginal tax rates (and therefore in average tax rates) will however be from $5\frac{3}{4}$ per cent to $40\frac{3}{4}$ per cent (if we include national-insurance contributions) for those at the bottom but from 35 per cent to 40 per cent for those at the top of the standard-rate band.

This effect was well illustrated by the Royal Commission on Distribution of Income and Wealth in their report on higher incomes. The Commission estimated the percentage increase in net salary which would come about through a 15 per cent increase in incomes before tax. In effect, they were considering how much living standards would drop if households at different levels of income received increases sufficient just to offset a 15 per cent rise in prices, but not for the extra tax to be paid on that increase. Their results are shown graphically in Figure 4.

On income up to the tax threshold, a 15 per cent increase in gross pay is reflected in an increase in net income of the same size (the calculations do not include national-insurance contributions or the withdrawal of means-tested benefits). If the pay increase takes the recipient through the tax threshold, it will represent a very much smaller rise in net pay – in the order of only 10 per cent. Above the tax threshold, however, the net benefit of a pay increase of 15 per cent rises as incomes rise above the tax threshold. On an income of just under £6,000 a year, the net benefit is 13 per cent, compared with only 10 per cent for the family with an income of £1,300 at the tax threshold. Beyond this point, however, increases in pay involve moving into higher rates of tax. This continues up to an income of £23,000 beyond which point the household remains at the highest tax rate and the net benefit of a 15 per cent rise increases once more.

'Fiscal drag' may provide governments with an administratively simple and apparently politically neutral means of raising revenue, but there are substantial redistributive implications of employing such a policy. If the increased revenue were raised through changes in tax rates or allowances, governments would be forced to choose how the tax burden should be distributed. It may

be that the political decision would still lead them to discriminate against larger families and low-income groups, and
therefore against the fundamental principles of a progressive
tax system, though it is doubtful whether the electorate would
condone such a decision if it were part of deliberate government
policy.

Tax Policy and the Average Wage-Earner

Our distinction between the deliberate and the automatic causes
of increased wage-taxation may therefore be somewhat tenuous,
but we can still identify a category of tax changes which are
overtly intentional and these relate mainly, though not wholly, to
tax rates.

The exceptional demand for revenue led to abnormally high
tax during and immediately after the war, but since 1945 there
has been a progressive reduction in the effective standard rate of
tax. Table 3 opposite shows how the rates of tax which affect ordinary wage-earners, the standard and reduced rates, have changed
since the war.

Until the introduction of the 'Unified Tax System' in 1973
wage-earners and salary-earners would claim earned income
relief equivalent to a given proportion of their income. The effective rates of tax, shown in the table, were therefore considerably
lower than the nominal rates. By the end of the war, the effective
standard rate of tax on earned income stood as high as 45 per
cent. The rate was cut drastically to 39 per cent in 1946 and was
lowered in stages throughout the years that followed. The standard rate reached its lowest post-war level in 1959 when it was
set at 30 per cent, and Conservative governments have never
since deviated from that standard rate. It has been Labour governments who in recent years raised it above the level of 30p in the
£. Throughout the 1964 administration, the standard rate remained at 32 per cent, was reinstated to 30 per cent by the Tories
and raised again by Labour after 1974 to 33 per cent and then to
35 per cent. The standard rate of tax is now the highest that it has
ever been for the last twenty years.

For many years, however, the standard rate of tax was not the

TABLE 3. Effective reduced and standard rates of tax, 1945–76

	1st reduced rate	2nd reduced rate	3rd reduced rate	Standard
1945				45
1946				39
1947				37·5
1948	12	24	—	36
1949	12	24	—	36
1950	10	20	—	36
1951	12	22	—	38
1952	12	22	29	37
1953	10	20	27	35
1954	10	20	27	35
1955	9	18	26	33
1956	9	18	26	33
1957	9	18	26	33
1958	9	18	26	33
1959	7	16	24	30
1960	7	16	24	30
1961	7	16	24	30
1962	7	16	24	30
1963	—	15	23	30
1964	—	15	23	30
1965	—	15	23	32
1966	—	15	23	32
1967	—	15	23	32
1968	—	15	23	32
1969	—	—	23	32
1970	—	—	—	32
1971	—	—	—	30
1972	—	—	—	30
1973	—	—	—	30
1974	—	—	—	33
1975	—	—	—	35
1976	—	—	—	35

only rate relevant to the majority of working people. Before 1970, the first slice of taxable income attracted tax at a reduced rate. If we look at the table for the year 1950, for example, we see that the first £50 of annual income above the tax threshold was taxable at an effective rate of only 10 per cent. The next £200 still fell due for tax at a rate of only 20 per cent, with the full standard rate of 36 per cent payable on any income above that level. In 1952, under pressure from the TUC, a third reduced rate was introduced. The first £100 of taxable income was rated at 12 per cent, the next £150 at 22 per cent and the next £150 at 29 per cent. This meant that the standard rate of 37 per cent was charged only on income in excess of £400 above the tax threshold – a level of income reached by few manual and clerical workers at that time.

As with the standard rate, the reduced rates of tax were lowered throughout the period of Conservative rule until 1963. In that year, the first reduced rate was withdrawn, and taxpayers were compensated by a widening of the bands at which the remaining two reduced rates were paid. This situation persisted until 1969. In that year, the second reduced rate was abolished and the amount of income which was taxable at the remaining lower rate was increased. The first £260 of taxable income now attracted an effective rate of 23 per cent. The last reduced rate was finally withdrawn in 1970.

In retrospect, it is puzzling to many that a Labour government should have been responsible for abolishing the reduced rates of tax – a step which considerably modified the progressiveness of the income-tax system and subsequently increased the tax burden of the low-paid. But in public policy, intentions and results can often move in opposite directions. The abolition of the reduced rates was intended as a progressive measure. Very little revenue was raised from those paying only at the reduced rates and the administrative costs of collecting it was high. In addition, the reduced rates were of most benefit to the rich, who stood to gain most from a lower tax bill. It was therefore decided to lift all those low-paid workers paying only at reduced rates out of tax altogether. Inflation ensured, however, that before long all those who had been exempted by this generosity were pushed back into the tax net – except this time they found themselves paying at the full standard rate.

We have argued that two factors have operated to increase the tax burden of the ordinary wage-earner: the effects of inflation reducing the value of tax allowances and pushing more families

TABLE 4. Standard-rate threshold as a percentage of average earnings, 1945–76 (two-child family)

Year	Standard or threshold basic rate for earned income as percentage of average earnings* per cent	Standard or basic rate (excluding effect of earned income relief) per cent
1945–6	142·9	50·0
1946–7	148·4	45·0
1947–8	154·7	45·0
1948–9	193·0	45·0
1949–50	187·3	45·0
1950–51	177·7	45·0
1951–2	169·7	47·5
1952–3	218·1	47·5
1953–4	205·7	45·0
1954–5	190·6	45·0
1955–6	179·3	42·5
1956–7	168·2	42·5
1957–8	159·2	42·5
1958–9	156·2	42·5
1959–60	148·0	38·75
1960–61	137·8	38·75
1961–2	131·8	38·75
1962–3	127·5	38·75
1963–4	128·7	38·75
1964–5	119·0	38·75
1965–6	109·8	41·25
1966–7	106·0	41·25
1967–8	100·7	41·25
1968–9	89·6	41·25
1969–70	82·0	41·25
1970–71	57·6	41·25
1971–2	58·6	38·75
1972–3	59·9	38·75
1973–4	52·4	30·0
1974–5	51·1	33·0
1975–6	44·6	35·0
1976–7	47·1	35·0

*The earnings figures used in the calculations are annual equivalents of the average weekly earnings of full-time adult male manual workers in manufacturing and certain other industries at October each year, except for the year 1945–6 when the figures related to July 1945.
Estimated figure for 1976–7.
SOURCE: *Hansard*, 22 May 1975, Cols. 565–6.

into the tax machinery and deliberate changes in tax rates. Let us consider the combined effect of these two influences. Table 4 shows how the tax threshold has fallen in relation to average earnings over the past thirty years. A typical (two-child) family paid no tax in 1950 unless they earned the average wage or more. But even when they started paying tax, it was only at a rate of 10 per cent. In 1975, the same type of family started paying tax on earnings of less than half the average and the rate at which they began to pay had risen to 35 per cent. The table below shows how the standard-rate tax threshold (the level of income at which the standard rate of tax becomes payable) has fallen, taking the example of a two-child family.

In 1950, this family would have started paying tax at slightly less than average earnings, but they started to pay at the standard rate only once their income had reached $1\frac{3}{4}$ times the average. In the early fifties the tax threshold rose to a high point well above average earnings, and the standard rate was payable only by those receiving more than twice average income. By the late sixties, however, the standard-rate threshold had fallen to a level equivalent to the average wage. In the mid-seventies, the standard rate is payable on less than half the average. Changes in tax rates over the period have therefore reinforced the effects of inflation on the tax burden of the low-paid. While the standard rate of tax has fallen, until very recently, the rate at which tax is paid by the low wage-earner has increased dramatically, from 10 per cent in 1950 to 35 per cent in 1975–6.

Tax Policy and the Rich

A rather different picture emerges if we consider what has happened to the tax burden of the very rich over the years since the war. This group has also been hit by the effects of inflation, but in this case deliberate tax changes have tended to mitigate, rather than to reinforce, the inflationary impact. Nominal surtax rates have remained virtually unchanged throughout the whole of the post-war period. The one exception to this was a reduction in the highest rate from $12\frac{1}{2}$ per cent to 10 per cent after 1951–2. In addition, a 10 per cent surcharge was levied on the bills of surtax-payers in the years 1965–6 and 1972–3. This rigidity of tax rates however conceals important changes which were made during that period to lighten the load of the high-income groups.

Up to 1957 the starting point for surtax remained at £2,000. In that year, however, personal allowances (over and above the single person's allowance) were allowed as a deduction from income for surtax purposes for the first time. Then in 1961 a special 'earnings allowance' was introduced for surtax payers. This raised the surtax threshold for earned income from £2,000 to £5,000. Further surtax concessions had to wait until 1970, when Roy Jenkins raised the threshold for all surtax-payers. The surtax 'exemption' was raised to £2,500 of chargeable income (after accounting for allowances and reliefs), although once this level was passed tax was assessed on all income in excess of £2,000. Mr Barber raised this exemption to £3,000 in 1972 (although beyond this point surtax was still payable on income exceeding £2,000). The number of surtax-payers was thus restored to its 1968–9 level.[20] The impact of these changes, combined with the factors tending to increase the tax burden of the lowest-income groups was illustrated in Figure 5, presented by Professor Kaldor in his evidence to the Select Committee on Tax Credit.

The graph shows the proportion of income paid in tax of married couples at different points on the earnings scale (expressed in relation to average earnings). The most surprising results emerge from a comparison of the situation in 1938–9 with that of 1971–2. At the lower end of the income range the curves representing the later years are significantly further to the left than that representing the pre-war situation. This reflects the fact that tax is payable at a much lower level of income and that a higher proportion of income is taken in tax at each income range. But as one moves up the income scale, the curve for the earliest year begins to converge with that of the latest. Hence, at the highest level of income shown on the graph, there is very little difference between the proportion of income taken in tax in the early seventies from that taken before the war.

The year 1973 saw the introduction of the New Unified Tax System, which merged income tax and surtax into one. A basic rate of tax was levied over a wide band of income and additional

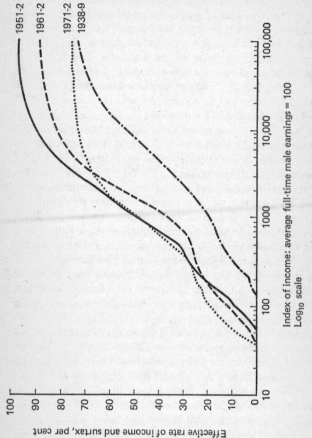

Fig. 5. Proportion of income paid in tax in various years (married couple, income all earned). (Source: *A Critique of the Green Paper Proposals*, Evidence to the Select Committee on Tax Credit, 29 March 1973, HMSO, 1973)

increments of taxable income above this level attracted higher rates. The higher-rate tax threshold was set at a level equivalent to £5,000 of taxable income (after deducting the various allowances and reliefs).

Comparing effective tax rates during the first year of operation of the new system (1973–4) with those applicable in 1970–71, John Hughes noted a substantial drop in the tax burden of the highest-income groups compared with only a moderate reduction for those lower down. A married couple with an equivalent real income of £20,000 (that is, adjusting the figures for inflation) paid 55·2 per cent of their income in tax in 1973–4 compared with 62·7 per cent in 1970–71. The concessions granted to the wealthy by the Conservative government over the period 1970 to 1973 had similarly reduced the proportion of income paid by married couples with an equivalent real income of £30,000 from 72·2 per cent to 61·7 per cent. Inflation and the Labour government together had some impact in restoring the pre-1970 tax contribution of higher-income groups. When they came to power in 1974, they lowered the higher-rate tax threshold from £5,000 to £4,500 and introduced an intermediate tax rate of 38 per cent on incomes between £4,500 and £5,000 a year. They also increased each of the higher rates of tax (as with the standard rate) by 3 percentage points. The highest rate was raised from 75 per cent to 83 per cent. Apart from the lowering of the higher-rate threshold and the introduction of the intermediate band of income at 38 per cent, the other higher-rate tax bands were left unchanged. As a result, inflation effectively increased the progressive nature of the tax structure at the higher end by narrowing the width of the bands in real terms and lowering the points at which they became effective. But even this was not sufficient to withdraw from the very rich the concessions granted in the period 1970–74. Even by 1975, Hughes estimated, the married couple receiving the equivalent (at 1970 prices) of £30,000 paid the same proportion of its income in tax as in 1970. Those with incomes above this level still paid proportionately *less* than five years earlier.[21] The rich therefore felt the pinch of an increased tax burden under the Labour government, while the very rich maintained their position. By 1976, however, even that government felt the need to restore the balance. The higher-rate threshold was raised again to £5,000 of taxable income and each of the bands of income above that level increased by £500. The extent of the concession was, however, restricted to those with a taxable income of less than £10,000.

Inevitably, the tiny proportion of taxpayers who are at the top of the income-tax pyramid tend to attract the generosity of Conservative governments and the antipathy of Labour. But the opposing policies have neutralized each other. If we look, as Professor Kaldor does, over the whole period since the war we find that their tax burden has increased only moderately. The biggest increases have been shouldered for them by those lower down the income strata.

Conclusion

The post-war period has seen a significant shift in the burden of direct taxation away from the company sector and towards personal income tax. This has meant that wage-taxation has increased out of proportion to the increase in public spending. Before the war, it is estimated, there were approximately 3·7 million income-tax payers, representing mainly the better-off sections of society. Today the situation is very different. The army of taxpayers now numbers 20·7 million – over 85 per cent of the working population – including virtually all manual and clerical workers. Amongst the recruits to this ever-growing army, as we will see in Chapter 3, are those families whom the government itself defines as poor. At the same time, the average wage-earner, who paid no tax even twenty-five years ago, now pays between a third and a half of his income to the Inland Revenue.

This massive extension of the system of wage-taxation has brought with it fundamental changes in the incidence of personal income tax. This is largely because governments have chosen to raise the increased revenue necessary by allowing the erosion of tax-free allowances by inflation rather than through overt changes in tax rates. As a result the distribution of the tax burden has shifted increasingly towards those with the lowest incomes and the largest families, so that the principles of vertical and horizontal equity on which the tax system is based have been eroded, like everything else, by inflation. At the same time, however, governments have undertaken deliberate adjustments to the structure of income-tax allowances and rates which have reinforced the regressive effects of inflation. The progressive structure of income tax was severely modified, for instance, with the reduction in the effective width and eventual abolition of the reduced-rate bands. This adjustment, though designed to increase administrative efficiency of the system, produced a significant rise in the tax burden of the lowest-paid, who had been dragged into the tax system through the effects of inflation. At the other end of the income scale, however, the deliberate policies of governments have mitigated the effects of inflation on the tax burdens of the rich. The net result has been a shift in the burden of personal taxation from rich to poor, the effect of which we consider in the next chapter.

References

1. B. HANSEN and W. SNYDER, *Fiscal Policy in Seven Countries, 1955–1965*, Organisation for Economic Cooperation and Development, Paris, 1969.
2. Royal Commission on the Distribution of Income and Wealth, Report No. 2, *Income from Companies and its Distribution*, Cmnd 6172, HMSO, July 1975, p. 80.
3. M. A. KING, 'The United Kingdom Profits Crisis: Myth or Reality?', *Economic Journal*, March 1975.
4. *Hansard*, 12 November 1974, Vol. 881, Col. 264, and 6 April 1976, Vol. 909, Col. 247.
5. A. GLYN and B. SUTCLIFFE, *British Capitalism, Workers and the Profits Squeeze*, Penguin Books, 1972. See also the debate in the *Bulletin of the Conference of Socialist Economists*, Department of Economics, Birkbeck College, University of London, Spring and Winter 1972, and Spring 1973, and C. J. BURGESS and A. J. WEBB, 'The Profits of British Industry', *Lloyds Bank Review*, No. 112, April 1974.
6. KING, March 1975, op. cit.
7. Transport and General Workers Union, *Inequality: Evidence to the Royal Commission on the Distribution of Income and Wealth*, Spokesman Books, 1976.
8. R. J. NICHOLSON, 'The Distribution of Personal Incomes', *Lloyds Bank Review*, No. 83, 1967, reprinted in A. B. ATKINSON

(ed.), *Wealth, Income and Inequality*, Penguin Books, 1973, p. 105.

9. ibid., p. 106.

10. A. J. WALSH, 'Tax Allowances and Fiscal Policy', in P. Townsend and N. Bosanquet (eds.), *Labour and Inequality*, Fabian Society, 1972.

11. Royal Commission on the Distribution of Income and Wealth, Report No. 1, *Initial Report on the Standing Reference*, Cmnd 6171, HMSO, July 1975, p. 68, para. 173.

12. Organisation for Economic Cooperation and Development, *Expenditure Trends in OECD Countries, 1960–1980*, Paris, 1972. Cited in DUDLEY JACKSON, H. A. TURNER and FRANK WILKINSON, *Do Trade Unions Cause Inflation?*, Cambridge University Press, 2nd edn, 1975, pp. xi–xii.

13. Royal Commission on the Taxation of Profits and Income, Final Report, Cmnd 9474, HMSO, 1955, Memorandum of Dissent, p. 359.

14. *Hansard*, 22 March 1976, Vol. 908, Col. 49.

15. F. W. PAISH, 'The Real Incidence of Personal Taxation', *Lloyds Bank Review*, January 1957, reprinted in Paish, *Studies in an Inflationary Economy*, Macmillan, 1966, and updated in 'Inflation, Personal Incomes and Taxation', *Lloyds Bank Review*, April 1975, No. 116.

16. F. WILKINSON and H. A. TURNER, 'The Wage Tax Spiral and Labour Militancy', in Jackson, Turner and Wilkinson, op. cit.

17. C. POND, 'The Attack on Inflation: Who Pays?', *Low Pay Paper* No. 11, Low Pay Unit, July 1976.

18. *Libra*, Journal of the Chartered Accountant Students' Society of London, Vol. 2, No. 5, March 1976.

19. R. I. G. ALLEN and D. SAVAGE, 'Inflation and the Personal Income Tax', *National Institute Economic Review*, No. 70, November 1974. See also C. TRINDER, 'Comment on Indexing Personal Income Taxation', in T. LEISNER and M. KING (eds.), *Indexing for Inflation*, Institute for Fiscal Studies, Heinemann, 1975.

20. *Report of the Commissioners of Her Majesty's Inland Revenue*, No. 170, Cmnd 5804, HMSO, December 1974.

21. J. HUGHES, *Income Tax and the Labour Government: The Inflation-Adjusted Arithmetic*, Trade Union Research Unit, Technical Note No. 27, Oxford, June 1975.

3 The Myth of the Progressive Tax System

It is commonly assumed that Britain's system of income tax is progressive – that the higher the income of the individual the larger the proportion of that income which he is called upon to contribute to public funds. In this chapter we shall consider first the justification for a progressive system of taxation, then whether the principle of progressive taxation commonly thought to apply to the British tax system is reflected in the reality.

The Principle of a Progressive Income Tax

In Chapter 1 we saw that the growth of the tax system in the early years of this century brought with it the development of the principle of progressive taxation. By 1920 this principle was so firmly established that the Royal Commission which reported on the workings of the tax system in that year found it unnecessary even to consider whether or not progression was the correct principle to be applied. Similarly, the second Royal Commission reporting in the mid-fifties was satisfied that 'not merely progressive taxation, but a steep gradient of taxation, is needed in order to conform with the notions of equitable distribution that are widely, almost universally accepted'.[1] This notion of a progressive principle has carried through into the official literature of the seventies. The casual observer seeking information on the workings of the tax system is told that 'as a long-standing government policy, personal income taxation in Britain is levied *progressively* so as to fall proportionately more heavily on those with larger incomes'.[2] The principle is therefore firmly established. But before turning to consider whether or not the system with which we are confronted today conforms to this principle let us examine the arguments which have been put forward in favour of progression.

Two principles lie at the heart of the argument for a progressively graduated income tax. The first is that of 'ability to pay'. This employs the notion of a subsistence income defined either in absolute terms, as the income required to acquire the minimum necessary requirements of an individual or family, or in relation to the general standard of living accepted by society as a whole. The Royal Commission on the Taxation of Profits and Income expressed the concept in this way: 'There should be no income tax levied upon any income which is insufficient to provide the owner with what he requires for subsistence.'[3] By definition the poor have incomes which are inadequate to provide even the basic essentials of an acceptable standard of living, and it is logical that those defined as poor should not have their income reduced still further by income tax. Since the 'ability to pay' increases more than proportionately with income, it is regarded as proper that the rich should pay a greater proportion of their income than the poor. By the same logic the minimum necessary income required by a family is higher than that for a single person or a childless couple. Equity therefore demands that families without children should pay a larger proportion of their income in tax than families on the same level of income but who have children to support.

The notion is therefore essentially one of 'surplus income' over and above what is necessary to maintain a socially determined minimum standard of living. The larger the surplus enjoyed by each individual, the larger should be their contribution to public revenue.[4] The Canadian Royal Commission on Taxation, reporting in 1966, accepted the same principle: 'Because we believe that non-discretionary (i.e. essential) expenses absorb a much larger proportion of the annual additions to the economic power of those with low incomes than of the wealthy, in order to obtain the proportionate taxation of discretionary economic power, we recommend that a base that measures total economic power be taxed at progressive rates.' The Commission therefore argued that the principle that each individual should contribute in proportion to his income – a principle with such compelling apparent logic – was not necessarily discarded by the introduction of a system of progressive taxation. Such a system merely ensures the proportionate taxation of *surplus* income. The Commission went on to argue that 'progressive rates would reflect the diminishing relative importance of non-discretionary expenditures for those with larger gains in economic power'.[5]

At this point the second concept, that of 'equality of sacrifice', enters the argument. The aim here is to ensure that the tax burden is distributed in such a way that each individual is called upon to make an equal sacrifice. Traditional economic theory tells us that the utility derived from each increment of additional income is smaller than that derived from the last. It follows that equality of sacrifice will be achieved only if a larger tax liability is imposed on those with higher incomes, who lose relatively little utility from the marginal units of income taken in tax. The British Royal Commission (1954) acknowledged that 'in general, and in the absence of special need, there is a presumption that to take £1 from a man with a large income will cause less sacrifice than to take the same sum from a man whose income is smaller. Taxation should therefore be laid predominantly upon the wealthy, and a progressive income tax is justified as a means of bringing about this result.' This conclusion, however, troubled the Commissioners. 'It would seem to follow from it that (at least in the case of two men whose other circumstances are similar) no tax at all should be levied upon the man with £500 a year so long as there is another man who is left with more than £500 a year after paying tax. In other words, the State should fix a certain permitted level for the maximum of income after tax, and should confiscate all income above that level ... the least sacrifice principle, literally applied, leads not to progressive taxation but to confiscation.'[6] The Commission therefore concluded that no precise tax formula was available by which to assess the 'fairest' distribution of the tax burden. Nevertheless the Commissioners agreed that the burden of taxation should be distributed with the greatest weight shouldered by those with the highest incomes, and that this could best be achieved by a system in which rates of tax were steeply progressive. This remains the criteria on which Britain's system of income tax is based. Are these criteria, firmly established in principle, reflected in the practical workings of the system of income tax?

Taxing the Poor

Let us first consider the proposition that, following the concept of 'ability to pay', the poor should be exempt from the system of income tax. To begin, we need a definition of what we mean by 'poor', and since we are concerned about the administration of the tax system by the government it is appropriate to use a governmental definition of poverty. In Britain today there are two official poverty lines: the supplementary benefits level and the level of eligibility to family income supplement. Supplementary benefit is payable to any family or individual who is not in full-time work. The aim is to 'top up' the family's income to a level prescribed by Parliament. In addition, those receiving supplementary benefit are entitled to have their rent (or mortgage interest) and rates met in full by the Supplementary Benefits Commission who administer the scheme. The second poverty line, which applies to the poor at work, is determined by the eligibility levels for family income supplement (FIS). FIS was introduced in 1971 by the Conservative Administration specifically in an attempt to mitigate the effects of the low-pay problem. It is payable to any family with children in which the head is in full-time work but whose earnings are regarded as inadequate to meet certain minimum requirements for the family. Again FIS is intended to 'top up' the income of such families.

Taking these two poverty lines – one for the poor out of work and one for the poor in work – we see the extent to which the criteria of poverty are acknowledged in the system of income tax. In Chapter 2, we discussed the phenomenon of the falling tax threshold caused by the effects of inflation and the (apparent) paralysis of administrators who fail to adjust the tax system to take account of its effects. Table 5 illustrates one of the consequences of the sinking threshold, showing the supplementary benefit level (plus an addition for average rent and rates which are paid in full for families on SB), the prescribed limits for family income supplement, and the tax threshold. In each case the figures, which apply to 1976, are given for a single person, a married couple with two children and married couples with three and four children.

TABLE 5. The tax threshold and the poverty line

	Tax threshold[1]	Prescribed[2] amount for FIS	SB[3] scale rate
Single person	14·13	—	19·15
Married couple	20·87	—	27·10
Married couple (one child)[4]	26·63	39·00	30·70
Married couple (two children)	31·40	43·50	35·05
Married couple (three children)	36·85	48·00	40·40
Married couple (four children)	42·87	52·50	48·20

NOTES:
1. Applicable from April 1976.
2. Applicable from July 1976.
3. Ordinary scale rate applicable from November 1976, plus an addition of £6·45 for average rent and rates.
4. In each case, the youngest child aged 4; second youngest 8; third 11; fourth 16.
SOURCE: *Hansard*, 14 May 1976, Vol. 911, Cols. 313–14.

The principle that the poor should be exempt from income tax no longer applies. In each case, the tax threshold stands at a level which is lower than both the supplementary benefit level (the minimum income to which the poor out of work are entitled) and the prescribed limit for family income supplement. This clearly says a great deal about the consistency of government policies and the logic with which such policies are pursued. But the situation also has very real consequences for the living standards of families at the lower end of the income scale. These consequences vary according to the definition of poverty used. Taking first the supplementary benefit level, we find that the government guarantees a minimum level of income (inadequate as this may be) for households which have no income from full-time employment. But for those families in which the head of the household works a full week income tax has to be paid even on earnings which are below this level. This means that for many low wage-earners with children their net income after taking into account tax, national-insurance contributions and the expenses of getting to and from work may be less than the family would receive if relying on the bare subsistence income provided by the Supplementary Benefits Commission. For a great many more, a full week's work may afford their family a standard of living which is only marginally higher than if they were unemployed.[7] That is not to say that the level of income provided for those who are dependent on supplementary benefit is generous. Indeed, there is evidence that, for those families finding themselves in this position, life is drab, precarious and characterized by hardship.[8] Even these paltry standards are not, however, applied when deciding who will contribute to the funds of the Inland Revenue.

A consideration of the second poverty line – the prescribed limits for family income supplement – brings the sheer force of the contradiction into sharp focus, because in this case it is the same families to whom different criteria of need are being applied. The eligibility level for FIS is higher than the starting point for tax. This means, of course, that over a wide band of income, families will be defined as poor by one government department but as having income sufficient to contribute to public funds by another. We therefore have the absurd situation in which families are paying tax and receiving family income supplement *at the same time*. Hence a married couple with two small children earning £35 a week were eligible (at July 1976 rates) to receive a poverty wage supplement of £3·50 from the Department of Health and Social Security on the grounds that their income from employment was inadequate. At the same time, they would be required to pay £3·80 to the Inland Revenue in the form of income tax and national-insurance contributions.

This situation is the creation of inconsistent policies which have come home to roost in the 1970s, but the situation is not a new discovery. The Royal Commission on the Taxation of Profits and Incomes considered proposals that 'in a situation in which two state agencies exist side by side, engaging in broadly similar transactions with the same group of citizens' some duplicated effort might be saved if the systems of income tax and social security were merged.[9] Again in 1972, a Select Committee was established to consider the possibility of reshaping the income tax and social-security systems where they overlapped: 'The present relationship with the two systems is unsatisfactory,' the Committee concluded, 'the principles on which each separately rests are different, and the results are not always consistent . . . The government give with one hand and take with another.'[10] Despite the rigorous investigation of the proposed tax credit scheme which the Committee was considering, no such merging was ever implemented. Whatever the criticisms of the proposed reform (and as with any major reform there were bound to be many)[11] it would have overcome the basic problem that the present tax system effectively neutralizes some of the beneficial aspects of the 'welfare state'.

A third implication emerges from this entanglement of taxation and welfare benefits, and that is the now well-recognized problem of the 'poverty trap'. It is commonly believed that disincentives caused by high marginal tax rates affect only the better-off, who find themselves at the pyramid of a progressive system of income tax. Paradoxically, however, the marginal 'tax' rates faced by the low-paid are in many cases substantially higher than those faced by even the most successful business executive. In 1974, the latest date for which figures are available, the government estimated that 20,000 low-income families faced a marginal 'tax' rate in excess of 100 per cent at a time when the maximum rate of income tax payable on earned income was 83 per cent and on unearned income 98 per cent.[12] *The Economist* has estimated, however, that 'the government may have miscalculated by a factor of ten', giving an actual figure of 200,000.[13]

This remarkable situation has two causes. First the poor, as we have seen, pay tax on a very low level of income, and the rate at which they begin to pay tax has increased substantially (see Chapter 2). In addition, low-paid families may have their income supplemented by a number of means-tested benefits. Because eligibility for these benefits is dependent on income, they carry a high implicit marginal 'tax' rate. That is, an increase in earnings may be offset by a loss of benefits and payment of tax. In their evidence to the Select Committee on Tax Credits, the Department of Health and Social Security listed forty-two means-tested benefits administered either by central government or local authorities.[14] A low-income family receiving an extra £1 in earnings will lose 35p straight away in tax, plus another 5¾p in national-insurance contributions. If they are claiming FIS they could lose another 50p (since the amount of benefit is calculated as half the difference between the family's income and its entitlement). Taking these three main elements alone, therefore, the family already faces an implicit marginal 'tax' rate of 90¾ per cent – above the maximum payable on earned income. Rent and rate rebates carry a 'tax' rate of between 23 and 33 per cent, so that if the family is also claiming these they could be more than £1 worse off after a £1 rise in earnings.

In addition to this however, extra earnings may lose families their eligibility for free school meals and free welfare milk, and if this happens their weekly income will be reduced by a further £1·41 for each child. As Field and Piachaud have pointed out, 'for millions of low-paid workers very substantial pay increases have the absurd effect of increasing only marginally their families' net income and in some cases are actually making the family worse off'.[15] The poverty trap has created a situation in which it is impossible for low wage-earners to improve the standard of living of their families by achieving an increase in earnings. Such an increase may indeed leave the family with a lower net income than if they had never received it at all. In times of high rates of inflation, the existence of the poverty trap represents an especially critical situation. Any attempt by the low-paid even to maintain their living standards against the rising cost of living will be frustrated first by the demands of the Inland Revenue and the parallel contributions to the National Insurance Fund, followed by the progressive withdrawal of the income support on which the family may have been forced to rely.

The first principle of a progressive system of income tax has therefore been discarded in practice as far as the administration of the British tax system is concerned. We have also seen the implications of this in terms of the living standards of low-income families. Such families may receive benefits from the government in recognition that their income is inadequate, but at the same time be called upon to contribute to government revenue through taxation. One of the results of this is that the poor face higher marginal tax rates than the rich – something of an anomaly in a supposedly progressive tax system. What of the second principle we have identified – that the tax burden should be distributed in such a way that each taxpayer bears an equal sacrifice? How progressive is Britain's system of income tax in this respect?

How Progressive is the Income Tax?

A progressive graduation in the system of income tax is achieved in two ways. In the first place, a number of tax-free allowances are allocated in acknowledgement of particular circumstances which may reduce the taxpayer's ability to pay. These have the effect of reducing the average tax rate (tax as a proportion of total income). The larger the proportion of the taxpayer's income which is accounted for by these allowances the lower will be the average tax rate. For instance a man on £20 a week pays the same marginal rate of tax as a man on £100 a week (35 per cent). For the first taxpayer however, approximately three quarters of his income will be treated as tax-free (assuming that he is a single person with no children) and only the other quarter of his income will be taxable. In the case of the £100 a week man only one eighth of his income will be treated as tax-free, the other seven eighths being taxable. Their effective (average) tax rates will be 10 per cent and 30 per cent respectively. An additional element of progression is introduced into the system of income tax through the graduation of marginal tax rates. That is, those with a higher income are subject to a higher marginal rate of tax. Developments have occurred in recent years in both these elements of progressive graduation which have significantly modified the redistributive effects of the system of income tax. Let us consider first what has happened to tax rates.

As we noted in Chapter 2, nominal rates of income tax were progressively structured in the 1950s. After crossing the tax threshold, three bands of income were taxed at reduced rates before the full standard rate of tax became payable. This was supplemented by the progression of surtax rates payable on higher incomes. Today's system of income tax is basically proportional. Over a very wide band of income (at present £5,000) tax is payable at the same marginal rate of 35 per cent. A single man earning £735 a year pays at the same rate as a man earning £5,735; a man, wife and two children on £1,633 a year at the same rate of income tax as a similar family with an income of £6,633. True progression of marginal tax rates is only applied to incomes above this level, that is, in the surtax rates which were only recently unified with the income-tax system itself. This means that only 6·5 per cent of all income-tax revenue is collected on a progressive basis. Figure 6 shows the marginal rates of tax faced by a typical family with different bands of income.

We can justifiably consider income tax and national-insurance contributions together. Both have a significant effect on the living standards of families and their collection has now formally been merged under one agency. If the family's income is more than £13 a week, its marginal tax rate will be 5¾ per cent and will continue at this level until its income reaches £31·40. At this point the rate of tax payable on additional earnings will jump to 40¾ per cent – a larger leap in marginal tax rates than any faced higher up the income scale and with a consequentially detrimental effect on living standards. The rate of tax will remain at 40·75 per cent up to an income of £96 a week (the ceiling beyond which national-insurance contributions are levied at a flat rate – see Chapter 4). Beyond this point the marginal rate of tax *falls* to a rate of 35 per cent until earnings reach approximately £127·50, at which point the rate rises again to 40 per cent. However, the marginal rate of tax faced by a family on £1,633 a year will not actually be exceeded other than by those taxpayers earning more than £7,000 a year (when the rate rises to 45 per cent). Beyond this level tax is levied at progressively higher rates but, as we have shown, such rates effect only 2 per cent of all taxpayers.

The higher-rate tax structure does indeed approximate to the traditional conception of a progressive tax system, in which marginal rates rise in steps with increases in income. But only a very small part of the direct tax system is structured in a progressive way. If we look at that part of the income-tax structure which affects the majority of taxpayers, we find that, contrary to popular belief, nominal marginal rates of tax are in fact regressive.

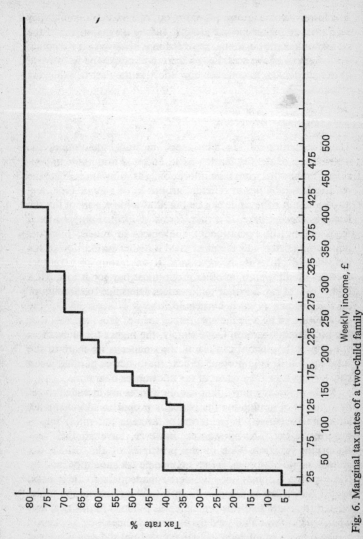

Fig. 6. Marginal tax rates of a two-child family

The lower-income groups pay more out of each extra pound they earn than do higher-income groups. Taking the major part of the system of income tax alone, progression is achieved only through the system of allowances. Let us therefore turn to the framework of tax allowances to consider how effective they are in achieving this end.

Tax Allowances

The distribution of tax allowances inevitably determines the distribution of the tax burden itself, and it is important to consider who benefits from their allocation. Tax allowances affect the relative tax liabilities of different groups in two ways. First, any given amount of revenue can be raised at a lower *rate* of tax the larger is the tax base. If certain forms of income are exempted from tax by the operation of allowances or reliefs, then the remaining taxable income must yield a higher proportion of tax than would otherwise be necessary. If one group of taxpayers receives an allowance, another group must pay for it through a higher rate of tax. Secondly, allowances determine the amount of taxable income of each household, and it is according to the distribution of taxable income, rather than of gross income, that the tax system operates. Quite simply, the higher the allowances which each household can claim, the smaller is its share of the total tax bill. It is important to bear these factors in mind when considering how the system of tax allowances operates.

We have already noted that tax allowances are intended to act as a means of graduating the basically proportional income-tax structure to convert it (in terms of average tax rates) into a progressive tax. The allowances, however, have another very important function. One of the principles of the British tax system, as we have seen, is that no income tax should be paid by those whose incomes are considered inadequate to fulfil basic needs. As we saw in Chapter 1, until 1920 an 'exemption limit' existed to ensure that this principle was pursued in practice, and when the limit was abolished the basic allowances took its place.[16]

The Royal Commission in 1954 pointed out the disadvantages of using tax allowances to fulfil this dual role in the tax system.

The two functions of the allowances – of exempting certain minimum incomes from tax and acting as an instrument of progression – are fundamentally in conflict. 'The practice of looking to the personal allowances and earned income relief (since abolished) to provide effective exemptions has had the effect of distorting the tax structure at the lower end of the scale, in that the starting point of liability is lower than it could reasonably be expected to be if the needs of subsistence are borne in mind.'[17] If that was true twenty years ago, Table 5 shows it to be even more so today. The Commission explained that this system of allowances could not act as an effective exemption limit without excessive cost in lost revenue. Whereas an exemption limit applies only to those at the bottom of the income scale, allowances are granted to taxpayers throughout the system. The cost of raising these allowances to maintain their value as an effective exemption is therefore very costly. At that time, it was estimated that the cost of raising allowances sufficiently to maintain their real value would have been almost eight times the actual cost of the tax lost from those taken out of tax at the bottom. The rest would have been distributed as a benefit to all taxpayers, no matter what their level of income.

The Commissioners therefore proposed that a specific exemption limit be reintroduced to overcome this problem. Low-income groups could thereby be protected from the effects of inflation pushing them into the tax system, at a fraction of the cost involved in using allowances for this purpose. Their proposals have never been adopted, despite more recent demands from the TUC for a reintroduction of an exemption limit. In 1968 they argued 'the General Council take the view that the point at which taxation starts to be paid, and also the point at which the standard rate is reached, are too low and that adjustments should be made at the lower end of the income-tax scale, not by a general increase in personal allowances but by the introduction of some form of minimum earned-income allowance.'[18]

The problem of using tax allowances as an exemption device is brought into sharp relief in Table 6. One of the purposes of the allowances is to reflect ability to pay between different taxpayers. Higher allowances are given to families than to single people and childless couples. Certain groups are excluded altogether on the grounds that they have an income insufficient to meet their basic needs. The table, which shows the current value of personal and child tax allowances to households with different levels of income and family responsibilities, illustrates how effective the present system of allowances are in achieving this differentiation between households with different needs.

TABLE 6. The value of tax allowances, 1976–7 (£ per week)

	Half average earnings	Average	5 times average
Single person	4·94	4·94	10·60
2-child family	10·99	10·99	23·55
4-child family	—	14·33	30·71

Average earnings estimated at £75 a week. All children aged 11 years or under.

One of the essential features of the present system of tax allowances is that their value increases as income increases. This is because each pound of income which is treated as tax-free is offset against tax at the highest marginal rate paid. For most wage-earners they are therefore worth 35 per cent of their nominal value in reduced tax payments. As the taxpayer moves into the higher-rate tax bands, however, the value of tax allowances increases to a maximum of 83 per cent on earned income and to 98 per cent on unearned income. For most wage-earners, therefore, the allowances are of substantial benefit: £4·94 to a single person; about £11 a week to the married couple with two children; £14·33 to those with four. To those families with incomes five times the average, however, the benefit is substantially greater. At this level of income, the allowances are worth approximately twice the value to the average wage-earner.

From these results, we can see that the system of tax allowances, themselves intended as an instrument of progression, are in fact regressive in their effects in terms of the benefit they confer on different groups. Tax allowances are worth more to high-income groups than to those lower down the earnings scale, because they lower the amount of income which would otherwise be taxable at higher rates.

In Chapter 2, we describe the fall in the tax threshold over the years since the war from a level significantly above average earnings (for a two-child family) to well below half the average. The threshold to which we referred was that made up of the personal and child tax allowances shown in the table above. In effect, however, the tax threshold for different families may vary widely according to the other allowances and reliefs to which they are eligible. Table 5 (p. 53) showed that a married couple with two children would start to pay tax on an income of £31·40 – well below the official poverty line. But if fortune had given this family sufficient income for it to buy a house on a mortgage, the tax threshold would be considerably higher. If they held a voluntary life-insurance policy, the threshold would be higher still. In fact, there are probably almost as many different types of allowances which can be claimed against tax as there are means-tested benefits, including relief for interests on loans, alimony, life-insurance policies, fees to professional bodies and so on.

To Him Who Hath

As we are concerned with the distribution of tax allowances, which in itself decides the incidence of the tax burden, it will be useful to divide the allowances into two types. First there are those claimed by all taxpayers, the personal allowances for single and married people, and the child tax allowances for families – which we have discussed so far. Secondly there are a number of forms of expenditure, like life-insurance premiums and mortgage interest repayments, which are traditionally regarded as necessary or desirable by the State, and which are therefore deducted from income for tax purposes. This second group of allowances, though formally justified in terms of a household's ability to pay according to its commitments, cannot act as an instrument of progression. Indeed, this group of allowances works in the opposite direction. As the TUC pointed out, 'the progressivity implicit in the different rates of the income tax is very much reduced when account is taken of the allowances which can be set off against it'.[19]

The basic allowances claimed by the ordinary wage-earner and

TABLE 7. Cost of certain tax allowances and reliefs, 1975–6

	Cost to Exchequer £m	Amount claimed at higher rates £m
Personal allowances		
Single person	2,185	32·8
Married person	4,210	168·4
Wife's earned income relief	1,080	32·4
Child allowances	1,250	50·0
Dependent relative (and daughter's service)	34	0·7
Additional personal allowance	30	0·3
Additional personal relief	235	
Housekeeper allowance	1·5	0·03
Age allowance	200	
Expenditure reliefs		
Mortgage interest relief	950	80
Life assurance relief	240	N/A
Bank loan interest (for house purchase)[1] (for other purposes)[3]	31	
Superannuation and retirement pension[2] on employee contributions on employer contributions	155 290	DK
Relief for provision of medical insurance[1] (claimed by firms)	10	
Fees to professional bodies and work expenses	105	25

NOTES:
1. Latest available figures are for 1974–5.
2. Latest available figures apply to 1971–2.
3. Latest available figures apply to 1973–4.
SOURCES: *Fourth Report from the Expenditure Committee, Session 1975–6,* House of Commons Paper No. 299, HMSO, March 1976; *Hansard,* 4 February 1976, Vol. 904, Cols. 664–5; 23 February, Vol. 906, Col. 66; 10 May, Vol. 911, Col. 46; 17 May, Vol. 911, Cols. 329–30; 19 May, Vol. 911, Cols. 565–6; 20 July, Vol. 915, Cols. 437–8; and a letter to Lord Vaizey from the Treasury, 15 October 1976.

those at the bottom of the income scale have been eroded by inflation in recent years. This has had the effect of pulling even greater numbers of the lowest-paid into the tax system for the first time. Not so with the array of other allowances, reliefs and concessions which have proliferated over the years and which by their nature are of greatest value to the 'better-off'. The report of the 1955 Royal Commission explained the changing burden of taxation in terms of an 'erosion of the tax base'. The various concessions and reliefs which have been granted in recognition of special situations had meant that the amount of income effectively taxable had been reduced significantly. Such concessions and allowances, the Commissioners argued, 'have the effect of shifting the tax burden in a manner which is no less far reaching for being unobtrusive . . . neither the public, nor the legislature, nor the courts are conscious of the extent to which the tax system, behind a façade of formal equality, metes out unequal treatment to the different classes of the tax paying community.'[20]

Such allowances and reliefs are indeed innumerable, and the Inland Revenue itself cannot calculate their full cost in terms of the revenue lost. Nevertheless, it is certain that the cost of these 'benefits' to high-income groups is considerable. The most important of those for which official estimates are available are set out in Table 7, together with the amount claimed at higher rates where possible.

The list of allowances in Table 7 are by no means exhaustive, but represent only those for which estimates are available. It is interesting in itself that the total cost of most forms of public expenditure can be itemized, but that governments have only fragmented and inexact information on the range of tax allowances which are permitted. Nevertheless, the total cost of the allowances listed was at least £11,006·5 million (remembering that in a few cases the figures apply to earlier years). The figures on the amount of revenue lost through the claiming of allowances at the higher rate is even less complete, but we know that almost £400 million was allocated to high-income groups as an extra subsidy in this way.

The functions of graduating the tax system and acting as an exemption limit can be performed only by the primary and secondary personal allowances set out in the top half of the table. The estimated cost of these allowances was £9,225 million in 1975–6. About £285 million of this was again distributed to the 2 per cent of taxpayers who pay at the higher rates as an *additional* subsidy.

The reliefs shown in the lower half of the table are granted in acknowledgement of 'outgoings'. The intention is again to distinguish between the 'ability to pay' of different taxpayers, but in effect these allowances are highly regressive. Perhaps the most contentious amongst this group is the massive subsidy awarded to home-buyers. In 1975–6, this allowance cost the general body of taxpayers £950 million – sufficient to reduce the basic rate of tax on wage-earners by 3p in the £. In addition, those who chose to buy their house through a bank loan received (in 1974–5) a further £31 million in tax relief. It is interesting to note that the resources devoted to helping people buy houses are equal to more than two thirds the value of those directed to families to help them bring up children.

As with all allowances granted through the tax system, the benefit is greatest for high-income groups. No less than £80 million (nearly 10 per cent of all mortgage interest relief) was granted to the minority of taxpayers who pay at more than the standard rate. The relief is granted against the interest paid on a mortgage up to a value of £25,000. So for a standard-rate tax-payer, the effective rate of interest on a mortgage is reduced from 11 per cent to 7·2 per cent. To someone paying at a rate of 60 per cent, the cost of buying his house is reduced to 4·4 per cent. It has been estimated that a person paying the highest rate of tax plus the investment income surcharge would pay an effective interest rate of less than a quarter of 1 per cent.[21] Similarly, a twenty-five-year mortgage on a £15,000 house (borrowed at an 11 per cent rate of interest) would be subsidized to the tune of £10,300 if the occupier paid tax at the standard rate, but £24,425 if he paid at the highest rate on earned income. If he paid the investment income surcharge, his house purchase would attract a subsidy of £28,840.[22]

A second major subsidy to the better-off is provided in the form of relief on life-assurance policies, which cost the Exchequer a further £240 million in 1976–7. In this case, the relief is granted only at the standard rate – a reform which we have argued elsewhere should apply to all forms of tax allowance. Nevertheless, it is a concession claimed mainly by the better-off. Of £190 million granted as relief in 1974–5, £52 million was claimed by those earning more than £5,000 a year.[23]

In many respects, the system of tax allowances is analogous to that of social-welfare benefits. Both serve to increase the disposable income of the recipients and are granted in recognition of social needs. As Webb and Sieve have persuasively argued, tax allowances are merely 'fiscal benefits' which are intended to fulfil the same role as other forms of welfare provision.[24] Such benefits, however, largely because of their covert nature, do not confer the same stigma on the recipients as their cash equivalents.

Official recognition was given to the overlap of fiscal and cash benefits, especially those granted to provide support for children, with the publication of the proposals for a tax-credit scheme in 1972. As a result of the complexities involved in having a dual system of income maintenance, the Green Paper pointed out, the system of family support was both more costly to administer and more difficult to understand.[25]

Nevertheless, the two systems of welfare provision remain side by side, one for the rich and one for the poor, representing, as Field and Meacher pointed out in their evidence to the House of Commons Expenditure Committee, two welfare states. 'Yet now that massive cuts in public expenditure are being planned, debate is exclusively concentrated on the likely cuts in the provision of help to the poorest. It appears that the Government has no plans to cut the benefits paid to richer members of society through the tax system.'[26] These views were subsequently endorsed by the Expenditure Committee itself, who drew attention to the tenuous distinction between tax allowances and public expenditure in their report on the 1976 White Paper which proposed massive cuts in public spending: 'It would assist rational assessment of Government policy if tax reliefs in relation to housing, children or investment were considered in conjunction with housing subsidies, family allowances or investment grants.' They went on to give the specific example of housing: 'Some part of housing is in public expenditure, some part of it is, in effect, in tax allowances, and it becomes difficult to form a coherent political discussion when, on a subject as important as that, the two halves of the argument are in different places.'[27]

Although the two parallel systems represent equivalent forms of social-welfare provision, they do differ in significant respects. As we shall see in Chapter 8, the administration of the two systems in terms of control and punishment of abuse varies greatly – abuse of the tax system is several times greater than that of social security, yet the incidence of detection and punishment immeasurably lower. In terms of generosity also the second welfare state outshines the first. The examples we have already cited illustrate the point well, but a few further comparisons will show the relative generosity of the State in its provision to the rich through the tax system compared to that intended to mitigate real hardship amongst those at the lower end of the income scale.

The provision for dependent children is one example. Child tax allowances cost the Exchequer £1,510 million in 1976–7 compared with £285 million for family allowances and £18 million for FIS.[28] We have already discussed the very large housing subsidies paid through mortgage interest relief costing £950 million in 1975–6. By contrast the rent and rate rebate scheme intended to benefit low-income households cost the community a total of only 40 per cent that amount.[29] The administration of the two welfare states is very different in another respect. The cash benefits intended for low-income families either diminish in value (as in the case of family allowances) or are withdrawn altogether (as with the various means-tested benefits) as the household's income rises. The consequences of this, reflected in the poverty trap, were outlined earlier. This is not the case however for the benefits payable through the tax system. Here, as we have seen, the value of the allowances rise as income increases.

Conclusion

We began this chapter by outlining two of the basic principles of British income tax: that the poor should be exempt and that the fairest distribution of the tax burden can be achieved through a progressive system of income tax. The first principle has clearly been discarded in the practical administration of the tax system, with the result that the tax threshold is lower than both the supplementary benefit level and the level of eligibility to family income supplement. This has provoked three consequences: first, there are many families dependent on a low wage who are little or no better off working a full week than they would be if dependent on the meagre provision of the Supplementary Benefits Commission. Second, we have the absurd situation in which such families receive supplementary payments from the State but pay all or part of it back as income tax. Third, the low level of the tax threshold, combined with the range of benefits which are subject to a means test, have created the problem of the poverty trap, whereby an increase in money wages could leave the household with less than if they had never received it.

The second principle too has been treated with little respect. It has been agreed in principle that the fairest distribution of the tax burden can be achieved through a progressive system of income tax. In effect however the progressive nature of the British tax system is severely modified. For the great bulk of taxpayers, excluding less than 2 per cent who pay tax at higher rates, the system of income tax is a proportional one. The only element of progression is introduced through the system of tax allowances. But as we have seen these are themselves regressive in their effects, being of greatest benefit to high-income groups. While the personal allowances which can be claimed by all taxpayers do introduce a mild element of progression, this is outweighed heavily by the effects of the many other reliefs and allowances which can be claimed by high-income groups to offset their effective tax burden. We conclude, therefore, that the belief in the progressive system of income tax is more firmly rooted in myth than in reality.

References

1. Royal Commission on the Taxation of Profits and Income, Second Report, Cmd 9105, HMSO, April 1954, p. 33, para. 108.

2. Central Office of Information, *The New British Tax System*, HMSO, May 1973.

3. Royal Commission on the Taxation of Profits and Income, op. cit., p. 48, para. 158.

4. See, for example, M. WYNN, *Family Policy*, Penguin Books, 1970.

5. Royal Commission on Taxation (Canada), Vol. 1, reproduced in R. W. HOUGHTON (ed.), *Public Finance*, Penguin Books, 1970.

6. Royal Commission on the Taxation of Profits and Income, op. cit. p. 32, para. 104.

7. For a fuller discussion of this point see R. HOWELL, MP, 'Low Pay and Taxation', *Low Pay Paper* No. 8, Low Pay Unit, December 1976.

8. See, for instance, F. FIELD, *Poverty: The Facts*, CPAG, 1975.

9. Royal Commission on the Taxation of Profits and Incomes, op. cit. p. 9, para. 154.

10. *Proposals for a Tax-Credit System*, Cmnd 5116, p. 31, para. 121–2.

11. For detailed criticisms of that scheme from a redistributive point of view see *Minutes of Evidence to the Select Committee on Tax-Credit*, N. Kaldor, 29 March 1973, and A. B. Atkinson and Child Poverty Action Group, 12 April 1973.

12. *Hansard*, 12 February 1976, Vol. 905, Col. 335.

13. 'Tax and Poverty', *The Economist*, 24 July 1976.

14. Minutes of Evidence to Select Committee on Tax Credit, 8 February 1973, p. 47.

15. F. FIELD and D. PIACHAUD, 'The Poverty Trap', *New Statesman*, December 1971. For recent examples see Howell, op. cit.

16. An exemption limit was reintroduced in 1935 and lasted until 1952 but was not used as an essential part of the income-tax system.

17. Royal Commission on the Taxation of Profits and Income, op. cit., p. 49, para. 161.

18. TUC, *Economic Review, 1968*, p. 80, para. 259.

19. TUC, op. cit., p. 79, para. 255.

20. Royal Commission on the Taxation of Profits and Income, Final Report, Memorandum of Dissent, Cmnd 9474, HMSO, 1955, p. 355, para. 3.

21. Consumers' Association, *Which? Tax Saving Guide*, 1975–6.

22. *Hansard*, 12 December 1975, Vol. 902, Col. 323.

23. *Hansard*, 7 August 1975.

24. A. L. WEBB and J. E. B. SIEVE, *Income Redistribution and the Welfare State*, Occasional Papers in Social Administration, No. 41, Bell, 1971, pp. 75–6.

25. *Proposals for a Tax-Credit System*, Cmnd 5116, HMSO, 1972.

26. F. FIELD and MOLLY MEACHER, 'Rich Law', *Guardian*, 21 October 1975.
27. *Fourth Report from the Expenditure Committee*, Session 1975–6, House of Commons Paper 299, HMSO, March 1976, p. xiii and p. 19.
28. *Hansard*, 29 June 1976, Vol. 914, Col. 128.
29. *Hansard*, 7 August 1975.

4 The Welfare State: The Poor Man's Burden

In the last chapter we looked at the growth in the tax-allowance welfare state. We now turn to examine those Acts which from 1908 onwards helped to form the other welfare state. Most of the accounts of the growth of the welfare state detail the group of claimants benefiting from each measure, but equally important for the theme of this book is who was called upon to pay for each successive reform. Indeed it is remarkable that few studies even bother to detail the contributions required, let alone go on to consider their distributionary effect. In the first part of this chapter we attempt to answer these questions. We then go on to look at the changing burden of financing the welfare state since 1945. The final section concludes with an examination of why the national-insurance scheme still fails to prevent poverty.

The Rise of National Insurance

The pre-First World War Liberal government introduced two measures which concern our study. The first was the payment of old age pensions in 1908. The second measure was the National Insurance Act of 1911. These Acts are important for two reasons. In the first place it is generally agreed that they form the beginnings of the modern welfare state, but also they contrast two radically different ways of paying for welfare reforms which have a central bearing on our present study.

In 1908, the Old Age Pensions Act made provision for the payment of pensions in the following year of 5 shillings a week to each pensioner who was at least 70 years of age, who had been resident in the United Kingdom for twenty years or more and who had not been in receipt of poor law relief during the last two years. The full pension was payable to those with incomes of £21 a year or less, and a reduced pension was paid to those with incomes rising to £31 a year. The scheme was non-contributory, and by 1913 the annual cost was £12·5 million, which was borne from general taxation.

This reform may seem modest today, but as one authority of the period has commented, 'At the time, non-contributory pensions were regarded as a wildly extravagant piece of class lawmaking. Moreover, as an exemplary piece of social legislation, as a way of transferring wealth from one group to another, tax-supported old age pensions were of almost unequalled effectiveness.'[1] The pensions were non-contributory, not because the Liberal government wished to see an important redistribution of income between classes, but because there were insuperable barriers to a contributory scheme. First and foremost amongst these obstacles was the objection of the Friendly Societies to any scheme which would attract the savings of their working-class clients away from private insurance schemes. That the Liberal government would have preferred a contributory scheme can now be seen from the Cabinet papers of the time. Moreover, when the Liberals came to introduce their second reform they opted for a contributory base and met stiff opposition from some left-wing members of the Labour Party. This small handful of members realized that welfare reforms paid for from general taxation could result in a redistribution of income between classes, whereas the proposed poll tax for the 1911 National Insurance Act meant that the reform would be paid for largely by working people themselves. The significance of the way welfare reforms are paid for has still not been grasped by the full labour movement.

The 1911 Act was divided into two parts. Part One was concerned with the payment of sickness benefit (at 10 shillings a week for 13 weeks for men, and 5 shillings for the next 13 weeks), of a disability pension (of 5 shillings a week), of a maternity benefit (paid at 30 shillings), and the right to treatment in a sanatorium and to seek medical treatment from a GP as a panel patient. All workmen over 16 and earning less than £160 a year were compulsorily insured, as were all manual labourers irrespective of their earnings. Other workers could insure voluntarily, but only by paying both the employer's and employee's contribution.

Workpeople were required to pay 4d a week, the employer 3d a week and the State contributed a further 2d – hence Lloyd George's winning slogan of '9d for 4d'.

The second part of the 1911 National Insurance Act provided unemployment pay to insured workpeople in selected trades.[2] Benefit was paid at 7 shillings a week after one week's waiting period for a maximum of 15 weeks in any twelve-month period. For this benefit both the employer and employee contributed $2\frac{1}{2}$d per week, and $1\frac{2}{3}$d a week came from the Treasury. In total $2\frac{1}{4}$ million men became eligible for unemployment pay out of a total labour force of slightly over 10 million.

Inter-War Reforms

The National Insurance Act passed in 1916 made it possible to extend unemployment insurance to nearly every industry in the UK. Coverage could be made by government order for any enterprise engaged in work for war purposes. However, the Act met with strong resistance from both workpeople and employers and by 1918 only 4 million out of a total of 14 million workers were covered. From 1918 onwards there was a succession of Acts attempting to give some form of welfare payments to those made unemployed during the inter-war years. The last major unemployment Act to reach the Statute Book before the Second World War was passed in 1934. Its major purpose was to establish two boards. The first was the Unemployment Insurance Statutory Committee, which had the power to oversee the national insurance fund. The second board was named the Unemployment Assistance Board and was responsible for the payments of those who were disqualified from a contributory unemployment benefit. However, none of the Acts during the inter-war period changed the financial contributory principles of the 1911 Act. By 1931 employers, workpeople and the State each contributed 10d a week into the national insurance fund.

Lloyd George originally intended to include a widow's and orphan's pension as part of the 1911 reforms. But pressure from the Industrial Societies, bodies like the Prudential, which had developed a massive and very profitable industry in selling funeral policies and who feared that a widow's pension would lessen their attractiveness, resulted in the idea being dropped. The proposal was not resuscitated until 1925, when widows and orphans received a pension as part of the reforms brought forward by Neville Chamberlain. For the theme of this chapter it is important to note why the extension of benefit to widows and orphans, as well as the introduction of a contributory old age pension, should have occurred at this time. Bentley Gilbert has summed up the political motivation behind this measure, noting that it gained widespread support from Conservatives because there 'was the possibility – more than a likelihood, indeed a threat – that the alternative to a contributory pension financed by the working class would be a non-contributory pension financed, it was intimated, by capital levy'.[3]

Chamberlain's Act also dealt with old age pensions. The original 1908 Act had been slightly modified in 1916 when the Government paid a 2s 6d weekly allowance to those who were deemed to be suffering special hardship. In the following year this concession was removed and the means test liberalized by excluding the income from military allowances and certain voluntary savings, while at the same time raising the basic permissible earnings for a full pension to 30 shillings a week. In 1919 the old age pension was raised to 10 shillings a week and the pauper disqualification clause was removed. Chamberlain believed that the ideal pension reform would be one in which the beneficiaries would pay the entire cost of their own pensions.[4] In a very large measure he was successful in this goal. Under the 1925 Act a contributory pension was paid between the age of 65 and 70, at which point people were transferred automatically to the non-contributory pension. Those entering the scheme at 16 would pay the entire cost of their insurance-based pension covering their lives between 65 and 70 as well as 21 per cent of the cost of the 1908 old age pension. It was also calculated that the proportion of the total pension costs supported by new entrants would increase as rates of contribution were raised at regular intervals. The government of the day estimated that by 1956 workers coming into the scheme would pay not only for the entire cost of their own pension, but also the pensions of those still drawing the 1908 benefit. A contributor could expect 10 shillings a week pension, and his widow would be eligible for a similar sum at the age of 65. The contribution principle continued to remain a tripartite one, with 4d a week coming both from employers and from male employees and 3½d a week from the State.

The 1929 Pensions Act allowed benefit to be paid to widows at the age of 55 if their husbands were in the scheme and had died before 4 January 1926. The 1937 Widows' Orphans' and Old Age Contributory Pensions Act extended pension rights to independent workers with incomes of over £250 a year but less than £400 a year (£250 for women). This was the last addition to the national-insurance scheme before the outbreak of the Second World War.

The Post-War Period

At the beginning of *Social Insurance and Allied Services*, Beveridge wrote: 'All the principal causes of interruption or loss of earnings are now the subject of schemes of social insurance. If, in spite of these schemes, so many persons unemployed or sick or widowed are found to be without adequate income . . . this means that the benefits amount to less than subsistence . . . To prevent interruption or destruction of earning power from leading to want, it is necessary to improve the present scheme of social insurance in three directions: by extension of scope to cover persons now excluded, by extension of purpose to cover risks now excluded, and by raising the rates of benefit.'[5] The basic premise of the Beveridge report was that 'the abolition of want requires a double redistribution of income, through social insurance and by family needs'. Family needs were to be met by 'a generous system of children's allowances, sufficient to meet the subsistence needs of all dependent children when the responsible parent is in receipt of any insurance benefit or pension, and of all such children except one in other cases'. In addition, Beveridge said there should be the provision for all children of free school meals and welfare milk and foods.

The redistribution of income through social insurance was to be brought about by the payment of national-insurance benefit which would guarantee claimants an income above the State poverty line. Family allowances were first paid in 1945. The new national-insurance scheme came into force in 1948. The scheme was again financed on a tripartite basis. Flat-rate contributions were collected from workpeople, employers and the government. Working men were required to pay a poll tax of 25d a week and working women who had not opted for the married women's option paid 19d a week. In 1948, for each £2 contributed by both employees and employers, the State contributed £1. However, this level of contribution was maintained for only a single year. The history of the financing of the welfare state in the post-war period can be summarized very briefly. From 1950 onwards the progressive elements in the financing of the welfare state – the Exchequer contribution – was steadily reduced until it reached about 17·2 per cent in 1973–4.

This retreat from progressive taxation was brought about in two ways. At various points of time, the Government made a straight cut in the Exchequer subsidy. For example, in 1952 it amounted to a fraction over 25 per cent. In the following year it was reduced to 14·6 per cent. The declining percentage contribution to the national insurance fund from general taxation can be seen from Figure 7. The second way by which the government cut the progressive element in the financing of the welfare state was by the introduction of and then the increasing reliance on graduated contributions. In 1961 the Conservative government brought in a graduated pension scheme. Workers earning between £9 and £15 a week were required to pay a graduated contribution as well as the flat-rate stamp. But whereas previously the government had made a contribution from the Exchequer to match the flat contributions from workpeople and employers, they made no such contribution to monies arising from graduated contributions. For this very reason graduated contributions began to play an increasing role in the financing of the welfare state and, as we can see from Figure 8, by 1974 the total sum raised from this source was greater than the flat-rate contribution. However, it would be wrong to think that the introduction of and increased reliance on graduated contributions resulted in shifting the cost of the welfare

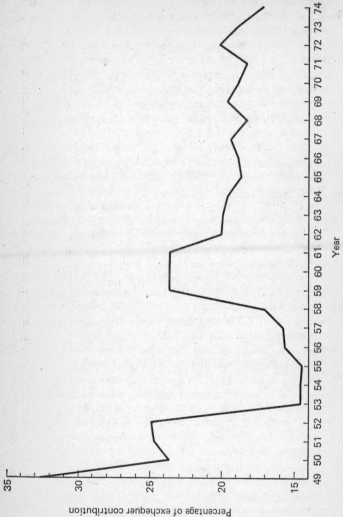

Fig. 7. The size of the Exchequer contribution to the national insurance fund, 1949–74

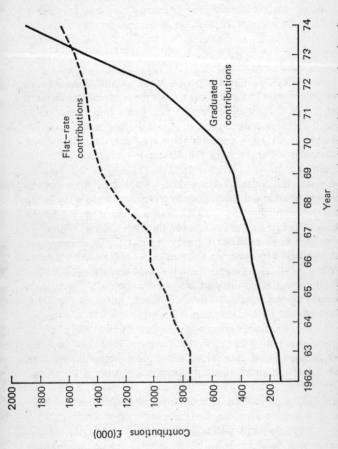

Fig. 8. The size of flat-rate (which carries an Exchequer subsidy) and graduated national-insurance contributions, 1962–74

state onto those with the broadest shoulders. We now turn to consider how the government prevented this happening and in doing so we examine the size of national-insurance contributions which workers on different levels of income have been required to pay since the Second World War.

Onto the Weakest Backs

At the end of the inter-war period national-insurance contributions represented less than 3 per cent of the adult man's industrial wage.[6] The Beveridge reforms, which came into operation in 1948, lifted this contribution to about 3·5 per cent of average earnings. In the early post-war years the trade-union movement was concerned more with the failure to implement fully the Beveridge proposals (which centred on paying generous benefits, for which the State paid one fifth of the cost from general progressive taxation) than with the regressive nature of national-insurance contributions. Indeed, immediately after the implementation of Beveridge's proposals, the trade unions 'offered' an increase in contributions 'if a sufficient increase in benefit could not be secured by restoring the Exchequer grant and by dipping into reserves'.[7] However, by 1954 the trade-union movement was drawing attention to the increasing burden placed on lower-paid workers by the national-insurance stamp. Although the TUC admitted that national-insurance contributions now represented '*on average* a smaller percentage of wages than they did when the scheme was introduced ... it is, however, important to stress that average wages conceal wide variations below the average, and the above statement is not necessarily true of lower-paid workers.'[8]

By 1958 national-insurance contributions amounted to 3·8 per cent of average male earnings. This upward trend continued when the national-insurance poll tax was modified in 1961. As we have already seen, in that year the government introduced an earnings-related pension for which contributors were required to pay earnings-related contributions. Initially those earning over £9 and up to £15 paid their flat-rate contribution together with a wage-related contribution. Those earning more than £15 still paid the same graduated contribution irrespective of their income. This stop is usually called the 'ceiling' in the national-insurance scheme. And it has been this ceiling which has been largely responsible for ensuring that the national-insurance contribution remained a regressive tax. This is a point that Wilkinson and Turner made in their study which covered this subject.[9] As we can see from their table, which is reproduced as Table 8: 'the high flat-rate element combines with the earnings' ceiling to ensure that the percentage of income taken by the contributions continues smaller as one moves up the earnings range. The new scheme did, however, make the contribution system a little less regressive

TABLE 8. Social insurance contributions as a percentage of various levels of male manual workers' earnings

Relative income level	National Insurance and graduated pension as % earnings	
	1960	1970
Highest decile	2·5	4·4
Upper quartile	3·0	5·3
Median	3·6	6·0
Lower quartile	4·5	6·4
Lowest decile	5·4	7·2

SOURCE: Jackson et al., p. 70.

at the middling or moderately high level of wages but this effect disappears as one moves out of wage-incomes normal range.'[10]

The analysis by Wilkinson and Turner covers the years up to 1970. We therefore bring the argument up to date by looking at the development of the national-insurance scheme up to and including the major reforms initiated in 1975. In order to examine this period in detail we look at the contributions for those on the lowest decile (the poorest 10 per cent of wage-earners), those on median earnings (the mid-point in the earnings distribution) and those on the highest decile (the best-paid 10 per cent of workers). And so that we can see the full effect of the ceiling on graduated contributions we look at the money and percentage contributions

TABLE 9. National-insurance contribution in money terms and as a percentage of earnings for male manual workers, 1970–75

Year	Contributions £ p				Contributions as percentage of earnings			
	Lowest decile	Median	Highest decile	3 times median	Lowest decile	Median	Highest decile	3 times median
1970	1·27	1·55	1·69	1·69	7·3	6·0	4·4	2·2
1971	1·36	1·65	1·70	1·70	7·0	5·8	4·1	2·0
1972	1·46	1·85	2·35	2·35	6·8	5·9	5·1	2·5
1973	1·62	2·19	2·73	2·73	6·5	5·9	5·1	2·4
1974	1·81	2·46	3·09	3·09	6·3	5·8	5·1	2·5
1975	2·02	2·93	3·79	3·79	5·5	5·5	5·9	2·4

made by those on three times the median income (see Tables 9 and 10).

The continuing regressive nature of the national-insurance contribution scheme can be seen by comparing both the size of the money contribution and this sum expressed as a percentage of total earnings. For example in 1970 those on the lowest decile

TABLE 10. National-insurance contributions in money terms and as a percentage of female manual workers' earnings, 1970–75 (not contracted out and paying the full stamp)

Year	Contributions £ p				Contributions as percentage of earnings			
	Lowest decile	Median	Highest decile	3 times median	Lowest decile	Median	Highest decile	3 times median
1970	0·75	0·75	1·19	1·56	8·5	5·8	6·4	4·1
1971	0·81	1·02	1·26	1·57	7·9	6·9	6·0	3·6
1972	0·88	1·12	1·42	2·22	7·7	6·8	5·9	4·5
1973	0·95	1·20	1·63	2·60	7·2	6·3	5·9	4·6
1974	1·05	1·38	1·88	2·96	6·6	6·0	5·7	4·3
1975	1·22	1·70	2·40	3·79	5·5	5·5	5·5	4·1

contributed £1·27p out of a weekly wage packet of £17·20p. A male manual worker on three times the median income was required to pay only £1·69p a week on earnings of £76·80p. In other words 7·3 per cent of the earnings of a male manual worker on the lowest decile went in national-insurance contributions, compared with only 2·2 per cent of income for those on three times the median earnings.

Exactly the same picture emerges if we examine the contribution to the insurance fund from manual women workers. A woman on the lowest decile in 1970 paid 75p a week (8·5 per cent of her income) in national-insurance contributions on a weekly wage of £8·80p. A woman worker on three times the median paid a weekly contribution of £1·56p (4·4 per cent of her earnings) on a wage of £38·40p a week.

By 1974 the poorest workers were paying a slightly smaller percentage of their income in contributions. In that year the male manual worker on a wage equal to the lowest decile was contributing 6·3 per cent of his income in contributions, compared with 7·3 per cent in 1970. A similar change occurred for women manual workers on the lowest decile; a fall from 8·5 per cent to 6·6 per cent of earnings. However, the percentage of income taken by way of the national-insurance stamp did not change at all significantly for either men or women manual workers on median earnings over the period 1970–74. But for workers earning the highest decile we can see that, because of the ceiling on graduated contributions, they continue to pay a smaller percentage of their income in contributions than lower-paid workers. This difference in contributions is even more marked if we examine those on three times the median earnings.

In 1974 Sir Keith Joseph piloted onto the Statute Book a bill which made a major change to the means by which working people financed the welfare state. The measure, which came into force in 1975, abolished the stamp and earnings-related contribution and substituted for them a social-security tax of 5·5 per cent of earnings (since increased to 5·75 per cent). However, the ceiling was reintroduced into the new scheme, and the social-security levy was applied to earnings between £11 and £69 a week. The ceiling has since been raised to £96 a week. And once again it is this ceiling on graduated contributions which continues to ensure that the social-security tax remains regressive for male manual workers. The extent of its regressiveness can be seen by looking in Table 9 at the contributions made by manual workers in 1975. Because of the ceiling, male manual workers earning the highest decile (£76·90 per week) contributed only £3·79 a week, which was equal to 4·9 per cent of their earnings, compared with 5·5 per cent for other workers. This difference is more marked if we examine those earning three times median earnings. Again because of the ceiling, the money contribution was pegged at £3·79 a week, which, on a wage of £159·6 per week, resulted in a contribution of 2·4 per cent of income. But for the ceiling, the higher-paid would have been contributing £8·78p a week.

The position in respect of women workers is somewhat different. Largely because women are paid at a much lower rate than men the ceiling on contributions, which is usually set at one and a half times male average earnings, ensures that most females pay 5·5 per cent of their earnings in contributions.[11] It is only when one examines women on three times median earnings (see Table 10) that we find them paying a smaller percentage of their income, in this case 4·1 per cent, in the social-security tax.

Two major conclusions can be drawn from this analysis. The first is that despite the Sex Discrimination Act national-insurance contributions remain a poll tax for most male workers, but, because of their lower wages, and because the ceiling on contributions is the same for male and female workers, national-insurance contributions have been converted into a proportional tax for the overwhelming majority of workers. Second, the cost of financing the welfare state rose appreciably during the Labour Party's period in office from 1964, and this was disproportionately borne by the poor. Likewise the welfare tax burden on the poor was eased somewhat during the Heath administration's tenure of office from 1970 to 1974. A further lessening of the burden occurred in 1975 when the Tory measure scrapping the national-insurance contribution and card system and replacing it by a proportional social-security tax came into effect. However, the ceiling on contributions remained and so ensured that the richest taxpayers paid a smaller percentage of their salary in contributions than other groups of workers.

Why the Scheme Failed

The financing of the welfare state is regressive both because of the nature of the contributions placed on working people and the steady reduction of the Exchequer contribution to the insurance fund throughout the post-war period. And because of this very significant reduction to the fund from general taxation, the national-insurance scheme has not had the resources to abolish poverty. Beveridge envisaged that insurance benefits would be paid at a level above the State poverty line. He proposed a 24-shilling allowance for single people and 40 shillings for a married couple's weekly benefit, irrespective of whether the claimant was drawing sickness or unemployment benefit or an old age pension. These sums were based on the assumption that prices would rise by 25 per cent during the war years. The incoming Labour government fixed benefits at 26 shillings and 42 shillings for single persons and married couples respectively on the grounds that the cost of living would be held at 31 per cent above the pre-war level. In setting these benefits the government claimed that the new level of benefits would provide 'a broad subsistence basis' on the lines proposed by Beveridge.[12] However, as one of the first critics of the post-war welfare state has observed, 'prices had already risen by far more than 31 per cent [when benefits were introduced], the general price level throughout 1946 was at least 54 per cent above the pre-war [level]'.[13]

The essence of the Beveridge scheme was its insurance base. In other words contributions were set at a level which, if people entered the scheme at 16, would ensure that they had built up sufficient contributions to finance the benefits they would draw throughout their working and retired life. But the Attlee government believed it wrong to introduce a major reconstruction of the welfare state which would exclude many older members of the community. Such political pressure to modify the Beveridge scheme was foreseen when the Government Actuary reported on *Social Insurance and Allied Services*. In order to keep the scheme financially sound the government would be required to pay an increasing Exchequer contribution to cover the costs of paying benefit to those who had an incomplete insurance record. The Government Actuary's original report in *Social Insurance and Allied Services* estimated that by 1965 the Exchequer would be contributing 46 per cent of the social insurance budget.[14] In fact as we have seen the reverse has occurred. In 1974 the Exchequer

contribution was exactly 17·2 per cent. The failure of the government to keep its side of the bargain in the financing of the welfare
state for those who had been unable to pay the necessary contributions has meant that for many years the insurance fund
has not had sufficient monies to pay out benefits which would
guarantee claimants an income above the State poverty line.
Indeed, on the rare occasion when the insurance fund has built
up a surplus, this has been used as an excuse for a further
reduction in the Exchequer supplement to the fund, rather than
in attempting to implement fully the Beveridge proposals.

Even had successive governments fulfilled their commitment to
finance the payment of benefits to those with inadequate contributions, so allowing the insurance fund to pay out adequate
benefits, we would still have had poverty in the post-war world.
This is because the Beveridge scheme excluded the two groups of
claimants who, because their earnings are interrupted, are unable
to earn an income above the State poverty line. As Ruth Lister
has written: 'Beveridge glossed over completely the problem of
those disabled from birth or childhood who had never been able
to work and build up a contribution record. He did propose "an
end of marriage allowance" for women akin to widow's benefit,
but with the proviso that this would not be payable if the marriage
"ended through her own fault or voluntarily without just
cause".'[15] The difficulties associated with establishing a person's
'fault', or 'just cause', ensured that this proposal was not
implemented.

The second main group excluded from the national-insurance
scheme was the long-term unemployed. As the original scheme
was drawn up 'all the principal cash payments – unemployed
disability and retirement, will continue so long as the need lasts'.
However, this was not accepted in respect of unemployment
benefit, which was originally limited for a duration of 7 months
to which further days could be added, depending on the claimant's
insurance record, so that benefit could be drawn for a maximum
of 19 months. In 1966 this provision was changed. An earnings-
related unemployment benefit was introduced payable to
claimants for 6 months. A flat-rate benefit continues to be paid
for up to the first year of unemployment.

The result of this failure to implement Beveridge fully, and to extend insurance coverage to those groups at present outside its scope, has resulted in a massive increase in the numbers of people dependent on means-tested benefits. The number of households drawing supplementary benefits has risen by over 150 per cent. In addition there has been a growing dependence on other means-tested benefits. Under the Housing Finance Act Mr Heath's

TABLE 11. Major unclaimed means-tested benefits, 1975

Benefit	Number eligible	Numbers not claiming	Value of unclaimed benefits £m
Supplementary benefit:			
OAP, households	2,125,000	450,000 *	129·2
families	1,588,000	470,000 *	361·7
Rent rebates and allowances:			
council tenants	1,100,000	273,333	40·5
private unfurnished tenants	550,000	412,500	51·7
private furnished tenants	125,000	112,500	16·4
Rate rebates	3,500,000	1,050,000	40·9
FIS	93,000	23,000	4·8
Free school meals	940,800	156,800	13·0
		TOTAL:	658·2

* 1974 estimates.
SOURCE: Parliamentary answers to Richard Wainwright.

administration introduced a national system of rent rebates and allowances. At the present time something like 1·9 million households are deemed too poor to pay their rent in full and are therefore eligible for a means-tested rebate. Full details of the importance that means tests play in the welfare state can be seen from Table 11.[16] This also gives information on the ineffectiveness of means tests as a weapon against poverty. Where figures are available, we give details of the take-up of the benefit. We also estimate the value of benefits which go unclaimed.

Conclusion

In this chapter we have shown that the contributory system of national-insurance benefits has failed in a number of important respects. It does not give complete coverage, nor does it guarantee claimants an adequate income above the State poverty line without the need to resort to means-tested assistance. What it has managed to ensure is that much of the welfare state's income maintenance proposals are paid for by working people themselves, and that the poorest workers are called upon to pay a significant part of their income to help finance not only their own benefits but of those who were brought into the scheme without full contribution records. It is in this respect that the financing of the welfare state has added to the growing regressiveness of the British tax system.

References

1. BENTLEY B. GILBERT, *The Evolution of National Insurance in Great Britain*, Michael Joseph, 1966, p. 159.
2. The selected trades covered were building, construction works, shipbuilding, mechanical engineering, iron founding, construction of vehicles and sawmilling trades.
3. BENTLEY B. GILBERT, *British Social Policy 1914–1939*, Batsford, 1970, p. 235.
4. ibid., p. 244.
5. Cmnd 6404, HMSO, 1942.
6. KATHERINE HOOD, *Room at the Bottom*, Lawrence & Wishart, 1960, p. 33.
7. *TUC Report*, 1953, reporting a meeting in 1951.
8. *TUC Report*, 1954, p. 143.
9. DUDLEY JACKSON, H. A. TURNER and FRANK WILKINSON, *Do Trades Unions Cause Inflation?*, Cambridge University Press, 1972.
10. ibid., p. 70.
11. For an analysis of low pay among women see the essay by CHRIS POND and STEVE WINYARD in *Are Low Wages Inevitable?*, ed. FRANK FIELD, Russell Press, 1977.

12. *Hansard*, 6 February 1946.
13. HOOD, op. cit., p. 14.
14. Cmnd 6404, HMSO, 1942, p. 209.
15. RUTH LISTER, *Social Security: The Case for Reform*, Child Poverty Action Group, 1975, p. 27.
16. For more comprehensive information see FRANK FIELD, *Poverty: The Facts*, Child Poverty Action Group, 1975.

5 The Structure of Indirect Taxes

We have seen in Chapter 1 that income tax is ostensibly based on the principle that a person should be taxed according to his ability to pay. The same cannot be said of expenditure taxes, where egalitarian principles seem to have been consistently lacking over the centuries. The earliest expenditure taxes – excise duties payable to the State on articles manufactured under licence – were first introduced in 1660 on ale, beer, cider, spirits, tea and coffee, and have since fluctuated according to the needs of the Exchequer. The choice of taxable items appears in the early days to have deliberately excluded those consumed by a quarter of the population referred to as 'cottagers and paupers', who could clearly not afford to contribute to the National Exchequer. On the other hand, even in the seventeenth century, expenditure taxes were unduly concentrated upon items consumed by the less wealthy sections of the community, with half of excise taxes being levied on the national beverage, beer. The regressive nature of excise taxes (which raised £26·9 million in 1688–1702) contrasted strongly with the clearly progressive principle behind the poll tax (also introduced in 1660). The only serious attempt to tax the rich therefore was the land tax, which applied primarily to wealthy landowners and provided the Exchequer with £19·1 million in the same period. A similarly inconsistent pattern will emerge as we look at the recent history of expenditure taxes and examine the range of goods covered and the amount of revenue thereby raised. In this chapter we examine the importance of excise duties, the role of selective employment tax and the introduction of purchase tax and its replacement by the value-added tax. In the following chapter we examine the incidence of indirect taxation.

Excise Duties

A considerable proportion of total revenue in this country is derived from excise duties on a very few items, notably tobacco, beer, spirits, wine and hydro-carbon oils. The weight of these excise duties is clear from Table 12, which gives the information

TABLE 12. Value of customs and excise duties 1973 and 1976

	1972–3 £m	1975–6 (*provisional*) £m
Purchase tax	1,387·8	1·0
VAT	—	3,455·0
Hydro-carbon oil	1,553·7	1,544·1
Tobacco	1,182·9	1,680·3
Spirits, wine	582·0	909·6
Beer	491·7	652·1
Betting, gaming	171·3	265·0
Car tax	—	180·0
Protective duties	368·7	559·4
Other revenue duties	7·1	8·5
Total customs and excise duties	5,745·2	9,255·0
Income tax	6,477·0	15,018·2
Corporation tax	1,533·1	1,995·4
Motor vehicle licence duties	490·0	632·7

NOTE: The excise duties on hydro-carbon oils, tobacco, spirits, wine and beer account for more than half of all expenditure taxes (£4,786m) and amount to nearly one third of income-tax receipts.
SOURCE: *Financial Statistics* No. 168, April 1976, pp. 27–9.

just before the replacement of purchase tax by VAT and for 1975–6.

Excise duty on tobacco represented 64 per cent of consumers' expenditure on tobacco in 1973; the percentage in the case of alcohol was 33·6 per cent and in the case of motor running costs 44·2 per cent. It is the regressive impact of the tax on tobacco together with the neutral impact of the other excise duties and

VAT throughout the income range which very largely eliminates the advantage to low-income families in Britain of the exemption of food and fuel from taxation. Significantly, purchase tax and, as yet, VAT have had a neutral effect upon the distribution of income in this country.

Why then are excise duties levied at ever-increasing rates by both Labour and Conservative Chancellors? Three powerful arguments have been put forward: medical, environmental and financial. The justification for heavy taxes on alcoholic drinks is easily found in the increasing numbers of people with a drinking problem. The most recent official estimate of serious-problem drinkers in England and Wales is 400,000, though this is almost certainly a very conservative one in view of the tendency of many alcoholics or 'very heavy drinkers' to hide their plight for as long as possible from the medical profession and the world at large.[1] Drink is undoubtedly a problem, but taxes are not imposed on alcohol in the expectation of a subsequent fall in demand. On the contrary, it is the inelastic demand for alcoholic drinks and other goods subject to excise duties which seduces successive Chancellors to increase the rates of duty charged. Any Chancellor knows that an extra penny on a pint of beer will not lead to a proportionate drop in demand. He can therefore be assured of additional revenue from this source.

In the case of tobacco the government's dilemma is more marked. In 1976 the Labour government sponsored a major publicity campaign to discourage smoking while knowing that in revenue terms the success of the campaign would be a disaster! The health hazards of smoking extend far beyond the more emotive cancer risk. Any government therefore finds it easy to justify the astronomical excise on tobacco. But a cynical observer might be excused for drawing the conclusion that the publicity campaigns are a piece of window-dressing behind which even Labour governments have sought to raise taxes on the poorest members of society: pensioners, disabled and unemployed men who the government knows will sooner do without food or warmth than forgo their pipe or packet of cigarettes. The resilience of the demand for tobacco was illustrated by a recent estimate that a tax increase of 5p on tobacco would raise fully £200 million of additional revenue,[2] and again by the Chancellor's budget speech of the same year when he predicted an increase in revenue of £275 million as a result of an additional 7p on a packet of twenty cigarettes.[3] In terms of equity it is hard to justify an indirect tax system under which the average tax ranges from 15 per cent in the case of non-smokers and non-drinkers to as much as 30 per cent in the case of heavy smokers and drinkers.

Environmental considerations have been put forward in defence of the prohibitive oil excise duty: the need to preserve oil supplies and to curb the ever-increasing popularity of the private motor car, for example. Recent increases in petrol duty have no doubt played a part in the recent drop in consumption. In 1975,

TABLE 13. Selective consumers' expenditure in the UK (current prices £m)

	1971	1972	1973	1974	1975
Alcoholic drink	2,602	2,910	3,416	3,927	4,910
Tobacco	1,691	1,808	1,945	2,237	2,741
Betting and gaming	367	397	443	508	581

NOTE: All the figures are estimates. The bases for making them are described in *National Accounts Statistics: Sources and Methods*, HMSO, 1968.
SOURCE: *Hansard*, 6 March 1976, written answers, Vol. 906, Col. 176.

for example, consumption was about 10 per cent below the level expected on the basis of pre-1973 trends.[4]

Nevertheless, a more honest argument for the preservation of high excise duties on the items concerned is the potential of these items as revenue producers. Not only are they consumed in very considerable quantities by many millions of people (Table 13) but, as already noted, the demand for the goods is only marginally affected by an increase in price.

When we come to consider the costs of administering VAT and the problems of collecting and monitoring multiple rates of the tax on a variety of items which may be sold by a single stockist, it will be appreciated that from the administrative standpoint the collection of £4,786 million of revenue from a mere three categories of goods (alcoholic beverages, tobacco and oil) is indeed an achievement of some worth. But despite the apparent advantages of heavy duties applied to a limited number of items, harmonization of all indirect taxes within the EEC will profoundly affect the structure and rates of both excise duties and VAT in Britain. Before examining the effects of harmonization within the EEC, which are detailed in the following chapter, we will outline the past and present structure of the indirect taxes, including purchase tax, the selective employment tax and value-added tax.

From Purchase Tax and SET to VAT

The consumer's heyday was in the nineteenth century, when import duties were swept away in a tide of free-trade mania, leaving all necessities tax-free by 1860. The tide was reversed however in October 1940, when the needs of war led to the introduction of purchase tax. It is perhaps unfair to judge the equity of purchase tax during the war years when the revenue requirements and shortage of basic necessities led to the imposition of astronomic rates of tax, reaching a peak of 125 per cent of cost on a number of items during 1947–8. Within ten years, however, the rates and exemptions were rationalized and an attempt was made to achieve a number of objectives, notably: to tax consumers in accordance with their ability to pay; to derive more than £500 million in revenue; to minimize administrative costs and inconvenience to the taxpayer; to avoid hindering exports; and to provide a means of contributing to the management of demand.

An essential feature of the tax was its narrow base, excluding food and fuel and all services. Equally essential to the equity objective was the decision in 1958 to tax a range of items at three different rates. Items which might be regarded as essential (including clothing, footwear and furniture for example) were taxed at 10 per cent. Popular extras such as confectionery and ice cream carried an intermediate rate of 15 per cent while luxuries were penalized with a 25 per cent rate. The attempt to vary the tax burden according to the consumer's ability to pay may have succeeded in the early years, but increasingly items classed as luxuries became accepted as necessities for the elderly and disabled as well as for low-income earners. The incidence of purchase tax consequently fell to an ever greater extent on low-income families. Obvious examples of latter-day necessities are the radio and television, which were taxed at 25 per cent and yet are the lifeline of housebound elderly or disabled people and poor families in overcrowded conditions with few recreational outlets. Despite this trend, the exemption of food and fuel, which account for such a high proportion of low-income households' expenditure, ensured that purchase tax was never seriously regressive.

As a revenue raiser, purchase tax became increasingly ineffective as consumers' expenditure in this country on the goods subject to purchase tax steadily declined relative to total consumption. Since the rates of purchase tax were not increased to compensate for the decline in expenditure on the taxed items, the weight of purchase tax in the total tax bill declined steadily until the tax was replaced by VAT in 1973.

The most mourned features of the purchase tax since its replacement have been its administrative simplicity and low cost of collection. The tax was restricted to a selected group of items which together accounted for rather less than one quarter of total consumers' expenditure in 1962. Furthermore, the tax was a single-stage tax payable at the wholesale stage of distribution. Only when wholesalers or manufacturers (who were registered for purchase tax) sold goods to unregistered firms (usually retailers) was any tax paid. The tax collectors were therefore concerned with a comparatively small number of registered firms (approximately 80,000 collection points), so that the total cost of administration was maintained at about £4 million per year.

Amongst the untaxed items were food, fuel, children's clothing, household cleaning materials, books and newspapers, secondhand cars, cookers, lawn mowers and horticultural goods. In fact one could envisage a single adult surviving quite well with good food, central heating and even a fine garden without paying a penny in purchase tax.

In contrast to all this our European neighbours were struggling with an infinitely complex administrative nightmare called the 'cascade turnover tax'. The single advantage of this tax, which was more apparent than real, was the imposition of low rates of tax to achieve a sizable revenue. However, the other side of this coin was the fact that the tax was paid in full on each transaction at every point in the chain of production and distribution. There were three main disadvantages to a cumulative multi-stage tax of this kind: first, the tax encouraged vertical integration, that is, the takeover by one producer of firms involved in successive stages of the production process. Thus a car manufacturer would be wise to buy up producers of tyres, ball-bearings, glass for windows, steel-plating and so on, rather than pay tax on all these inputs. He would then reduce the tax bill still further if he owned his own retail outlets. Second, the tax fell equally on investment and consumption and thus penalized investment comparatively more than purchase tax or VAT. Thirdly, exports are not generally taxed in the country of origin, but under a cascade turnover tax it was impossible to calculate the amount of tax to be refunded, since the total tax paid on each product depended upon the amount of tax borne at successive stages of the production process. This could not be precisely known.

In Britain no such problems arose. Quite simply, registered firms paid no purchase tax on exports. No refund was necessary. Similarly a registered firm paid no purchase tax on imported goods until they were sold to an unregistered buyer. The distortion of trade was thus minimized in this country at least as far as the application of purchase tax was concerned.

The Selective Employment Tax

In the face of a steady decline in purchase-tax revenue as a proportion of GNP the Labour government sought, in 1966, to find a way to increase revenue without further penalizing manufacturing industry, the sector already subject to purchase tax and excise duties. The selective employment tax (SET as it came to be known), which applied to carefully selected industries, seemed to fulfil this central objective and was thus brought into effect in September 1966.[5]

The second and longer-term objective of the tax defined in the White Paper was the encouragement of economy in the use of labour in service industries, thus making more labour available for the expansion of manufacturing industry. This second objective has been strongly criticized on the grounds that economy in the use of labour in manufacturing industry itself would be more beneficial for the purpose envisaged than economy in the service sector alone, and certainly the implication that employment in a service industry is in some sense inferior to employment in manufacturing industry was bitterly resented.

The tax applied to the majority of service industries, though transport and communications and all self-employed persons were specifically excluded; the tax should not however be regarded as a tax on services only. On the contrary, it also applied to professional and scientific services and the distributive trades employed by manufacturing industry, thus spreading the burden of the tax over the great majority of consumer goods.

SET applied to 7·5 million employees (without full refund) or more than 33·2 per cent of all employees in Britain. The tax was levied at a flat rate for each employee regardless of income but varied according to the age and sex of each employee. In 1966 the same flat rate applied to every employee of a given sex over the age of 18, whether as little as eight or as many as forty hours were worked. The result was predictable: part-time workers were encouraged, and in some cases forced, to work either less than eight hours (when no SET would be payable) or full-time (when the SET burden would represent a smaller proportion of payroll costs). In 1967, in response to representations about the implications of the tax for part-time workers, the SET rate for employees working over eight but under twenty-one hours was cut to 50 per cent of the rate for full-time employees. Again in 1968 the relative treatment of part-time workers was improved when the full SET rate was increased while the part-time rates for men and women over the age of 18 were not. From 1968 until 1973, when SET and purchase tax were replaced by the value-added tax, the part-time rates for adults remained at one third of the full-time rates.[6]

The tax was collected from all civil employers in the private and public sectors but later refunded to those not defined as within the scope of the tax. Manufacturing enterprises not only received a full refund of the tax but also a premium of, for example, 37½p per week in 1966, for each male employed and smaller sums for women and young persons on the payroll.

In the public sector the main public utilities received rebates of the tax and publicly owned manufacturing enterprises such as the National Coal Board received premiums. Special arrangements were made in the case of the NHS, for example, where the tax payments were reimbursed to hospitals and other employers of NHS staff; and the armed forces, in respect of which the central government exempted itself from the tax.

The Social and Economic Effects of SET

The overall effect of SET upon the distribution of income is unfortunately not known. However, we do know that the tax did have a number of consequences, some of which were more acceptable than others. Firstly, the application of the tax to the distributive trades meant that the tax applied to almost all foods, contrary to the long-standing tradition in this country of exempting food from taxation. Secondly, SET applied to a range of services which were exported. However, this may not have been quite the disadvantage it was made out to be. If the demand for the exports concerned declined by a smaller proportion than the price increase caused by the tax, then the net effect of the tax would have been an improvement in the balance of payments. Only if the demand for the exports were elastic and fell sharply in response to the price increase were the results undesirable. Thirdly, the interference of the SET in the freedom of part-time employees to choose the number of hours they worked, although mitigated after the initial year, nevertheless remained a cause for discontent throughout the life of the tax.

In quantitative terms, even these effects were not great. In 1969 87 per cent of employees in large retail companies worked full-time (0·4 per cent more than in 1966, when SET was introduced). The impact of SET upon part-timers was clarified by the response of large retailers to the Reddaway Report survey. Fully 60 per cent of respondents to the survey reported that they had replaced part-timers for whom SET was liable (working eight to thirty hours) by those for whom it was not (those working less than eight hours). Only 25 per cent had replaced part-timers with full-timers.[7] For individuals whose working hours were reduced from, say, thirty-one to seven the income effect was considerable. Thus it was among the part-time workers, who represented 13 per cent of full-time equivalents in the labour force, that the brunt was felt and, in a minority of cases, felt deeply.

The employers however were not immune from the effects of the SET. Retail profit margins were reduced by more than half the cost of SET in the distributive trades, despite the considerable increase in the productivity of employees following the introduction of the tax and the consequent saving in payroll costs. If more than half the burden of SET in the distributive trades was borne by retailers, the remainder of the cost was shared between those who lost earnings (as a result of a shortening of the working week, for example) and consumers who paid higher prices. One estimate of the price effect of SET throughout the industries affected suggests that two thirds of the cost of SET was passed on to the consumer in the form of higher prices.[8] If this estimate is correct, the impact of the tax on employment patterns and profit margins will have been less severe in the construction industry, professional services and other establishments covered by the tax than was the case in the distributive trades studied by Reddaway for his First Report.

In conclusion, the selective employment tax earned £320·9 million of revenue for the Exchequer in 1971–2 at an administrative cost of a mere £11·9 million, thus achieving the first objective set out in the White Paper.[9]

At the same time the available evidence suggests that SET increased the productivity of labour in the service trades, at least in the short term. The tax was widely criticized on a number of counts but perhaps most vehement were the claims that the tax penalized service industries unduly. Not until the tax was replaced by VAT, which placed a heavier tax burden upon services, were the merits of the selective employment tax appreciated.

VAT in Britain

The value-added tax is a means of taxing final consumers' spending by instalments. In two important ways the new tax differs from its predecessors: firstly, it is a multi-stage tax (purchase tax was a single-stage tax); and secondly it is in principle a comprehensive tax levied on all final consumer goods and services *except* those specifically exempt. Both the purchase tax and SET, on the other hand, were levied on a narrowly defined list of goods and services. The value-added tax is paid at each stage in the production and distribution chain whenever goods are sold from one firm to another or ultimately to the consumer.

If we take for illustrative purposes a VAT rate of 10 per cent (the rate at which the tax was first introduced), we can illustrate how the tax is paid at each stage of production, is rebated to producers and ultimately paid in full by the consumer. Let us assume that the primary producer buys no inputs, so pays no VAT himself. He produces £100 worth of goods and sells them to a manufacturer. He will then collect £10 VAT (10 per cent of £100) from the manufacturer and will pay this to the Customs and Excise. He has gained and lost nothing as a result of this transaction. He has merely acted as a tax collector. Ten per cent VAT is chargeable to the manufacturer, who pays £110 for his £100 worth of goods. But then he can pass this cost on to the buyer of his goods – the wholesaler. If the value added to the goods by the manufacturer is £100, bringing total value to £200, then the tax payable at this stage is a further £10, bringing total VAT to £20. This the manufacturer charges to the wholesaler. The manufacturer too gains and loses nothing from the VAT. He merely collects £20 from the wholesaler, £10 of which he paid to the primary producer to cover VAT on his inputs and £10 of which he pays to the Customs and Excise. And so the chain continues, with each producer paying tax on his inputs and passing this on to the next buyer plus tax on his own value added, until the article is sold to the final consumer, who must pay the total price including all the VAT due. The consumer cannot pass the tax on to anyone and so the buck stops there. In the example given in Table 14 he pays £300 for goods plus £30 VAT. None of this burden has fallen on any of the producing firms. This is an 'ideal' case, and there are undoubtedly situations where a manufacturer or retailer may feel unable to pass on the full burden of VAT and some of the cost will be borne by him at least in the short run. For our purposes it will be assumed that the incidence of VAT falls squarely upon the consumer. This is the intention and in the long run is probably a fair assumption.

TABLE 14. How VAT applies at each stage of production and exchange

	Purchase price to seller exc. VAT £	Purchase price inc. VAT £	Selling price exc. VAT £	VAT liability £	VAT credit £	VAT due £
Farmer sells to manufacturer	0	0	100	10	0	10
Manufacturer sells to wholesaler	100	110	200	20	10	10
Wholesaler sells to retailer	200	220	250	25	20	5
Retailer sells to consumer	250	275	300	30	25	5
						—
						30

The total cost to the consumer is £330, of which VAT accounts for £30.

In the case of VAT, if the rate is 10 per cent then the *retail* price is inflated by 10 per cent. Purchase tax on the other hand was based upon the wholesale price, so that a rate of 10 per cent would inflate the retail price by less than 10 per cent. The cascade turnover tax inflated retail prices by a considerably greater percentage than the rate of the tax itself because of the cumulative effect of the tax.

In order to avoid serious opposition to the introduction of VAT, only 55 per cent of consumers' expenditure was covered by the tax and the traditional exemption of food and fuel from expenditure taxes was maintained by means of zero-rating. The immediate effects of the switchover from purchase tax to VAT were thus minimized. In addition to food and fuel, the list of zero-rated items included all exports, books and newspapers, journals, petrol (for a time), the construction of buildings, fares on public transport and drugs and medicines supplied on prescription. No tax is payable on zero-rated items and any tax payable on inputs can be reclaimed. ·

A somewhat different and less privileged category of goods qualifies for exemption from VAT. The significant difference between zero-rating and exemption is the fact that any inputs to exempt items are chargeable for VAT and no tax refund can be claimed. Items on the exempt list include land, insurance, postage, finance, education and health services and finally betting and gaming (which bear excise duty). When VAT was first introduced, popularly consumed goods such as confectionery, soft drinks, ice cream and potato crisps were also exempt, having been subject to purchase tax. On its return to power in 1974 the Labour Party made a number of changes, the effect of which was to reduce, if only marginally, the regressive effects of VAT. The standard rate was reduced from 10 to 8 per cent in July 1974 and the higher rate of 25 per cent on petrol was extended to a wider range of luxury items in April 1975, though the rate on luxury goods was subsequently reduced to $12\frac{1}{2}$ per cent in April 1976.[10] The contentious issue of defining a 'luxury' item returned to the political arena. The very considerable imports of electrical goods, radios and television sets (see Table 15), for example, induced Mr Healey to impose the higher rate of VAT on these items despite their widespread use by low-income families, pensioners and the disabled.

The anomalies produced were numerous and the arbitrary nature of the distinction between standard and luxury items can be illustrated by selecting just a few examples. Why, for example, are ironing boards regarded as necessities (VAT 8 per cent) if irons are luxuries (VAT $12\frac{1}{2}$ per cent)? How can films be neces-

sities (VAT 8 per cent) if cameras are luxuries and taxed at the
luxury rate? And is a vacuum cleaner (VAT 12½ per cent) any
less of a necessity than a cooker (VAT 8 per cent)? Less contro-
versial however is the 12½ per cent VAT rate on furs, jewellery,
goldsmiths' and silversmiths' wares, boats, aircraft and caravans.

TABLE 15. Imports, 1974

	£m
TV sets	89
Tape players	59
Cameras	26
Radios	74
Records/tapes	43
Films	25
Fridges	29
Other gadgets	16
Heaters	24
Washing machines	23
Shavers	4
	£412

SOURCE: Mary Goldring, 'VAT and Super VAT', *Investors' Chronicle*,
April 1975.

Arguments for the Changeover from Purchase Tax to VAT

There were five main reasons supporting the changeover from
purchase tax to VAT. Firstly, it was argued that the broader-
based VAT would enable an increase in revenue without a substantial increase in the standard rate of the tax. However, if
VAT can be broadened to include an ever-increasing number of
items, probably ultimately including food, then the same applied
to purchase tax and its companion tax, SET.

Secondly, proponents of the tax argued that VAT does not
penalize exports and so will assist Britain's balance of payments.
However, exports were not subject to purchase tax either. The
only element of tax affecting exports under a purchase-tax

system was the tax on business expenditures such as office furniture, which were not recoverable. It has been estimated that the net effect of the switchover to VAT has been an increase in exports to the value of £20 million, but balanced against this has been the loss in purchase tax and SET revenue from foreign purchasers of some £40 million. The bulk of the latter could be accounted for by services subject to SET. It has been argued that exporters under VAT are in a very similar position to exporters under a purchase tax, with the important difference that an exporter under VAT is obliged to lend to the fiscal authorities his tax on inputs which is later repaid to him.[11] The Federation of British Industry therefore concluded in 1962 that 'we do not understand how the rebate system can be described as having an export incentive effect not promised by purchase tax, nor do we understand the psychology or logic behind the suggestion that it is better to pay tax and later have it refunded than never to pay tax at all'![12]

Thirdly, the full impact of VAT rests on the consumer, so, it was reasoned, the tax would promote investment and economic growth. As already noted, if we assume some decline in demand in response to price increases, both purchase tax and VAT would have a depressing effect upon demand and hence upon investment. One estimate suggests that two thirds of SET was passed on in the form of higher prices, but in the manufacturing sector where investment is needed and where purchase tax applied the tax was almost certainly passed on in full to the consumer in normal circumstances.[13]

The fourth important argument for VAT was put in the following terms: a single rate of VAT on all commodities would not distinguish between different commodities and would not distort the market in favour of one group of commodities against another. However, the introduction of the higher rate of VAT in April 1975 and the existence already of a zero rate on some goods undermined the neutrality principle, though to a somewhat smaller extent than the purchase-tax rates had done previously. (Purchase-tax rates prior to the budget of 1972 had been 45, 30, 18 and 11·25 per cent. As from 1972 the four rates were reduced to three: 25, 18 and 11·25 per cent.) Again there is no reason why VAT should be limited to a smaller number of rates than a single-stage purchase tax.

Lastly, it was argued that the VAT does not distort investment policy as it produces no difference in costs between relatively capital-intensive and relatively labour-intensive methods of production, or between vertically integrated firms and those which specialize. This argument applied equally well, however, to purchase tax.

None of the five major economic arguments in favour of VAT stands up to examination. The adverse administrative implications of the tax, on the other hand, are indisputable. In contrast to the single-stage purchase tax, *all* transactions of goods subject to VAT at every level of production must be invoiced for VAT, even though the tax on inputs is later returned to the company. Tax calculations have to be made on many millions of invoices each year.

Only 1,500 civil servants were required for the administration of purchase tax and a further 600 for SET, whereas 10,500 people were employed to administer VAT in 1975 to raise £2,500 million for the government. One estimate of the total additional burden falling on the country in the form of additional collection and administration costs to industry and government is £300 million a year.[14] This estimate is based on the assumption that industry has had to employ at least 50,000 extra people for administration and accounting purposes.

Evasion of VAT

It has been argued that a multi-stage tax is more difficult to evade than a single-stage one.[15] However, in view of the small number of companies subject to purchase tax, this allegation probably does not hold water. The monitoring of some 65,000 taxpayer registrations was manageable – much more so than the two million or so involved in the collection of VAT.

An indication of the problems already encountered was given by the Public Accounts Committee report in 1975, which pointed to an annual loss of revenue of £35–40 million in VAT underpayments (a 1·5 per cent shortfall). The Customs and Excise

Group General Secretary, Jack Morrish, declared that their own estimates indicate a degree of avoidance and evasion several times the figure quoted. He believes that a proportion of traders regard VAT as a voluntary tax – 'if they can avoid it they will'.

It is commonly assumed that we have a somewhat higher degree of tax morality in Britain than exists on the Continent. Nevertheless, it is worth noting that Italy estimates a 50 per cent revenue loss through tax evasion. In France, M. Fourcade, the Finance Minister, singled out the VAT as being a particularly expensive tax in terms of tax evasion. 'What we want to track down particularly,' he said 'are the fraudulent practices such as sales without proper billing, to evade the impact of the VAT. Such practices are universal in France and tax evasion is reckoned to rob the state of some 60,000 million francs a year, or 20–30 per cent of revenue from all taxes.'[16] The experience of our European neighbours does not induce a sense of confidence in VAT as an unavoidable tax.

The main opportunities for evasion seem to be through the failure to invoice sales to final consumers or tax-exempt purchasers (how tempting for the decorator to offer his customer a handsome reduction in the cost of his work if the bill can be paid in cash); the misclassification of goods in tax returns (this method can be used only when there are multiple rates of tax); false statements of sales; and excessive tax credit claims, not fully backed by purchase invoices.

VAT is hard to evade in the manufacturing sector however, where the double-invoice system will reveal discrepancies if monitored by a computer. Complicity of officials is therefore important in this sector. This is not true in the service sector, however, where evasion is rife and detection virtually impossible.[17]

In view of the extraordinarily heavy administrative costs of VAT, the burden both financial and administrative for companies and the weakness of the positive arguments put forward in defence of the new tax, it is perhaps surprising that Britain agreed to forgo her simple and effective single-stage tax. More importantly, for the theme of the book, we need to consider what effect this major change in our system of indirect taxation has had on the distribution of income. We examine this question in detail in the following chapter.

Conclusion

In this chapter we have attempted to give a picture of the structure of indirect taxation in this country. Indirect taxes fall into two main groups. First there are excise duties, the main ones of which are levied on fuel, tobacco, drink and gambling. Overall, excise duties have a regressive effect which largely eliminates the advantage to poorer families of food and fuel being exempt from VAT. Purchase tax was introduced in October 1940 and proved to be an immensely simple (and therefore inexpensive) tax to administer. However, in 1974 it was replaced by VAT, the administration of which is a nightmare both to the taxpayer and administrator alike. In order to make VAT more acceptable, only 55 per cent of consumers' expenditure was covered by the tax and the traditional exemption of food and fuel from expenditure taxes was maintained by allowing them a zero rating. We now turn to examine the incidence of indirect taxation.

References

1. *Better Services for the Mentally Ill*, Cmnd 6233, HMSO, p. 62.
2. *Hansard*, 10 April 1975, Vol. 889, Cols. 473–4.
3. *Hansard*, 15 April 1975, Vol. 889, Col. 307.
4. *Hansard*, 15 April 1975, Vol. 890, Col. 309.
5. *Selective Employment Tax*, Cmnd 2986, HMSO.
6. W. B. REDDAWAY, *Effect of the SET, The Distributive Trades*, p. 310, Appendix 6; *Hansard*, 30 March 1971, Vol. 814, Col. 1395.
7. W. B. REDDAWAY, *Effects of the Selective Employment Tax, First Report, The Distributive Trades*, p. 137, Table XIV.6, HMSO.
8. *Observer*, 8 February 1970.
9. *Financial Statistics*, October 1972, No. 126, p. 29, Table 25.
10. *Hansard*, 6 April 1976, Vol. 908/909, Col. 256.
11. *Report of the Committee on Turnover Taxation*, Cmnd 2300, HMSO, March 1964.
12. ibid., p. 40.
13. *Observer*, 8 February 1970.

14. *Hansard*, 5 December 1972, Vol. 847, Col. 1108.
15. ALAN WATSON, 'What is VAT?', *Listener*, 1 June 1972.
16. 'The Ups and Downs of VAT', *Guardian*, 19 November 1975.
17. DAVID HAWARTH, 'VAT Fiddlers Get Away With It', *Observer*, 7 May 1972.

6 The Redistributive Effects of Indirect Taxes

Important changes have taken place recently in our system of indirect taxation. In the last chapter we looked at the replacement of SET and purchase tax with VAT. We now turn to an evaluation of the overall effect of indirect taxes on the distribution of income. We shall pay particular attention to changes in the burden of indirect taxation over the past few years, looking at how changes have affected different income groups as well as households of different sizes irrespective of their income. As Britain is a full member of the EEC, and thereby committed to harmonizing its indirect taxes with her partners', we shall also attempt to estimate the likely distributionary effect of a reduction in excise duties and an increase in VAT which will occur in the near future.

From Purchase Tax to VAT

The most recent analysis of the incidence of all indirect taxes in Britain suggests that the heaviest burden of indirect taxes falls on households at the lower end of the income scale and, in particular, on married couples of working age with an income below the poverty line, who in some cases contribute as much as one quarter of their income in indirect taxes alone.[1] Those receiving supplementary benefits will receive allowances to cover their rates. Nevertheless, for the 1·4 million households living at or below the poverty level, but who are not entitled to or are not receiving supplementary benefits, the indirect tax system is penal indeed. In contrast, households with incomes three times average earnings fare very well, contributing only 12–15 per cent of their disposable income in indirect taxes, less than half the proportion contributed by a number of the poverty groups.

Recent changes in the incidence of indirect taxes have if anything reinforced their regressive impact. The data relating to households of two adults with subsistence-level incomes in 1964 shows that these households paid 15 per cent of their incomes in indirect taxation. The same households in 1974 contributed 20 per cent of their incomes in indirect taxation. The following table also shows the increasing proportion of the incomes of low-income families with dependent children which are taken in indirect taxes. (It should be noted that the *Family Expenditure Survey* and thus the *Economic Trends* analysis of that survey do not provide data for each household type at subsistence level and it has therefore been necessary to take household types at the lowest income level for which the data are available for 1964. The tax position of these households has been compared with those at subsistence level in 1974.) A low-income family with one child paid 19 per cent of their income in indirect taxes in 1964; in 1974 they paid 26.6 per cent. Similarly, low-income families with two, three and four children all paid a higher proportion of their incomes in indirect taxes in 1974 than in 1964. With the exception of single-person households, the same pattern emerges from the comparison of households with average earnings, though here the increased burden upon larger families has been particularly marked. Only at the higher level of income of three times the national average has the trend been in the opposite direction.

It might be assumed that the changeover from the purchase tax to the value-added tax accounted for the increasingly regressive impact of indirect taxation in recent years. However, the table below suggests that the changeover in 1973 accounted for a small and fairly uniform increase in the incidence of indirect taxes upon households at every level of income. The increase in local rates has, on the other hand, been particularly regressive in recent years, and increasing tobacco duties have also affected some of the lower-income groups to a marginally greater extent than the rich during the early 1970s. Taking all household types together, the burden of indirect taxes has increased throughout the income scale by about 1·8 per cent in the three years 1971 to 1974, covering the period of transition from purchase tax to

VAT, and the general conclusion must be that much of the regressive shift occurred prior to the introduction of VAT. Only an examination of the incidence upon families with children reveals the more recent regressive changes. Families with

TABLE 16. Indirect taxes as a percentage of the disposable income of households with incomes at or below the poverty level, average earnings and incomes approximately three times average earnings, 1964 and 1974

	Income at subsistence level		National average earnings		Approx. three times national average earnings	
Retired households	*1964*	*1974*	*1964*	*1974*	*1964*	*1974*
1 adult		17·7		14·8		
2 adults		22·1		18·4		
Non-retired households						
1 adult	(20)	22·6	22	20·7	[19]	12·7
2 adults	15	20·0	20	22·8	13	15·2
2 adults, 1 child aged under 5	(19)	26·6	18	22·9	[20]	15·3
2 adults, 2 children aged 5–10, and under 5	(19)	(25·2)	17	23·4	16	14·3
2 adults, 3 children aged 13–15, 5–10, and under 5	(16)	41·4	15	22·9	[12]	14·8
2 adults, 4 children aged 13–15, 11–12, 5–10, and under 5	(17)	20·7	14	21·6	[18]	13·3

SOURCE: *Economic Trends*, August 1966 and February 1976. (The estimates are based largely upon information from the *Family Expenditure Survey*. Where the information was not available at any income level, either no figure has been given or, where appropriate, the data for the income level closest to that in question have been used for comparative purposes. In these cases brackets have been used; round brackets to indicate that the figure relates to the household group at the lowest level of income for which the data are available; and square brackets indicating that the figure applies to the household group at the highest level of income for which the data are available.)

one child and below-average incomes paid a maximum of 23 per cent of their incomes in indirect taxes in 1971, whereas in 1974 this had increased to 27·1 per cent. Similarly, families with three children and below-average earnings in 1971 paid up to 19 per cent of their income in indirect taxes; in 1974 they paid up to 23·2 per cent (or in an extreme case, 41·5 per cent).

In conclusion to this section, the regressive nature of the existing structure of indirect taxes in Britain is partially accounted for by the still heavy rate of excise duty on tobacco, but more particularly by the heavy burden of rates upon poor families, many of whom do not claim the rebates to which they are entitled and

TABLE 17. Change in the percentage of disposable income paid in indirect taxes, 1971–4

	Under 381	381+	557+	816+	1,194+	1,749+	2,561+	3,750+
All households								
Purchase tax (1971) to VAT (1974)	+0·7	+1·0	+0·8	+1·1	+0·8	+0·7	+0·9	+0·8
Duties on beer, wines and spirits	+0·3	+1·0	+0·5	+0·3	+0·4	+0·5	−0·2	−0·5
Rates	+1·5	+0·6	+1·1	+1·3	+1·0	+0·9	+0·7	+0·6
Duties in tobacco	+0·5	+0·1	+0·6	−0·2	+0·2	+0·4	+0·1	+0·7
Other	−1·0	−2·0	−1·7	−0·4	−0·4	+0·1	+0·9	0·0
All indirect taxes	+2·0	+0·7	+1·3	+2·1	+2·0	+2·6	+2·4	+1·6

SOURCES: *National Income and Expenditure 1964–74* HMSO, p. 36, Table 31; *Family Expenditure Survey*, 1972, Table 8; *Economic Trends*, February 1976, p. 84, Table f.

many more of whom do not qualify for rebates. As will be seen below, the value-added tax is, as yet, neutral as between high and low income earners, whether or not they have dependent children, and excise duties on drink and oil likewise. How will the structure and redistributive effects of our indirect taxes be affected by harmonization with our EEC partners?

The Redistributive Effects of the Introduction of VAT

A systematic attempt has been made to measure the redistributive effects of the changeover from the purchase tax and SET to the value-added tax.[2] However, in order to obtain an accurate result, the proportion of each household's expenditure on items subject to the VAT and on those items which are zero-rated would need

to be known. In fact the *Family Expenditure Survey* categories
do not coincide perfectly with the VAT categories so a number
of simplifying assumptions were necessary. The figures given in
Table 18 are therefore rough approximations and should be
treated with some reserve. Nevertheless, the results of the study
are of interest.

TABLE 18. The net effect on income of the changeover to
value-added tax

Range of original income £ per year 1973	£816–£987	£1,194–£1,446	£1,749–£2,116	£3,099–£3,750	£4,537–£5,490
1 adult	−1·9%	−1·9%	−3·0%	−3·7%	—
2 adults	−1·6%	−2·1%	−1·8%	−2·3%	−1·6%
2 adults + 2 children	−0·1%	−0·7%	+0·1%	−0·3%	−0·4%
2 adults + 4 children	—	−0·3%	−0·7%	—	—

As can be seen from the table, families with two children at
certain income levels appear to have gained marginally from the
changeover, but the authors maintain that in most, if not all,
such cases the gain can be accounted for by the sources of error
of the calculations (for example the failure to take into account in
the calculations the VAT payable on inputs to goods which, as
final goods, are exempt). Despite the admitted bias in favour of
VAT in the above results, in almost every case households appear
to have suffered a marginal reduction in their net income level
as a result of the introduction of VAT. No clear pattern of
redistribution emerges in either direction – the new tax does not
appear to favour one end of the income scale any more than the
other, though it does seem that, as VAT stands, it is more
favourable to families than to childless households (largely owing
to the zero-rating of food, fuel and children's clothing, which
together account for such a high proportion of family expenditure).

We need to look a year or two further back if we are to understand how so marginal a redistributive effect was achieved at the
time of the changeover to VAT. In 1972 the high rates of pur-

chase tax were drastically reduced, at a cost to the government of about £175 million in a full year. The 45 and 30 per cent rates were both cut to 25 per cent and a year earlier purchase-tax rates had been reduced by 18 per cent. Those who benefited most from the 1971 and 1972 changes were the higher-income groups, and the changes were almost certainly made in preparation for the abolition of purchase tax.

If, therefore, purchase tax in the years prior to 1971 is compared with VAT as it was first introduced, it is clear that VAT brought with it advantages for the higher-income groups. Nevertheless, even with two rates of VAT (0 and 8 per cent) up to April 1975, we have a relatively progressive expenditure tax, as *The Economist* has pointed out.[3] The proportion of low incomes spent on three zero-rated items was estimated to be 57·4 per cent, whereas the proportion of high incomes spent on the same three items was a mere 34·0 per cent. In contrast, the proportion of low incomes spent on items subject to the 8 per cent VAT was 42·6 per cent, much less than the 66·0 per cent of high incomes spent on the same items. The situation has since been affected by a series of budget changes, including the introduction of a 25 per cent higher rate of VAT on 'luxury' items in 1975 and its subsequent reduction to $12\frac{1}{2}$ per cent in April 1976. The effect of these changes has been an increase in the burden of VAT on higher-income groups and a subsequent modification of this increase. In concluding the first half of the discussion of the redistributive effects of introducing VAT therefore, it seems clear that there is nothing inherently regressive about the new tax. The redistributive effects of the VAT depend upon the number and level of the different rates applied as well as the items exempt from the tax.

As noted above, the existing regressive structure of indirect taxes in Britain is largely accounted for by the still heavy rate of excise duty on tobacco (which takes twice the proportion of a low income than a high income); and the burden of rates on poor families, which can be three times as great as the burden on the rich. Even before the introduction of a higher rate of VAT, this tax was very mildly progressive, rising from 2·3 per cent of income at the lower end of the income scale to 3·3 per cent of income in the case of households earning £5,490 or more, and today this trend will be marginally more marked.[4] But this situation will change as Britain has to harmonize her system of indirect taxes in line with her European partners'. We now turn and examine this issue.

The Effect of EEC Membership

The implications of the Treaty of Rome for our tax system are far-reaching. As soon as the decision was made that Britain should join the EEC, it was perfectly clear that we would be obliged to comply with Article 99 of the Treaty which requires the harmonization of indirect taxes. More specifically, on 11 April 1967 the EEC Council of Ministers issued two directives. The first required the removal of fiscal distortions of competition by the institution of the common VAT system; the second required that not only the system but also the *rates* of tax should be aligned, thus eliminating the 'tax frontiers' between member countries. It was certainly no surprise therefore when Mr Barber (as he then was) in 1971 announced that purchase tax and SET would be replaced by VAT as from April 1973. Britain was merely conforming with the six founder members of the EEC, all of whom had adopted the new tax by 1972.

An even greater contribution to the National Exchequer than that of VAT is made by excise duties in Britain, and the harmonization programme applies equally to these. In 1971 a Draft Council Directive made clear that full harmonization of both the structure and rates of excise duties was a necessary prerequisite of the free circulation of goods between member states, without any distortion of competition. Just what will this mean in Britain?

At present, excise duties in this country are three times as high as they are in the EEC on spirits; nine times as high on wine; and over four times as high on beer. The British duty on tobacco is double that in Europe, and the only excise duty remotely comparable in this country with those in Europe is the duty on hydro-carbon oils, the burden in Britain being on average a mere 25 per cent higher than in the rest of the EEC. European exchequers, however, make up for the loss of revenue from excise duties with a swingeing VAT, higher and wider-ranging than Britain has yet contemplated.

Three basic principles are put forward as a basis for the harmonization of excise duties and Britain had already complied with the first two of these at the time of entry into the Community:

1. that excise duties should not be levied on products of basic necessity, that is products quasi essential to life;
2. that excise duties should not, as far as possible, be levied on products used as raw materials in industry;
3. that excise duties should be harmonized in order to maintain equal conditions of competition as between competing products at Community level.

Mineral oils, manufactured tobacco and alcohol are all subject to excise duties in all member states, and these commodities fall

TABLE 19. The estimated revenue loss from the harmonization of excise duties within the EEC

Excise duty on:	Reduction in revenue £m
Spirits	253·5
Wine	93·3
Beer	384·0
Tobacco	605·0
Hydro-carbon oils	+73·0
Other excises	10·0
	£1,272·8 million

SOURCE: *Excise Duties in the UK and EEC*, CBI, November 1972.

within the principles outlined above. The Commission recommends that excise taxes should be retained and harmonized. The 1972 CBI report suggested that if the harmonization of the rates of excise duties is based upon weighting by production, then the reduction in revenue to the British Exchequer would be as shown in Table 19.

The figures given are estimates only, but they suggest an increase in VAT of some 9–10 points if the revenue were to be recouped.

This would come about only gradually, since the first stage of harmonization will concern the structure of excise duties: for example, the substances to be taxed, exemptions, whether the tax should be specific or proportional and so on.

A somewhat surprising fact is that the burden of expenditure taxes in Britain today is very little below the average burden in the six original EEC countries – a total of 226·3 units of account per inhabitant in Britain compared with 234·8 units in the EEC. The overall burden of our expenditure taxes can therefore be expected to remain fairly constant throughout the period of harmonization. What we can expect is a marked shift in the tax burden from cigarettes and alcohol to items such as food and fuel, for example.

At present food is zero-rated in Britain, whereas in Europe a reduced rate of VAT is applied to food. This discrepancy will be allowed to continue throughout Britain's transitional period, but we will be expected to impose a tax on food in due course. Perhaps we can consider 1980 as a deadline, since by that date the Community budget will be financed in part by a payment by member states of 1 per cent of the base of VAT. Clearly, it will be regarded as vital that the base or coverage of VAT is similar in all member countries in order to achieve comparable contributions from each member.

The British standard rate of 8 per cent VAT (with a zero rate on food) lies well below the low extreme of the EEC range. France has a 20 per cent standard rate (and 7 per cent on food) and Luxembourg at the other end of the spectrum has a mere 10 per cent with a 5 per cent rate on food. In terms of luxury rates too, Britain's 12½ per cent appears remarkably lenient when compared with the swingeing 36¾ per cent in Ireland, the 33⅓ per cent in France and the 30 per cent in Italy. The idea of a single rate has given way to that of a 'fourchette' or fork of rates ranging from 12–18 per cent initially in order to avoid drastic changes in a short period of time for any member country. The ultimate objective is a range of only three to four points and thus the elimination of fiscal frontiers.[5] A broadening of VAT and a steady increase in the standard rate can therefore be anticipated in exchange for a steady reduction in the rates of excise duties.

But what will these changes mean in terms of the distribution of income?

If Britain increases the standard rate of VAT by some 5 to 10 per cent and extends the tax to items such as food, in line with our EEC partners, quite clearly the lower-income groups will be adversely affected. About a third of a low-income family's expenditure goes on food (in contrast with about one fifth of the expenditure of a high-income family). The introduction of even a 5 per cent VAT on food would also discriminate against families as against single persons or married couples without dependants.

TABLE 20. The impact of price changes from 1970 to 1974 upon different household structures (£)

	1970–71 price increase	1971–2 price increase	1972–3 price increase	1973–4 price increase	Total price increase
1 adult	1·25	1·05	1·51	2·70	6·51
2 adults	N/A	2·23	3·23	6·65	
2 adults (head over 65; income £30 p.w.)	N/A	1·34	1·85	3·05	
2 adults 2 children	3·05	2·39	3·62	7·28	16·34
2 adults 4 children	N/A	N/A	3·86	7·98	

SOURCE: Letter from the Secretary of State for Prices and Consumer Protection to Sir Brandon Rhys Williams, MP, 19 June 1975.

Families with children spend a significantly larger proportion of their incomes on necessities such as food. The combined effect of inflation and a new food tax upon the standard of living of families would undoubtedly need to be taken into account in family benefit policy. (Just how inadequate family policy is in this country can be seen from the comparisons which are made in Chapter 10.) Recent price effects (even without a food tax) emphasize this point, as we can see from Table 20.

The unusual rate of price increases during recent years has consistently affected families with children considerably more than households without dependants. Over the four-year period in question, single-person households have had a 6·51 point price increase, whereas two-child families have suffered a 16·34 point increase. A food tax on top of this would undoubtedly hit the living standards of families hardest.

The picture is by no means complete, however, until we add the impact of the harmonization of excise duties. Here the effects are the reverse – a reduction in duties on beer and tobacco would add a sizable sum to the pockets of some poor people. The most

TABLE 21. Taxes as a proportion of consumers' expenditure on specific items

	1963 %	1973 %
Tobacco	69·1	84·0
Alcohol	37·2	33·6
Motor running	38·0	44·2
Durables	11·7	11·5
Other household goods	6·0	9·8
Chemists' goods	12·6	9·8
Clothing	6·1	9·0
Entertaining and recreation	5·2	5·5
Food	1·7	1·1
Fuel and Light	0·5	0·6
Travel	6·0	5·0
Communications	0·0	0·1
Books etc.	10·2	31·0

SOURCE: NI and *Expenditure Blue Book 1963–73.*

heavily taxed item in the British economy is tobacco – a commodity which consumes a higher proportion of very low wages than high incomes (because of the limited degree to which demand varies with income). A second heavy tax is that on alcohol – also a commodity absorbing a relatively high proportion of low incomes.

At present the wage-earner in a family with 2·4 members and an income of about £35 per week (little more than half of national average earnings) pays £1.20 in tax on the tobacco or cigarettes he buys each week, and a further 47p on his beer (assuming he both smokes and drinks to an average extent). If a 5 per cent tax is introduced on food and fuel and the standard rate of VAT is increased from 8 per cent to 12 per cent, we can calculate the effects on the family income at the top and bottom ends of the income scale (Table 22).

TABLE 22. Effects of harmonization upon the net income of families with an average of 2·4 members

	Income level £30–£35 per week	Income level £120+ per week
5% tax on fuel	11p loss	17p loss
5% tax on food	44p loss	95p loss
Increase in VAT by 4% in clothing, footwear, durable household goods, other goods, transport and vehicles and services	48p loss	£2·28 loss
Total loss from these changes	£1·03 (3·1%) loss	£3·40 (2·8%) loss
Effects upon consumers of tobacco and alcohol		
Reduction by 50% of excise duty on tobacco	60p gain	£1·04 gain
Reduction of excise duty on beer by 80%, and on spirits by 50%	38p gain	£1·13 gain
Net effect of all changes (including the reduction in excise duties on tobacco and alcohol)	5p (0·1%) loss	£1·23 (1·0%) loss
Net effect of harmonization upon consumers who do not purchase tobacco or alcohol	£1·03 (3·1%) loss	£3·40 (2·8%) loss

SOURCES: *Family Expenditure Survey 1974*, p. 14, Table 1; *VAT NEDO Report*, 1971; *Excise Duties in the UK and EEC*, CBI, November 1972.

To the low-income family which consumes an average quantity of tobacco and alcohol each week, the gains from the harmonization of excise duties on tobacco and beer go a long way towards offsetting the losses which would result from a general increase in VAT and its extension (at a lower rate) to food and fuel. The net loss of income would amount to 5p or 0·1 per cent of income. At the higher end of the income scale the net loss would amount to £1.23 per week or approximately 1 per cent of income.

To low-income families who neither smoke nor drink, however, the harmonization of UK expenditure taxes with our EEC neighbours would cost £1·03 per week and the income loss would amount to 3·1 per cent, or a higher percentage of income than would be forgone by families at the highest levels of income.

Conclusion

While excise duties are regressive – low-income households spend 8 per cent of their income on alcohol and tobacco while higher-income groups' expenditure is around 6·5 per cent of income – the replacement of purchase tax and SET by VAT had little effect on the distribution of income. We saw however that major reductions were made in purchase tax in the years preceding its abolition and replacement by VAT, and these changes were advantageous to higher-income groups. Further changes in our system of indirect taxation are likely to take effect in the next few years. The Treaty of Rome will require a reduction in the level at which excise duties are levied, together with a raising of the rate of VAT in Britain and its extension to food and fuel. As far as the effect on income distribution is concerned, therefore, harmonization of both excise duties and the VAT with our European neighbours will increase the regressive nature of our tax system. In the light of these findings two issues surely deserve a full public debate prior to any agreement to harmonize our taxes along the lines suggested: the first is whether or not the British public wishes to see yet another twist of the regressive screw on the overall impact of the British tax system; and the second is whether the British people wish to see a substantial shift of the tax burden from commodities widely recognized as having deleterious health effects to items such as food, fuel and clothing.

References

1. *Economic Trends*, February 1976, p. 83, Table D, reproduced in Table 1.
2. P. M. JACKSON and J. W. McGILVRAY, *The Impact of Tax Changes on Income Distribution: The 1973 Budget*, IFS.
3. 'Don't Multiply These VAT Rates', *The Economist*, 6 July 1974.
4. *Economic Trends*, February 1976, p. 84, Table F.
5. DOUGLAS DOSSER, 'Taxation', in *Economics of Europe*, ed. John Pinder.

7 Local Taxation and the Distribution of Incomes

The size of local-government expenditure and the weight of taxation required to cover it have come under increasing fire in recent years. In this chapter we look at the way in which local authorities raise the finance for their increasing expenditure and the incidence of local taxes on different economic groups. We then go on to examine the contribution from central government and the extent to which this support is concentrated upon those individuals and areas most needing it. In 1974 the government appointed the Layfield Committee 'to review the whole system of local government finance in England, Scotland and Wales, and to make recommendations'. While our analysis of the existing system and its redistributive effects differs in important ways from the analysis of the Layfield Committee report, nevertheless the data upon which the following pages are based is drawn substantially from the report,[1] and from the evidence submitted to the Committee.

Inevitably, as the cost of local-authority services has grown in relation to expenditure in other sectors of the economy, the strain upon the rating system has increased and government grants have grown in importance. In 1890, for example, when local government had already been established in its modern form, total local-government expenditure amounted to little over £50 million. This has since increased to some £14,600 million, owing partly to the increasing range of services provided by local authorities and the improvement in original services but also, of course, to the effects of inflation. Rates have, however, increased in line with money incomes and remain at $2\frac{1}{2}$ per cent of personal disposable income. Their contribution to total local-government income has declined from 34 per cent in 1945 to 28 per cent in 1973–4, and by 1976–7 rates produced less than half the revenue provided by government grants.

The Structure of Local-Authority Revenue

Local authorities have three main sources of income: in addition to rates and government grants a sizable proportion of revenue is levied through fees and charges. Our discussion will concentrate primarily upon the rating system and its effects upon the distribution of income and possible reforms. The structure of government grants and local-authority fees and charges will be analysed in somewhat less detail.

The Poor Relief Act of 1601 is generally regarded as the origin of rating (though in fact the tradition of taxing property in order to provide revenue for local expenditure goes back still further). Despite the many changes in the types of property subject to rating and changes in the method of assessment, present-day rates have developed directly from the original 1601 property taxes, and today the yield of rates, both domestic and non-domestic, is second only to that of income taxes. Rates provide more revenue than corporation tax, VAT or excise duties.[2] Despite consideration from time to time of the possibility of replacing what must be regarded as an antiquated system of taxation (the latest thorough examination of the whole issue being that of the Layfield Committee), no government has yet seen fit to end this three-and-a-half century old tradition. Three attributes of rates perhaps account for their apparent invincibility: the yield of rates is readily predictable (a disadvantage during rapid inflation); evasion is extremely difficult; and the cost of maintaining the rating system is low in relation to the yield. At £86 million a year, the cost of administering the rates is equivalent to 2 per cent of the yield.

Nevertheless, the tax based upon the rateable value of property has been severely criticized on several counts. One of the major debates over the centuries has been how far rates should be payments in return for benefits received in the form of services. Today the tax in no way relates to the benefits received by the taxpayer. A clear example of the lack of any relationship between the burden of rates and receipt of the benefits which they finance is that of education, which accounts for 36 per cent of local-authority current expenditure and yet is of no value to pensioners, whose rate burden tends to be particularly heavy. Secondly, the rateable value of property is purported to be the rent which the property might be expected to earn, assuming the tenant bears the costs of repairs, insurance and maintenance generally. However, this rent rarely relates to existing free-market rents because of the many imperfections of the property market arising from, for example, fair-rent schemes, rent control and also the decline in the number of privately rented properties available. The rateable value is, therefore, 'assessed' by the valuation office of the Inland Revenue. It has been shown that the 'assessed rents' on properties are a declining proportion of 'actual rents' as the value of the property rises. The rateable values of cheaper properties thus represent a higher proportion of the actual value of the property than do the rateable values of more expensive properties.

A third source of criticism has been the lack of buoyancy of the rating system. The revenue from an income or expenditure tax increases automatically as incomes and expenditure respectively increase over time. The consumption of property, on the other hand, remains relatively static over time and the revenue from rates can be increased only as a result of new and improved building or a revaluation of all properties. New and improved properties have accounted for an annual growth in rateable value of only 2–2½ per cent in recent years. The revaluation of 1973, however, showed an overall increase in rateable values of 153 per cent or 10 per cent per annum compound since the previous revaluation of 1963. The sharp increases in rates resulting from the latest 1973 revaluation gave rise to widespread ill-feeling about the rating system as a whole, and brought the issue of reform of local-government finance to the forefront of political debate. The fourth, and for the purposes of this book the most serious, criticism of the rating system is the regressive impact of the tax upon individual taxpayers.

In 1937 the Fitzgerald Committee evidence showed that 'the burden of rates upon working-class households was clearly regressive in relation to household expenditure', though we are told that at that time a somewhat more complex pattern emerged from the middle-class sample.[3] Thirty years later the regressive impact of rates had become more marked and consistent. The Allen Committee reported in 1965 that rates were regressive with respect to both household original and disposable income, with low-income households contributing about 8 per cent of their income in rates and those with the highest incomes contributing ·ust under 2 per cent as shown in Table 23.[4]

TABLE 23. Impact of rates according to income, England and Wales, all households, 1963–4

	Under £312	£312 but under £520	£520 but under £780	£780 but under £1,040	£1,040 but under £1,560	£1,560 and over	All
Rates as percentage of household income	8·1	6·0	3·8	2·9	2·4	1·8	2·6
Rates as percentage of disposable income	8·2	6·2	4·1	3·2	2·7	2·2	2·9
Housing costs as a percentage of household income	26·6	19·8	13·4	10·3	8·5	6·4	9·0

SOURCE: *Allen Report*, p. 277, extract from Table 200.

The Allen Committee findings are supported by *Family Expenditure Survey* data analysed to show the incidence of rates and other taxes on different income groups for the years 1959 to 1974. The results of this work, to which we will return in more detail in Chapter 9, are published each year by the Stationery Office in *Economic Trends*. It should be said that all the available evidence on the incidence of rates is based upon the assumption that rates are borne by the occupiers of a property. In the case of owner-occupiers, for example, it is assumed that the burden of rates is not shifted back to the property developer, and in the case of tenants the assumption is that the landlord shifts the rate burden forward to his tenants. In view of the many imperfections of the housing market (including, for example, the fair-rent procedure, rent control and the restricted supply of housing) this assumption is widely accepted as more realistic than any other, though there may be cases, where for some reason, a landlord may not pass on the rates of a property to a tenant in their entirety, at least in the short run.

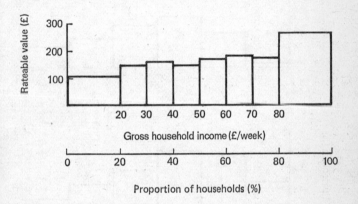

Fig. 9. Average rateable value by income group. (Source: *Layfield Report*, p. 156)

The evidence available reveals, not only that households with low incomes pay a significantly larger proportion of their income in rates than do households with higher incomes, but also that rates are inequitable between households of different size at a given level of income. The wide variation in the rateable value applicable to households in three different income groups is illustrated in Figure 10. The variation within these income groups exceeds the variation in the average rateable value between the top and bottom of the income scale, as shown in Figure 9. These variations can be explained by a number of factors. Retired

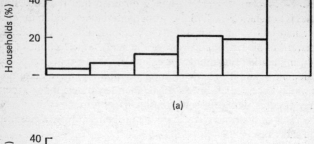

(a)

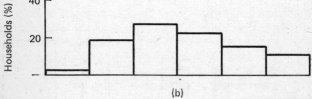

(b)

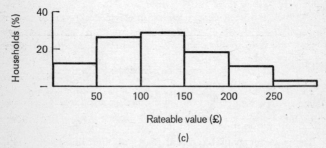

(c)

Fig. 10. Distribution of rateable values within selected income groups, England and Wales, 1974. (a) Gross household income over £80 per week; (b) gross household income £40–60 per week; (c) gross household income under £20 per week. (Source: *Layfield Report*, p. 157)

people, for example, notoriously hold a high proportion of their wealth in housing relative to the rest of the population. In many cases people continue to live in 'the family home' long after their housing needs have declined, as children have grown up and established their own homes elsewhere. Consequently, at most levels of income retired households pay a higher proportion of their income in rates than other households at the same level of income.

Families with dependent children, on the other hand, tend to pay a smaller proportion of their income in rates than single people or married couples at the same level of income. The only exceptions to this rule are families in the highest income bracket. This suggests that families with average or below-average earnings are constrained to live in relatively small properties or in less desirable areas where rateable values and rates are more modest. Only when the children leave home can many couples enjoy the 'luxury' of adequate housing. The heaviest rate burden is borne by single non-retired people (who pay 7·3 per cent of their disposable income in rates). In marked contrast, single non-retired people in the highest income bracket pay the smallest proportion of their incomes in rates (1·9 per cent). Throughout the income scale retired people are amongst the highest rate-payers, while families appear to fare somewhat better. However, the most consistent trend is the decline in the burden of rates as incomes rise. This is true of households of every size and of every tenure group throughout the range of income (see Table 24) and has been true since the war. (This data is obtained from unpublished *FES* data for the first two quarters of 1974. The raw *FES* data is given by gross household income, but Taylor reduced this to disposable income by subtracting income tax and national-insurance contributions, thus arriving at the figures in the table.)

The table shows the regressive burden illustrated in the earlier evidence of the Allen Committee and the 1968 NBPI, but the rates throughout are marginally higher than for the earlier years on record.

Should we be concerned if the incidence of rates *is* regressive? This question has been raised by Professor Wiseman,[5] who correctly points out that a regressive rate structure is perfectly compatible with a progressive overall tax system. What his argument neglects is the individual impact of a tax such as rates upon families and pensioners with incomes below the poverty line who find themselves paying a higher proportion of their incomes in rates than households with ten times their incomes.

At this level 50p paid in rates means 50p less spent on food or heating. Whether or not the rest of the tax system is progressive, this 50p will not be restored – except perhaps in the form of a means-tested benefit. A system which taxes low-income families and then requires the same families to submit to a means test in order to receive compensation for their poverty is neither efficient

TABLE 24. Rates as percentage of disposable income for households ranged by gross income, Great Britain, 1974

Range of gross weekly income £	All households	Owner-occupied	Mort-gaged	Fully owned	Local-authority tenants	Other tenants
10	11·0	12·0	16·8	8·2	13·1	9·0
10–15	8·2	8·5	14·0	8·2	8·8	7·3
15–20	7·2	7·6	5·7	7·7	7·9	5·4
20–25	6·1	5·9	6·8	5·7	6·5	5·7
25–30	5·1	5·6	4·0	5·8	5·1	4·3
30–35	4·7	5·2	4·3	5·2	5·1	3·5
35–40	4·3	4·5	4·4	4·6	4·2	4·2
40–45	3·6	3·5	3·8	3·2	4·0	3·0
45–50	3·4	3·6	3·5	3·8	3·5	2·9
50–60	3·3	3·3	3·3	3·5	3·4	2·9
60–70	3·0	3·2	3·3	3·0	2·9	2·5
70–80	2·7	2·9	3·0	2·5	2·4	2·4
80+	2·3	2·4	2·5	2·3	2·0	2·0

SOURCE: P. J. Taylor, *A Survey of the Evidence of the Burden of Rates*, Table 23.

nor socially acceptable. Furthermore, rates are a tax on a necessity and cannot, as such, be avoided by low-income households. As has been noted in an earlier chapter, excise duties are regressive, but it can be argued in their favour that low-income households can, in theory at least, choose not to spend their money on goods subject to excise duties. This cannot be said of rates.

Attempts to Offset the Regressive Impact of Rates

A number of measures have been introduced to counter the regressive nature of rates. These are the rate support grant, the rate rebate system and the payment of an allowance for rates to recipients of supplementary allowances and supplementary pensions. We now turn to consider how effective the first two measures are in securing a more equitable tax system.

By far the most important in terms of the cost involved is the rate support grant, which provided just under £7,000 million, or 87 per cent of the total Exchequer grant to local authorities, in 1976–7. The purpose of government grants was originally to reimburse local authorities for the 'national services' which they provided. However, in 1948 the more important function of compensating for the disparities in both the resources and needs of different regions was recognized and the 'Exchequer equalization grant' introduced.

The resources element of the rate support grant is calculated on the basis of the resources of each local-authority area, that is the value of industrial, commercial and domestic property upon which the yield of rates depends. Clearly an area with offices and factories of substantial rateable values will receive a smaller resources grant than an area with little commerce or industry. The second or needs element makes allowance for the variation in the population structure of local-authority areas. For example if a borough has a disproportionate number of school-children and people aged 65 plus, and therefore has a heavy demand for educational and social services, the needs element of the rate support grant will be increased accordingly.

The third and somewhat more dubious element is the domestic rate relief, which enables all rates levied on domestic and mixed properties (those which are used for both commercial and domestic purposes) to be reduced by a specified amount in the pound. This amount has increased substantially over time from, for example, 3·6 per cent of average rate bills in 1967–8 to 27·5 per cent in 1975–6. The benefits of the relief are received in proportion to the rateable value of the property, so that the higher the rateable value of an individual's property the higher the cash value of his rate relief from the government. People living in an area with high rateable values but low rate poundages will benefit more from the domestic rate relief than people living in poorer areas where rateable values are low and rate poundages relatively high.

Whereas the resources and needs elements of the rate support grant go a long way towards equalizing the impact of rates between areas, the domestic rate relief has a neutral or in some cases a regressive effect, providing less help where it is most needed. The precise impact of the grants on individual ratepayers is not known. We do know, however, the incidence of rates upon individuals after the distribution of the rate support grant. It is the regressive effect of rates net of grants which the rate rebate system was designed to reduce.

The Rate Rebate System

Rate rebates were first made mandatory on local authorities in 1966–7, when the earlier discretionary rate relief powers (first introduced in 1926) were replaced. The original rate rebate scheme was introduced in direct response to the finding of the Allen Committee that rates were a serious burden for low-income households and for old age pensioners in particular, many of whom were subject to rates amounting to 8 per cent or more of their incomes.

Under the original scheme all rebate recipients paid the initial £7·50 of their annual rate bill and rebate was paid at two thirds of the residual of the bill for a householder whose income was equal to or below the prescribed limit. If the gross household income exceeded the limit, the rebate was reduced by 25p in the £ for the excess. The significance of the tapering mechanism was its effect in producing a nominal marginal tax rate associated with rate rebates of 25 per cent, that is, a £1 increase in income would result in a reduction of rate rebate of 25p. This was a sizable component in the poverty trap.

One of the criticisms levelled at the old rate rebate scheme was the provision for rebate to be *reduced* if income exceeded the prescribed limits but the lack of any provision to *increase* rebate if income fell below the limit. The support for very low-income families where the rate bill was necessarily small in cash terms was, thereby, severely curtailed. (The minimum annual rate bill was £7·50 plus a third of rates.) Secondly, the income limits were never far above the supplementary-benefit level and the tapering of rebates was sharply applied so that the scheme was of very limited value.

The failure of the original rate rebate scheme was measured in terms of the take-up rate which, according to all the evidence available, was below 20 per cent of households eligible. A study of the circumstances of retirement pensioners in 1966, for example, estimated a take-up rate of only 10 per cent.[6]

As a result of the widespread criticisms of the functioning and take-up of the original rate rebate scheme a reformed scheme was introduced on 1 April 1974. The terms of the new scheme resemble those of the rent rebate scheme and take-up is encouraged in a number of boroughs by means of joint application forms which enable people claiming one benefit to receive both. Other new features of the scheme have also helped to increase the numbers benefiting from under 1 million in 1973 to about 2·5 million in 1974: first, the minimum rate payable of £7·50 plus one third of the residual of rates has been abolished under the new scheme. If income equals the needs allowance (or income limit) then the rebate equals 60 per cent of full domestic rates. Furthermore, the nominal marginal tax rate has been reduced substantially from the original 25 per cent level. Under the new scheme, if household income is greater than the needs allowance, the rebate will be reduced by 6 per cent of the excess. Also, if household income falls below the needs allowance, the rebate (of 60 per cent of rates) will be increased by 8 per cent of the shortfall of income. Under the new scheme it is, therefore, possible for a rebate to cover the full cost of rates if income is sufficiently low. And in addition to these changes, the new scheme is considerably more lenient towards a claimant's capital. The only assets now taken into account are liquid cash resources and these include only bank deposits on current account. Even national savings certificates and premium bonds are not regarded as liquid cash resources for the purposes of calculating entitlement to rate rebates. This reform represents a concession to the critics of the old scheme, who claimed, with some justification, that it penalized those pensioners who had saved throughout their lives.

Clearly these amendments have overcome some of the take-up problems of the earlier scheme. Rebates are more worthwhile for low-income households now that the rebate can cover over 60 per cent of the rate bill. Similarly the gentle tapering mechanism and the more lenient approach to capital make a rebate worthwhile for the many pensioners with small private pensions and some savings.

Nevertheless, it remains true that 30 per cent of the households eligible for rate rebates do not claim them, and the evidence available suggests that the households who do not claim means-tested benefits in general are those most in need of financial help. The Islington study examined the take-up of rate rebates in selected 'low-income areas' and amongst a more heterogeneous sample of households in the borough.[7] Following an intensive advertising campaign encouraging claims for rebates, the take-up in the low-income areas remained consistently below that in the broader-based sample. Within the low-income areas, too, it was the pensioners and families at the very bottom of the income scale who failed to claim, primarily because they remained unaware of the existence of the benefit (despite the advertising campaign) or did not realize that they would be entitled to help. Take-up was particularly low amongst private tenants, many of whom were not even aware that they paid rates as well as rent. It is difficult to envisage a rate rebate scheme which would effectively help the least articulate, least healthy and least mobile members of the community, that is those in greatest need.

The second major weakness of the scheme, despite the amendments introduced in 1974, is the consistently low level of the needs allowance (or income limits). Despite the substantial increase in the income limits in *money* terms during the past ten years, there has been no increase in the limits in relation to average earnings, and in the case of single persons the income limit has fallen as a proportion of real disposable average male earnings, as shown in Table 25.

It remains true, then, that in addition to the 1 million house-holds eligible for rate rebates and not claiming them, substantial numbers of households with below-average incomes are not entitled to rebates and pay rates which can amount to 10 per cent or even 20 per cent of income. Many others receive rebates but still find themselves paying a high proportion of their income in rates. For example, a married couple with £30 per week and a rate bill of £3.50 a week will pay 11·7 per cent of their income in rates if they do not claim a rate rebate and 5·3 per cent if they do. How-ever, a married couple with more than £5,490 a year and living in a similar property will pay only 2·2 per cent of their income in

TABLE 25. Income limits for rate rebates as a proportion of real disposable average male earnings 1966–7 and 1975–6

	Single person	Married couple	Dependent child
1966–7	35·5%	44%	6·6%
1975–6	32·0%	44%	6·6%

SOURCES: *Rate Rebates in England and Wales*, Department of the Environment and Welsh Office, HMSO; *Department of Employment Gazette*; NIESR calculation.

rates. Rate rebates reduce the regressive effect of rates but do not eliminate it.

A third major criticism of the rate rebate scheme is its failure to meet the needs of private tenants. The take-up of rate rebates by private tenants has consistently been below the take-up by either owner-occupiers or council tenants (Table 26). Although the private-tenancy sector is shrinking in relative terms, the numbers remain large in absolute terms and include many groups who are economically and socially deprived. These groups will always be difficult to reach by a scheme which is selective, is based on a claims procedure and requires the claimant to have command over a range of information.

The fourth and somewhat contrary criticism of rate rebates concerns the allocation of resources. The main beneficiaries of the rate rebate scheme are old age pensioners (in 1972–3 they accounted for 85 per cent of claimants), and particularly those who continue living in the family home for many years when they no longer need the space available. In urban areas with a severe shortage of accommodation, a more socially beneficial government subsidy would be a contribution towards removal costs or conversion costs for pensioners to enable fuller use of the limited accommodation available.

TABLE 26. The distribution of take-up rates by tenure of ratepayer, England and Wales, 1972–3

	Percentage of local authorities with the take-up rate shown		
Take-up rate	Amongst direct ratepayers	Amongst local-authority tenants	Amongst other indirect ratepayers
Under 3%	3·0	39·2	68·4
3 to 7%	54·7	52·4	24·7
7 to 10%	29·6	6·3	2·9
10 to 15%	10·9	1·8	2·0
over 15%	1·8	0·3	2·0

SOURCE: P. J. Taylor, *An Evaluation of Rate Rebates and Other Methods of Rate Relief in England and Wales 1966 to 1975*, Table 5. Submission to the Layfield Committee of Enquiry into Local Government Finance: adapted from *Rate Rebates in England and Wales 1972–3*, Department of the Environment and Welsh Office, HMSO, 1973, Table III.

For the above reasons it is perfectly clear that the rate rebate scheme has not transformed rates into a progressive or equitable tax system. Similarly, the allowance for rates which is added to supplementary pensions and allowances provides relief for those who claim, but for the one million households eligible for supplementary allowances but who do not submit to the means test involved no help with rates is available. The range of reliefs represent piecemeal tinkering with a fundamentally unjust system of tax, leaving those most in need of help unaided while allocating sizable government subsidies primarily for the benefit of higher-income property owners through the rate support grant.

If we assume that it is no longer satisfactory to continue depending upon the rating system for a substantial proportion of local-authority revenue, there are a number of reforms worthy of consideration.

Possibilities for Reform

The first concerns a possible increase in the dependence of local authorities upon fees and charges. At present local authorities raise approximately £1,400 million in fees and charges, half of which is derived from housing rents. Trading services, including municipal transport, account for a further £140 million, and charges levied on various services such as licence fees, charges for old peoples' homes, parking fees, trade refuse collection, library charges and the sale of school meals and milk raise a further £540 million.

During recent years the contribution of fees and charges to local-authority revenue has fallen sharply, particularly in the housing field, where the proportion of expenditure covered by rents has fallen from 61 per cent in 1973–4 to only 48 per cent one year later. The shortfall has been met primarily from an increase in the Exchequer subsidy (from 32 per cent to 40 per cent of housing revenue) but also to a smaller extent from an increase in rate fund contributions (from 8 to 12 per cent of housing revenue).[8]

Two overwhelming arguments can be levelled against any suggestion that fees and charges should be increased or extended to further services. Firstly, the individual benefit from many local-authority services cannot be identified. The preventive role of the police, for example, street lighting and the provision of zebra crossings are of general rather than individual benefit. Secondly, many of the services provided by local authorities are of benefit to households in particular need. It would be unacceptable and highly regressive to charge for such services. Obvious examples are the provision of services for the mentally and physically handicapped and the aged, which are used overwhelmingly by people with very low incomes. There may be a case for increasing charges for a number of services such as parking facilities, but clearly the scope for increasing revenue in this way is very limited.

The second possible reform centres on the extension of government grants. But before going on to consider how the government might extend its support for local-authority services while maintaining some autonomy for local authorities themselves, we should take into account the already sizable government contribution in this field. In 1976–7 the aggregate Exchequer grant amounted to £7,700 million, or 67 per cent of relevant local-authority expenditure. The rate support grant accounts for more than four fifths of the Exchequer grant, while the specific and supplementary grants account for 9 and 4 per cent respectively. Specific grants are earmarked for specified projects and must be used by the local authorities for these purposes. Supplementary grants are similarly tied to transport services and national parks, whereas individual local authorities have some discretion about the allocation of the rate support grant.

The main criticisms of the existing grant facilities may be summarized as follows. First, the domestic element of the rate support grant does not distribute resources to the areas in greatest need. As we have seen, the size of this grant is calculated on the basis of the rateable values in each local-authority area. A more appropriate basis for the calculation would be the average income of each area, thus relating the subsidy inversely to the ability to pay of the relevant population. Second, there are no statutory rules or formal criteria for determining the total level of grants. The amount is settled each year by the government after consultation with local authorities, thus providing no security to local authorities from one year to the next for planning purposes. Lastly, many services administered by local authorities are the responsibility of the government and are rightly regarded as national services, yet the government does not have a statutory obligation to cover the cost of providing the services. There is thus an undesirable degree of confusion about the division of financial responsibility between the government and local authorities. The result has been an uncontrolled expansion in local-authority expenditure and pressure upon the government to increase grants in order to avoid undue increases in local rates.

Control over local-authority expenditure is attempted in the following ways. The *Public Expenditure Survey* sets out a strategy for future expenditure for the short and medium terms, seen in the context of the general requirements of the economy. However, the recommendations of the survey are not mandatory on local authorities and therefore carry little weight outside the government itself. But local authorities have to obtain Ministerial sanction before raising a loan (with few exceptions). Ministers thus determine within narrow limits the amounts which local authorities can spend on capital each year. However, this system of loan sanction discourages a proper evaluation of the revenue consequences of capital expenditure. For macro-economic purposes it is essential that control should include the revenue element.

The rate support grant has traditionally supported increases in expenditure, even when these have been excessive, despite its obvious potential as a method of control. However, the Labour government in 1976 implemented its expenditure cuts in part through its control over the size of the grant, illustrating that existing arrangements do permit central control if governments are willing to accept the political odium involved.

The *Layfield Report* presents two possible alternative strategies either of which, in theory, would ensure adequate control over expenditure and stability within which local authorities could operate.

The first option would involve greater government responsibility for financing local services. This option is presented as an unattractive, dictatorial approach according to which the government would set the totals for local spending within fairly narrow limits and would determine how much each local authority would spend and for what purpose. The grant would be calculated, says the report, on a service-by-service basis but would be paid as a block grant in order to give local authorities some discretion in allocating the funds. This seems to suggest some confusion as to how far the government or local authorities would allocate funds under a 'centralized' system. However, the report does suggest that there would be a number of functions which local authorities could exercise with little government intervention and which could be financed adequately by the existing system of rates.

The second option, clearly favoured by the Layfield Committee, would mean a substantial reduction in the present level of government grants so that much greater responsibility for the control over expenditure would rest with local authorities. The central objective of the reform would be that local authorities which were considering proposals involving additional expenditure would be aware that the funds would have to be raised from local taxation. The government's role would be restricted to the overall management of the economy and the imposition of global limits to local-authority expenditure when this was necessary for demand management purposes. In addition to the existing rating system, local authorities would need to levy a local income tax to cover their increased share of expenses. The tax would be largely offset by a reduction in national income tax related to the fall in the value of government grants.

Having described the recipe for local responsibility and accountability to electors, Layfield recognizes the inevitability of considerable government control over the level of expenditure by individual local authorities and the equal inevitability of government grants totalling at least 40 per cent of total expenditure in order to compensate for disparities between local authorities in both the level of needs and available resources. The government grants (at any level) must necessarily be based upon an assessment of needs, implying a degree of control over specific as well as total expenditures.

Throughout the *Layfield Report* there appears a determination to opt for greater local autonomy, despite the logic of the arguments used which tends to support the opposite approach. The result is a considerable degree of confusion and a neglect of vital issues such as the need to ensure a satisfactory level of all statutory services in every local-authority area, which can be achieved only by a degree of central control over the services for which the government is responsible.

The cost of administering the 'Layfield proposal' would be in the region of £200 million a year, comprising the public and private costs of administering a local income tax (£50 million each) and the public cost of administering rates (£100 million). The cost would be justified, says the report, by the accountable management of some £13,000 million a year of public current expenditure.

An alternative and more logical view is that a middle way between the two extremes can be found which more naturally allows both for government control over the services for which it is responsible and a degree of local authority control in particular areas. Two alternative divisions of responsibility would be feasible: (1) a vertical division in which certain services, such as the police and education which account for a substantial proportion of local-authority expenditure, could be financed in full by the government, leaving all non-specified services to be financed by the local authority; or (2) a horizontal division based on the definition of minimum standards for which the government would bear financial responsibility. This would leave to the local authority primary responsibility for improvements in the services over and above the minimum standard.

The horizontal division of responsibilities is meaningful in that the provision of minimum standards in education, the police service, social and environmental services and public housing must be regarded as a national responsibility, and should therefore be financed out of a reformed national income tax (see the last chapter). Improvements or extensions to these minimum standards to meet particular local needs or demands would then appropriately be the responsibility of local authorities.

It is surely essential that a clear division of financial responsibility should be specified, so that electors at both national and local level know who is responsible for what; also that a clear definition of essential minimum standards be established even if initially this has to be done on the basis of manpower requirements, or inputs, rather than services provided, or outputs.

In this way the bulk of spending would be nationally determined, thus facilitating control over the total level of spending and over the even development of services across the country. This would be of particular value in some of the 'Cinderella' fields such as mental illness, mental handicap and services for the elderly, which in some areas have fallen far behind the minimum levels recommended by the government. At the same time, local authorities would have a stable base upon which to develop local features, for which they would be accountable to their local electors. A likely result would be that 'local authorities would enjoy an increase in discretion over some services at the expense of reducing it over others'.[9]

In the final chapter we discuss what reforms are necessary to bring about a progressive tax base in this country. One part of this package concerns the reform of local-government finance, which will need to go hand in hand with a major reform of the income tax system. Our discussion on a local income tax assumes an accompanying major reform in the structure of direct taxation.

A Local Income Tax

The Layfield Committee bases its proposals for reform upon the assumption that local-authority revenue must be sharply *increased*. They arrive at the conclusion that a local income tax is an indispensable *addition* to the existing rating system. However, the following discussion is based upon the assumption that local-authority revenue will be maintained at its present level or reduced so that a local income tax could *replace* the regressive domestic rating system.

If the entire rating system were to be abolished and replaced by a local income tax, the rate of tax would need to be at a level of 11p or 12p in the £. There are however several arguments for retaining non-domestic rating. Firstly, the revenue loss involved would be very considerable (non-domestic rates yielded more than £2,000 million in 1975–6) and even if not replaced entirely by local income tax the task of replacing the revenue from rates in full would be formidable. Secondly, industry and commerce are perhaps even more efficient than individuals at avoiding payment of taxes, but it is notoriously difficult to avoid paying rates. Thirdly, a local income tax would be flexible if based upon the 'major spending authorities' (the metropolitan districts, nonmetropolitan counties, London boroughs, the City of London, Scottish regions and the four unitary authorities). However, local income tax is not an administratively feasible proposition for the smaller authorities. Non-domestic rating could provide an independent source of revenue for these authorities, thus ensuring a degree of autonomy for them. Despite the disadvantages of non-domestic rates, in particular their impact upon prices, and thus their regressive impact upon incomes, it may not be politically feasible to eliminate both domestic and non-domestic rates.

If the domestic rate only were to be replaced by a local income tax, a rate of tax of about 4·5p in the £ would be required to raise the necessary revenue. After a consideration of alternative methods of administering rates, the Layfield Committee concluded that local income tax could operate satisfactorily only if it were administratively integrated with the national income tax system. Local income tax would thus be collected alongside and at the same time as national income tax. Local income tax could be distinguished from the national income tax in much the same way as national-insurance contributions are distinguished at present. This would increase local accountability by making any *changes* in local income tax apparent to the local taxpayer.

Differences in local taxes between employees of the same firm living in different areas could also increase consciousness. Local income tax would be subject to the same allowances and bands of taxable income as the national income-tax system. Similarly the local tax could be applied along with the national income tax to pensions, fees, profits from businesses, dividends and interest as well as to wages and salaries.

There are three main disadvantages to a changeover to local income tax. First, income tax is a key instrument of government demand management. The introduction of a local income tax could complicate the problems involved. For example, if the government reduced direct taxes in order to stimulate demand, this could be taken as an opportunity by local authorities to increase local income tax, thus blunting the effect of the government's action. Second, of the 24 million taxpayers, 22½ million are subject to a marginal tax rate of 40·5 per cent including income tax and national-insurance contributions, and approximately half a million households pay taxes at higher marginal tax rates. To impose still higher marginal rates could have serious implications, particularly for low-income households but also at the macro-economic level, upon the rate of inflation. Hence the added importance of the reforms recommended in the last chapter if the changeover to a local income tax is to be considered. Lastly, the yield of a local income tax would be less predictable than the yield of rates. Both the general level of activity in the economy and government changes in tax allowances and rate bands would affect the yield. However, no doubt the government could act as a buffer between the taxpayer and the local authority in order to ease the cash-flow problem.

None of the above problems is insurmountable and the advantages would appear to be of greater significance. A local income tax of 4·5p would raise sufficient revenue to compensate for the loss of domestic rates, and the burden of the tax would be related to income, taking into account family and other responsibilities through the tax allowance system, which we recommend in the final chapter should itself be changed fundamentally.

The tax would thus achieve a greater degree of vertical and horizontal equity than is achieved by the rating system. The vertical redistribution of income which would result from the changeover (in the absence of any other tax reforms) is illustrated in Figure 11. This is based on *FES* data for 1975 on the assumption that domestic rates are replaced by a local income tax. The figure suggests that those with very low incomes would be worse off as a result of the changeover. However, this conclusion is only valid if: (a) people claim the existing supplementary benefits and rate rebates to which they are entitled. In fact, as we have seen, about one million households do not claim the supplementary pensions (and rate allowances) to which they are entitled and 30 per cent of households entitled to rate rebates do not receive them. The local income tax would increase rather than reduce the incomes of these groups; (b) the existing low tax threshold and single rate of tax over a wide range of income were retained. If our recommendations for the reform of income-tax structure were introduced at the same time as local income tax, low-income households as a whole would benefit.

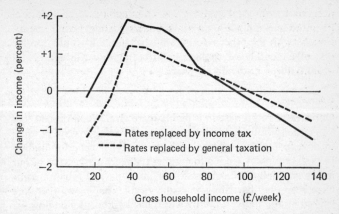

Fig. 11. The effect of replacing rates by taxes, 1975. Rates are domestic rates paid net of reliefs from rebates and supplementary benefits. The income whose change is being measured is income left after all national taxes and rates have been deducted. (*Source: Layfield Report*, p. 266, Fig. 8)

Even in the absence of any reform of the direct tax structure, for the great majority of households with below-average incomes the changeover to a local income tax would increase gross incomes, while households with incomes of about £100 per week or more would pay more tax under local income tax than under the existing rating system (as shown in Figure 11).

The primary advantage of local income tax would be that it would provide an independent source of revenue for local authorities which would be directly related to the ability of local electors to pay. Secondly, local income tax would be buoyant in a way that rates are not (the yield of the tax would increase automatically with the growth of economic activity and incomes generally). Thirdly, all taxpayers would be seen to be contributing to local revenue, whereas under existing arrangements non-householders who may earn considerable incomes contribute nothing to local rates. Fourthly, local income tax would be perceptible. Workers within the same factory would know if their own local income tax rate were higher than that of a colleague and would have the incentive to press for some justification from their local authority. Accountability would therefore be more meaningful than it is under existing arrangements. Finally, with the other reforms we advocate, this would become one of a number of changes contributing to an attack on inequality through the fiscal system.

Conclusion

Our present rating system is highly regressive. We have seen that the poorest households have to allocate 8·2 per cent of their income to rates, compared with only 2·2 per cent for higher-income groups. Attempts to counter the regressive nature of our rating system by the introduction of a national rate rebate scheme have been only partially successful. In this chapter we therefore looked at alternative ways by which local authorities could raise revenue. The Layfield Committee has proposed a local income tax. If rates were abolished entirely it would require the levying of an additional 11–12p as a local income tax. We rejected this proposal. Instead we propose that non-domestic rates should be retained, which will mean that local authorities will then only have to levy a local income tax of 4·5p in the £. Even without a major overhaul of the present system of income tax which we propose in the final section, this would result in a fairer local tax system. However, combined with a national income-tax system based on progressive principles, a local income tax would play an important part in helping to bring about a redistribution of the tax burden onto those with the broadest shoulders.

References

1. *Local Government Finance, Report of the Committee of Enquiry*, Cmnd 6453, HMSO, 1976 (referred to as the *Layfield Report* from now on).
2. *Layfield Report*, p. 150, Table 7.
3. J. R. and U. K. HICKS, *The Incidence of Local Rates in Great Britain*, NIESR, Occasional Paper No. 8, Cambridge University Press, 1945.
4. *Report of the Committee of Enquiry into the Impact of Rates on Households*, Cmnd 2582, HMSO, 1965.
5. J. WISEMAN, 'Local Government in the Twentieth Century', *Lloyds Bank Review*, No. 79, 1966.

6. *Financial and Other Circumstances of Retirement Pensioners*, HMSO, 1966. Similar results were found in a number of local studies: MOLLY MEACHER, *Rate Rebates: A Study of the Effectiveness of Means Tests*, Poverty Research Series No. 1, CPAG, 1971; C. PURCELL, *Prospects for Rent Allowances*, Wandsworth People's Rights, 1973; STUART MACPHERSON, *Poverty and Low Wages: Means-Tested Benefits and the Working Poor*, unpublished thesis.

7. MEACHER, op. cit.

8. *Layfield Report*, p. 135, Table 4.

9. PROFESSOR ALAN DAY, note of reservation to the *Layfield Report*, p. 311.

8   Tax and Social-Security Abuse

Feelings run high on the question of social-security abuse, but what are the facts? How much money is lost from public funds by people who illegally claim benefit, and how does this compare with the loss in revenue from taxpayers who commit abuse? This is the first question we try to answer in this chapter. We then go on to consider the measures governments take both to police the social-security system and to clamp down on tax abuse.

Extent of Fraud

Almost three quarters of known benefit fraud is by supplementary benefit (SB) recipients (see Table 27, p. 154). We therefore concentrate our attention on the main forms of SB abuse, which consist of claimants who refuse to take up work, those who draw benefit but work on the side, and those who claim to be heading a single-parent family when they are in fact part of a household where one of the partners is in full-time work.

Claimants who are unemployed may be eligible for unemployment pay. For the first six months of unemployment a claimant may be eligible for an earnings-related supplement in addition to the flat-rate benefit which is payable for up to one year to those claimants who have adequate contribution records. However, the level of income claimants derive from the flat-rate unemployment benefit is usually less than the official poverty line. They may therefore be eligible to have their income increased by what is now called supplementary benefits, but was called national assistance up until 1966.

Successive reports of the National Assistance Board (NAB) and the Supplementary Benefits Commission (SBC) have stressed how difficult it is for a layman to judge whether a person is workshy as opposed to suffering from a mental or physical disability which makes the undertaking of work difficult. Moreover, when detailed investigations have taken place the number of workshy claimants is found to be very small indeed.

The first detailed study on the attitude of unemployed claimants was carried out in 1951. After completing their inquiries the NAB officers, who were asked to judge if claimants were 'workshy', reported: 'In all, out of nearly 60,000 recipients who were classified as "unemployed" at the beginning of December, the Board's officers were not prepared to say firmly that more than 7,000 (5,500 men and 1,500 women) were persons who could be working if they wanted to work.'[1]

A much more detailed investigation of unemployed claimants was carried out in 1956 and the NAB reported similar findings. 'The results disclose many problems, but do not support any suggestion that workshyness is extensive, since three out of four of those interviewed, and more than four out of five of those who had been out of work for three or more years, were found to be under some sort of physical and/or mental handicap.'[2] Interviewing officers regarded 7 per cent of unemployed claimants as workshy, although on closer examination it was found that over three fifths of these claimants had physical disabilities or ill health. Moreover, it was reported that a considerable number of claimants, handicapped or not, whose attitude to work was considered unsatisfactory would probably have been unable to obtain employment even if they had been enthusiastic in seeking it, and in some cases lack of success over a long period may perhaps have contributed to a loss of enthusiasm.

Similar studies on the unemployed have been carried out in 1958, 1961 and 1964. All these studies reaffirmed both the smallness of the numbers of workshy claimants and, moreover, the extent of handicap amongst this small group who do not appear to be over-anxious to work. The most recent survey on the attitude of unemployed claimants was carried out in 1973. Interviewers were not requested to judge whether a claimant was workshy, but were asked to collect information on the unemployed's attitude to work. 'Although in the assessment of the local office staff a third of unemployed men appeared "somewhat unenthusiastic

for work" this does not mean that those men would in practice refuse a job if one was offered.'[3] The report noted that they would
be in danger of losing benefit if they did. Moreover, on closer
examination, the vast majority of these men lived in areas where
the Department thought the job prospects were bleak for all
unemployed workers. It is therefore difficult to judge to what
extent the unemployed claimant's enthusiasm had waned after
repeated failures to find work. Nor can we judge to what extent
this response given to interviewing officers was a cover for men
who feel rejected by a society unable to offer them worthwhile
employment. Indeed, it is worth noting that a follow-up study
six months later found a third of these men in full-time work.

There are also two other forces at work which may now make
it very difficult both to collect and interpret figures on supposed
workshyness. Recently we have witnessed an example of what now
appears to be an intermittent campaign against those claimants
who, it is alleged in the media, refuse to take work which is offered
them. As well as affecting the views of the general public, these
campaigns must be influencing the attitudes of supplementary
benefit officers and their opposite numbers working in the Department of Employment. It may be that local officers, when asked
to classify a claimant's attitude to work, are now over-anxious to
find the workshy about which they read and hear so much. Moreover, as many officers draw a wage which is less than the poverty-
line income for a two-child family[4] the need to feel and appear
separate from claimants might be partially achieved by stigmatiz-
ing many of those on the other side of the counter as not really
wanting to work, while forgetting that far fewer claimants are
now offered jobs once they have been unemployed for thirteen or
more weeks.

Secondly, we believe that we have witnessed during recent
years a changing attitude to work by many claimants. This is not
to say that large numbers of men do not still turn up and work a
full week for a wage which is less than the benefit they could
draw if they were not working. The most recent estimate published
by the government is for 1974. Reworking *Family Expenditure
Survey* data, government spokesmen have suggested that about
70,000 breadwinners are in this position. But our impression

is, and we stress it is only an impression, that increasingly young people are much more critical of the work they are asked to do. If their job opportunities extend only to boring low-paid work, there appears to be an increase in the numbers who either move from job to job, or who work only to tide them over their next period moving around the country. There has also been an increase in the number of family men who rightly refuse to take a job which will pay them less in net terms than they are currently drawing in benefit. Such a view has been officially approved by the Fisher Committee when it reported on the extent of supplementary-benefit abuse. The Committee recommended that men should not be required to take jobs which, even when one has added in all the means-tested benefits they will be eligible for once they start work, give them a lower net take-home pay.

Later in this chapter we will be examining the controls operated by the government which are aimed at getting people off benefit and into work. At this stage in our argument, all we need to note is that during 1974 577,676 claimants lost all or had part of their benefit reduced because they refused work, or left their last job without good cause, or had one or more of the regular control procedures applied against them (161,715 were sent for interviews with employment review officers, 383,000 were suspended from unemployment benefit, and 25,459 SB claimants lost all or part of their benefit because it was alleged they left their last job without good cause or refused to take suitable employment. 2,019 were sent to re-establishment centres and a further 5,483 were requested to attend for a medical examination.)

The second form of social-security abuse, and one which may cause the official figures to overestimate the numbers of people on low income, is the claimants' failure to disclose income which may disqualify them from benefit. Those on unemployment benefit are allowed to earn only 75p a day. Supplementary benefit claimants are entitled to benefit only provided their income and capital is below what are known as the prescribed limits. Claimants are allowed to have £1,200 capital before losing any of their entitlement to supplementary benefit, as well as earning up to £2 a week from part-time employment (£4 if they do not have to register for work).

How many claimants draw benefit while at the same time undertaking full or part-time employment which makes them ineligible for benefit? In 1974 the government investigated 9,961 cases where it was thought claimants were undertaking employment, together with 3,945 claimants who it was alleged were self-employed. Of these claimants 38 per cent and 41 per cent respectively lost their benefit after investigations were completed.[5]

In a recent study, Denis Marsden and Euan Duff reported in detail on some of these claimants who were working on the side. The Marsden survey was not a large or random one and this is a point which he stresses carefully. However it does allow claimants to speak for themselves. One claimant who was on the fiddle talked about the need to buy essential clothing for children when grants for shoes and other items had been refused by the SBC. Other men reported that fiddling started 'only after the failure of the search for work and with the build-up of the financial and other pressures from unemployment'. For many of the unemployed who had a job on the side, the extent of the extra income was limited. Marsden writes that: 'Fiddling was closely policed informally by local public opinion and by anonymous letters from neighbours (to the authorities), if a fiddler was thought to be getting more than his fair share of additional income.'[6] The greater the proportion of workless who took undeclared part-time jobs, the smaller were the rewards. This rationing must be operating even more severely at the present time with the growth in the numbers of long-term unemployed: 'It might be suggested that, paradoxically in times of high unemployment . . . the more tightly will the market forces operate to keep down fiddlers' gains from irregular work.'[7]

Unemployed claimants are not the only ones open to this temptation. The elderly, as well as the sick and those heading one-parent families, might be tempted to take a job without declaring it to the authorities. The DHSS assures taxpayers that each and every tip-off it receives from the general public about claimants working on the side is followed up and investigated. To a very large extent the government relies on neighbours reporting claimants who are drawing benefit as well as working at either a full- or a part-time job. However, the official figures which we have already quoted do not distinguish between these claimants and those who are registered as unemployed.

In 1974 287,000 families were headed by a single parent drawing supplementary benefit, and the public are concerned about two possible abuses committed by some of these families. The first concerns what is called 'fictitious desertion'. This occurs when a mother wrongly claims that she has been deserted by her husband and therefore is entitled to benefit as an unsupported mother. The second abuse is when a claimant is cohabiting or living as what is called a common-law wife. If the cohabitation occurs with another claimant, the woman is liable to have her needs assessed as a married woman, and her benefit correspondingly reduced. More commonly, cohabitation occurs with a man in full-time work, which makes a woman ineligible for benefit. (However, if the man's wage is below the new 'families' SB entitlement, benefit should be paid for the children.)

The Commission claims that in most instances claimants voluntarily disclosed that they were cohabiting and had their allowances altered accordingly. However, in a number of instances difficulties arise, particularly as it is very difficult to define what is meant by the term cohabitation. This is clearly seen from those claimants who appear in court on charges of fraud. Ruth Lister, who has conducted an independent piece of research into the operation of the cohabitation rule, reports that not only are claimants not told what is meant by the term cohabiting, but that when cases are heard before the courts the magistrates too have little interest in, and even less idea of the meaning of, the rule under which women have lost benefit. Instead, they content themselves with judging whether fraud has been committed on the basis of the woman's signed statements that there is not a man in the house.[8] In 1974 2,335 cases were investigated for fictitious desertion and 9,993 cases for undisclosed cohabitation. The investigations resulted in 45 per cent and 41 per cent respectively of allowances being reduced or withdrawn for each group of claimants who were investigated.

We will now try and estimate the amount of money wrongly claimed by claimants. This was an issue to which the Fisher Committee inquiring into the abuse of social-security benefits addressed itself. The Committee reported that 'abuse by wrongful claims is a serious problem. Although the *percentage of claims which are known to be fraudulent is not great, substantial sums of money are misappropriated each year.*'[9]

The Committee went on to define what is meant by 'substantial sums of money'. It obtained from the DHSS the net losses recorded in 1971–2 in respect of overpayments which were legally

TABLE 27. The amount of irrecoverable overpayment of all social-security benefit during 1974–5

	Total	Fraud on the part of the claimant or other person not being a servant of the Department
	£	£
Family benefits	205,805	32,310
Unemployment benefit	746,292	218,523
Sickness and invalidity benefit	1,754,832	299,243
Maternity benefit	29,840	8,139
Widow's benefit	148,914	65,747
Retirement pension	573,627	24,936
Industrial injury	178,149	20,242
Others	46,280	2,142
Supplementary benefit	5,010,139	1,405,676
Total	8,693,878	2,076,958

SOURCE: *Hansard*, 24 May 1976, Vol. 912, Cols. 79–80.

recoverable. The total overpayment in that year came to £1·5 million.[10] However, these figures include not only overpayment due to suspected fraud, but also others in which the question of fraud did not arise.

Since the Fisher Committee reported, the government has collected more accurate fraud figures. They can now break down the total of the amount of money which was irrecoverable owing to the overpayment of benefit, and to what extent this overpayment was fraudulent. The information for 1974–5 is detailed in Table 27. From this we can see that very nearly £8·7 million in benefit was recorded as irrecoverable overpayments. However, less than a quarter of the overpayments were due to fraud, and of that fraudulently claimed by far the greatest proportion occurred in the supplementary benefits system.

These figures should be approached with some caution. They record only the amount of detected fraud. To the extent that undetected fraud occurs the figures in the table above underestimate the true position. On the other hand, however, some people will argue that the figures released by the Department use the term 'fraud' all too loosely. Claimants are investigated and allowances are reduced or withdrawn, but the Department does not always feel that it has sufficient evidence to prove in a court of law that fraud has taken place. The Ruth Lister study, to which we have already referred, highlights the difficulties of mothers refuting a charge of fraudulently claiming benefit on grounds of cohabitation in that no one could tell them accurately what was meant by the term cohabitation. Further, it is worth comparing the amount of detected fraud with the sum paid out in benefit during the relevant year. For example, in 1975 £8·9 billion was paid out in social-security benefits alone. The amount of benefit fraudulently claimed is therefore £2 for every £8–9,000 paid to 'genuine' claimants.

Tax Abuse

Detected social-security fraud amounts to a fraction over £2 million a year. How does this compare with the non-payment of tax? We try to answer this question in two parts. The first looks at tax avoidance. This is legal, although we would judge socially very undesirable, and mainly concerns taxes on capital. We also examine the extent of tax evasion. This is illegal and mainly concerns taxes on income.

Until 1974 the main tax on capital was estate or death duty. This duty was charged on the capital value of property 'deemed to pass on death'. Capital valued under £15,000 was exempt.

Assets valued between £15,000 and £20,000 had a duty imposed upon them of 25 per cent. This rose to 75 per cent for estates valued above £1 million.

There were a number of special concessions associated with death duties. Agricultural property and business assets which were owned directly, together with gifts made four years before death, attracted reduced duty. Certain types of property, for example growing timber, were not aggregated with the rest of the estate, with the result that the property attracted a lower duty. A reduced duty applied if the estate came up for a second assessment of death duties within a five-year period. Moreover, some property was exempt altogether, including that settled on a surviving spouse, which bore duty on the first death, as well as certain gifts (up to £5,000 in consideration of marriage), property left to charities (up to £50,000 are exempt) and objects of national scientific and artistic interest.

When death duties were first introduced in 1894 they were said to 'throw into shade everything that had ever been done in the way of highway robbery'. The maximum rate was then 8 per cent. When the duty was replaced in 1975 by the capital transfer tax, the top duty was charged at 75 per cent. How effective was the duty in redistributing wealth?

Professor A. B. Atkinson has commented that the 'effectiveness of estate duty in reducing the transfer of wealth between generations depends sensitively on the way in which the rich react'.[11] He also noted how limited the redistribution of wealth had been this century and commented: 'What redistribution there has been is not between the rich and the poor, but between the very rich and the rich.'[12] He went on to explain that although the share of wealth owned by the richest 1 per cent had fallen this had been largely countered by a growth in the share of the richest 2·5 per cent wealth-holders. In other words, wealth was being spread more evenly within families and this helped to account for the large increase in wealth-holding of women which had taken place recently. But there had been no major redistribution from rich to poor.

One of the main reasons for this very limited redistribution of wealth was the ease with which a person could avoid paying death duties. There were five main avenues of avoidance. Certain assets bore lower rates of duty. Some forms of wealth were not aggregated with the rest of the estate when the duty was calculated (for example, timber growing, upon which, furthermore, the duty was not payable until the timber was sold. A third way of avoiding death duties was to export capital to places which levied lower or no death duties, commonly known as tax havens.

The two other ways of avoiding death duties were probably the most important. The first was by gifts *inter vivos* which, if given seven years before death, avoided all death duties. Reduced duty was paid on gifts made between four and seven years before death. However this method had one disadvantage. Once the money had been made over the power that ownership conferred was lost. Hence the growth of two forms of trusts. One form of trust settled property on a surviving spouse and so ensured that death duty was payable only when the first spouse died but not when the surviving spouse died. But there has also been a growth of what are called discretionary trusts. The essence of a discretionary trust is that beneficiaries are not entitled to any interest in the fund and have no enforceable claim on any part of the trust's income or capital. The person establishing the trust provides the trustees with a list of beneficiaries. These beneficiaries cannot be bound to act in accordance with the settlor's interest, although the settlor is able to choose who the trustees should be, and no doubt chooses those who will agree with his wishes.

Capital Tax Avoidance

Calculations have been made to estimate the extent to which people avoided paying death duties. Michael Meacher began his analysis by recalling that since 1909–14 estate duty rates on estates of £50,000 value have increased five-fold, and on estates of £1 million or more have increased six-fold. He went on to observe: 'This should mean that, subject to the maintenance during the ensuing sixty-year period of the same ratio between the number of estates at different capital ranges . . . the duty yield should have increased between five- and six-fold'.[13] Hence, he says, estate duty ought to have yielded £1·2 billion in 1969. Instead £381·9 million was raised in that year.

The second calculation has been undertaken by Professor Atkinson, who has commented that: 'One of the striking features of estate duty is the failure of the revenue to rise in line with the increase in the rates of duty.'[14] In 1911–13 the duties represented 0·25 per cent of total personal wealth. By 1966 this had increased to only 0·39 per cent – 'a very much smaller increase than one would have expected in view of the rise in the rates of duty'. In 1911–13 the highest rate of estate duty was 15 per cent, whereas in 1966 the rate was 75 per cent. Tony Atkinson therefore goes on to calculate that had the 1966 rate been enforced in 1912 the revenue payable would have been in the region of 1·5 per cent of total personal wealth. This implies that the total revenue from estate duty in 1966 should have been in the region of £1·2 billion rather than the £382 million actually raised.

We can present these conclusions in a different way. From the calculations of these two sources it appears that, at the time death duties were in force, for every £1 actually paid in death duties, something like £3 was avoided. This means that in the 1973–4 financial year death duties raised a little over £412 million instead of around £1·6 billion which could have been expected had the revenue from the duty kept in line with the rise in the country's wealth-holding.

In 1975 death duties were superseded by the capital transfer tax. In introducing the new measure the Chancellor remarked that the tax was 'to ensure that the estate duty fulfilled the function first laid down for it eighty years ago'.[15] The tax is levied at progressive rates charged on the cumulative total of gifts made during a person's lifetime with a further final cumulation of property passing on death. The transfer of assets between husband and wife is exempt from the tax but the special relief for agricultural land, business assets and woodlands has been withdrawn. A few small concessions to wealth-holders were made however. For instance farm land transferred by a full-time working farmer in his lifetime or on his death is subject to special rates of valuation, and any taxpayer can give away £2,000 annually without such sums being added to his cumulative total of capital transfers.

As with death duties there is no tax on the first £15,000 of capital transferred. For capital transferred valued between £15–20,000 the rate is 10 per cent, as opposed to 25 per cent which applied under the death duty rates. The full rate of 75 per cent applies only to capital transfers of £2 million or more, whereas on death duties this rate was reached at £1 million. Because the tax applies to all transfers of capital 'and will not be open to avoidance' the Chancellor optimistically expressed his firm belief that in the long term 'it will produce a higher yield than the existing estate duty despite the reduction in the rates and the exemption for transfers between husband and wife'.

Such optimism is unfortunately not borne out by the facts. Alongside traditional means of tax avoidance which have been adapted to suit the new tax, highly ingenious and totally artificial methods of avoidance have been rapidly developed by the two professions most concerned with advising clients on methods of tax avoidance – solicitors and accountants. Many of those methods are highly technical and involve the export of capital to a tax haven such as the Isle of Man, Channel Islands or Cayman Islands, and the setting-up there of some sort of trust. A typical second step would be a form of 'laundering' in which one or more layers of anonymity are grafted on through formation of local companies in which the capital is invested. Inevitably the transactions which follow are far less open to scrutiny by the Revenue than they would be in England since the provision of the Companies Act with respect to compulsory supply of information as to ownership, activities and accounts do not apply. Finally methods must be found to funnel profits back to the client. To quote from an article recently published by the official magazine of the Law Society (the solicitors' professional body charged with the statutory duty of overseeing the profession's standard of conduct) outlining the tax-avoidance possibilities of overseas trusts: 'in general it is true to say that in setting up a foreign trust in future the emphasis should be not so much upon removing assets from the United Kingdom or creating a foreign vehicle – or perhaps "receptacle" would be the better word – for future gains and the capital they may represent'.[16] The same article states: 'the problem in such schemes is getting the proceeds into the hands of the beneficiary. This might be done by means of loans from the company . . .' These types of avoidance schemes are, however, expensive to set up and are applicable only if substantial sums of money are involved. Less sophisticated, but highly effective methods are available much closer to home for anyone willing and able to consult a solicitor or tax accountant. All of them are to some extent artificial, in that they involve going through the motions of a transaction which is perfectly valid in law, but is not being used for its usual purpose, but rather in order to obtain a tax advantage. One example will suffice to illustrate the scope for wide-scale tax avoidance very clearly.

Most people would like to pass on their houses to their children and grandchildren and the tax threshold for capital transfer tax of £15,000 was doubtless chosen to reflect the price of an average home so as to enable an owner-occupier with a small house and a certain amount of savings to pass these on free of tax on his or her death. A house worth £80,000 is expected however to bear £19,250 worth of tax on transfer at a person's death to someone other than that person's spouse. It is possible to avoid the tax altogether by going through the motions of 'selling' the house to one's children or grandchildren, subject to one's right to the property for the remainder of one's life. This is known technically as selling a reversionary interest in the property. The 'purchase price' will be the value of the property discounted to take account of the seller's expectation of life. Suppose a woman in good health in her late fifties is widowed and left an £80,000 house in Sunningdale. She could sell the property to her son at a price of around £12,000. No money would in fact change hands, as the 'seller' could 'loan' £12,000 to her son and each year could then release him from payment of interest and part repayment of the capital. With present gift exemption a £12,000 loan at 12 per cent interest can be amortized within eight years. The resulting loss to the Exchequer on the death of the widow is nearly £20,000. It only requires 100 people each year to carry out this manoeuvre to produce a loss to the Exchequer equalling the loss due to all known social-security abuse. The scheme outlined above is in general use in 'tax-planning' offices in England together with many other ingenious schemes. Finally those whose consciences prick at the thought of tax avoidance can nevertheless mitigate the problem of capital transfer tax by insuring their lives for an amount which matches their estimated capital transfer tax liability. Insurance money paid out on death is exempt from capital transfer tax, and the insured can of course claim tax relief on the premiums paid.

What steps are being taken to deal with tax avoidance? The Inland Revenue has very extensive powers under the Income and Corporation Taxes Act 1970 and the Finance Act 1976 to investigate tax avoidance and levy taxes where an intent to avoid tax can be shown. Nevertheless there is little evidence that these powers are being effectively used. Only about thirty unskilled people are apparently employed by the Inland Revenue on administering these powers. Investigations have shown that in connection with one type of tax-avoidance scheme alone (involving discretionary trusts) control over billions of pounds' worth of investment in land was transferred to the Channel Islands with the result that no tax can be assessed on the income. As much as £1,000 million a year in income tax may be being avoided in this way. Even if the Inland Revenue succeeded in discovering the existence of such trusts, there is no provision for the capital to be subjected to capital transfer tax until the tenth anniversary of the trust, and in any case not before 1980. Most of these 'capital transfer tax-avoidance' trusts will remain untaxable until 1984–5. Before this there will have been at least one, probably two, general elections.

Tax Evasion

There was probably very little illegal evasion of death duties for the simple reason that it was so easy legally to avoid paying them. The same does not apply to taxes on income. We must therefore look at what information there is to help us to judge the size of this tax evasion. Our first piece of information comes from the Inland Revenue's own published reports. Each year the Commissioners publish data on the amount of tax remitted or written off as irrecoverable. The Commissioners also give reasons as to why the tax was not collected. The most recent report relates to the

year ending 31 March 1975. It gives details of the amount of tax
remitted or written off for each year since 1965 up to and including 1974. Adding the totals together for this period we find that
the Revenue gave up chasing a little under £119 million.[17] The
grounds least often accepted as a reason for remitting tax were
those of hardship. The most important reason why the Revenue
concluded that the tax was irrecoverable was that nearly half of
this £119 million was lost because the taxpayer had gone abroad.
We remain one of the few countries where people can emigrate
without presenting a tax-clearance certificate. This small change
in the way we conduct our affairs would have resulted in 1974 in
nearly £10 million additional revenue, and the lack of such a
measure is just one contrast with the battery of anti-abuse
measures on the social-security front.

Large as this sum is compared with the detected abuse of all
social-security benefits, it pales into insignificance when we look
at the extent of evasion of taxes by the self-employed. Here it is
useful to distinguish between those self-employed who employ
accountants, and the self-employed who practise what is commonly called 'the lump', who declare themselves self-employed but
have little intention of paying either tax or national-insurance
contributions.

The Commissioners of Inland Revenue also present data on the
numbers of under-assessments made by taxpayers. Their latest
report shows that 11,707 under-assessments were detected in
1975.[18] In an attempt to present this total in the best possible
light, the journal *Taxation* has written: 'When considering the
extent of evasion [by under-assessment] it is easy to overlook the
fact that only about 10,000 inquiry cases a year are settled . . .
but these figures are a very small proportion of the total number
of taxpayers, which is in the region of 20 million.' But as the
Inland Revenue Staff Federation has pointed out, in almost all
these 10,000 cases an accountant will have been acting. Further,
this total represents nearly one in a hundred self-employed taxpayers. The Inland Revenue Staff Federation calculated that these
accountants help their clients to under-assess their income by
about £45 million a year and so dodge about £15 million in
taxes.[19] If readers believe that this is overestimating the position

it should be remembered that only 70,000 self-employed declare an average wage of £60 a week or more and that only 250,000 of them admit to earning more than £30 a week. As one of the authorities on tax abuse has written, these 'low incomes to which the self-employed admit defy belief'.[20]

The second area of tax evasion on income concerns the massive growth in recent years of what is called 'the lump'. Attempts by politicians to counter the growth of this illegal practice are being supported by the whole of the trade-union movement; the building trade unions have been particularly keen on combatting the growth of the lump. Not only are they concerned with the loss of revenue resulting from this practice, but they also draw attention to the fact that safety standards are all too often ignored in the attempt to increase take-home pay.

By its very nature it is very difficult to estimate the amount of revenue lost by those operating the lump. This task however has been attempted by Anthony Christopher. He has written that with 'at least 415,000 men (and the Inland Revenue knows that there are at least that number) plus perhaps 200,000 about whom we know nothing, or who are using bogus companies, we may well be talking about £200 million or £500 million loss of revenue to the community'.[21]

Two Attitudes to Abuse

A little over £2 million a year is wrongly claimed from our social-security system. About £15 million a year is lost in revenue from the self-employed because of the skilled practices of accountants. Moreover we have just seen that one estimate is that up to £500 million a year is lost through operation of the lump. Given these figures one would expect both that the public would demand action, and that the government would reflect this demand in a whole battery of measures to prevent tax abuse, while one would expect little public disquiet about the extent of social-security abuse, and even less concern about the measures aimed at controlling it. But the reverse is true. We now turn our discussion to an examination of the methods by which the government seeks to combat both social-security and tax abuse, looking at the control procedures as applied to supplementary benefits unless otherwise stated.

Earlier we examined the three main areas of social-security abuse. These consisted of claimants who were workshy, those who claim benefits but worked on the side, and those who claimed a fictitious desertion or cohabited with a man in full-time work. To prevent abuse of benefit the Department has a whole battery of what are called control procedures. We will examine the range of these procedures against each type of abuse.

By far the most extensive battery of control procedures are applied against claimants thought to be workshy. First of all a claimant may be refused benefit at the outset of his claim. No figures have been collected on the number of claimants so treated, but experience from welfare rights agencies suggests that the numbers are not inconsiderable. Secondly, unless a claimant heads a single-parent family, is registered sick, or is over retirement age, benefit is payable only on registering for work. Furthermore, those claimants who it is judged have left or lost their previous job without good cause are suspended from unemployment benefit for up to six weeks, and on top of this will lose 40 per cent of their supplementary benefit entitlement. A claimant may also be suspended indefinitely from unemployment benefit if he places unreasonable restrictions on the kind of work he will take. Again, welfare rights organizations find that many claimants are wrongly penalized for allegedly leaving their work without just cause. The numbers of suspensions of unemployment benefit and reductions in supplementary benefit are substantial. Nearly 383,000 claimants were so penalized and were suspended from unemployment pay in 1974. Furthermore, 22,000 claimants also had their supplementary benefit entitlement reduced.

Thirdly, special efforts are made to find the long-term unemployed job opportunities, and for this the DHSS employs a group of unemployment review officers. In 1961 the first ten such officers were appointed because: 'It was found that an officer who had sufficient time to conduct long and repeated interviews with the man concerned, to arrange for him to receive offers of employment through the Ministry of Labour [now the Department of Employment], to make sure he went after jobs offered, to question him closely about the result of his application – confirming his story with the employer, where this seemed desirable – was often able to bring about greater and more decisive results than an officer who had normal area office duties to carry out at the same time.' Today there are 107 unemployment review officers, and since 1970 the numbers of unemployed who have been interviewed by these officers have more than doubled. The Department reports that, of those interviewed, very nearly half ceased to draw benefit shortly after the interview. They do not add, however, if the claimant was successful in finding work, or had just given up trying to claim benefit for fear of what many claimants regard as 'harassment' from some DHSS officers.

The fourth control procedure is operated by requesting claimants to attend a medical examination. It is a standard procedure for those claimants under the age of 55 who allege they are suffering from some sort of physical and/or mental disability and who have been claiming benefit for more than six months to be referred for a medical examination. In 1960, when this procedure was started, 46 per cent of claimants requested to attend the medical during the year found employment either before or shortly after the examination. There has been no research on why claimants refuse to turn up for the medical. Some may feel they could no longer 'swing the lead', while others may have found that during the time between seeing their own doctor and being requested to attend a medical their health had improved and they were therefore able to seek work. But there may well be other claimants who were still unfit for work but, judging that they were being sent for a medical examination because the authorities thought they were scrounging, ceased to draw benefit rather than have this label attached to them. There has been no work undertaken on the question of how large a group of claimants are scared off benefit by the application of this and other control procedures. What we do know is that in 1974 5,483 claimants were referred by local officers for a medical examination by the Department's regional medical service.

Fifthly, unemployed claimants may also be paid benefit provided they attend a re-establishment centre. These centres were first established in 1951 and there are now sixteen operating around the country. In 1975 2,043 persons attended one or other of these establishments during the year. The aim of a re-establishment centre is for a claimant to be 'reintroduced to a work routine'. If any one of these control procedures fails to get a claimant back to work, he may also be sued for the non-maintenance of himself and his family. In 1974 such action was taken against nearly 600 claimants. In addition, spot checks on unemployed claimants were announced in late 1976. Those claimants who it is thought might have a job on the side may find investigators turning up un-announced at their homes.

All these control procedures still operate, despite the post-war record level of unemployment and the government's policy of allowing unemployment to rise in an attempt to control inflation. Indeed, there is considerable evidence to show that official figures underestimate the numbers of unemployed. At the beginning of 1976 the DE monthly returns show about 1·2 million unemployed persons registering at their local offices. We know that large numbers of claimants do not register because they are neither eligible for unemployment benefit, nor is it likely that the Exchange will be able to offer them suitable employment. In early 1976 a more accurate unemployment figure has been put at 1·8 million.[22] However, when the official unemployment figures begin to fall the government will reintroduce an additional control procedure which will go under the name of the modified four-week rule. The old rule was in operation from the middle of 1968 until the three-day week in 1974. All fit, unskilled men under 45 living in areas where it was 'thought' work was available had their supplementary benefit claims limited to four weeks. Other claimants had their benefit limited to up to three months. During the period in which the four-week rule operated nearly 300,000 claimants were thrown off benefit.[23] In fact the four-week rule was reintroduced in a few areas in 1976 as cheap casual labour was required for harvest work or in the holiday industry.[24]

The new four-week rule procedures will operate in the following way. Once fit, claimants aged between 18 and 45 having drawn benefit for four weeks, the right to benefit will be reviewed, and claimants may be sent for an interview with an unemployment review officer. If the officer considers that the claimant has not made a serious attempt to find work, benefit may be withdrawn. This can happen even though the officer does not offer the claimant the name and address of an employer who is seeking additional workers.

For the other two forms of social-security abuse – working on the side or cohabiting – the DHSS assures the community that each and every tip-off received from the general public about such claimants is followed up and fully investigated. As we have already seen, to a very large extent the government relies on neighbours' reports on claimants, and for each of these tip-offs the Department has a squad of what are known as special investigators. These officers are in fact the Supplementary Benefit Commission's own police force. The first investigators were appointed in 1954 and twenty years later their numbers had risen to 471. These officers are vigilant in their duties.

In 1974 they carried out 13,906 investigations into claimants who were working while claiming to be unemployed. In addition, 12,328 women who it was thought were cohabiting or claiming a fictitious desertion had their circumstances investigated by this squad of officers. If taxpayers generally had as high a level of productivity as special investigators do in cracking down on abuse, our feeling is that there wouldn't be very much wrong with the performance of the British economy.

The control procedures aimed at preventing tax abuse look pretty weak when placed side by side with those connected with social-security fraud. Fortunately, over the last few years there has been the odd sign or two of a changing attitude to tax abuse. Amongst a number of groups the trade unions have been taking a much stronger line on the whole question. For example, the TUC in its *Economic Review* for 1976 wrote: 'Changing the structure of income tax is only one part of the reforms needed to ensure that the well-off pay their fair share. Of equal if not greater importance is the drive against the avoidance and evasion of tax.' A year previously they put their views in even stronger terms: 'The General Council classify tax evasion as theft and believe it should be treated as such.'[25]

We have already seen that the government has taken powers by way of the capital transfer tax to attempt to prevent tax avoidance on capital. The need for the Revenue to have increased power to track down tax evasion on income was finally conceded in the 1976 Finance Act. Introducing the new measure the Chancellor of the Exchequer commented: 'The amount of tax evasion uncovered by the Revenue has fallen by 80 per cent in recent years' and added stoically that he did not believe this was due to a greater honesty amongst taxpayers.[26] He then went on to outline the new powers. The first concerned the power of a tax inspector to issue a notice calling for documents which relate to an individual's tax liability. The Chancellor commented that with most taxpayers this happens automatically because they pay under PAYE .The second power concerns the right of tax inspectors to enter premises with a warrant. The relevant section of the Act provides that if a judge is satisfied by information presented by the Revenue on oath that there are reasonable grounds for suspecting tax evasion, he may issue a warrant to an Officer of the Board of Inland Revenue. The Officer will then be authorized to enter premises, search for and seize documents as well as other evidence which might be needed for proceedings against the taxpayer.

Conclusion

The Parliamentary debate on this section of the Finance Act illustrates the central theme of this chapter. Max Madden, the Labour Member for Sowerby, questioning the Financial Secretary to the Treasury, was reported as saying that the enormous cost of tax evasion to the nation is more widely resented by working people than are the new powers being given to Inland Revenue officers. He went on to add: 'In the examination of the handful of cases brought against those who evade tax, and in so far as losses are concerned, there seems to be a double standard portrayed compared to the enormous number of prosecutions for abuse of the social-security system.'[27] In replying, the Financial Secretary to the Treasury underlined this point, adding: 'There is a need for comparison between the ability of certain sections of our community to evade their responsibilities in the tax field, and the need to get into perspective some of the abuses that take place on a much smaller scale and amounts in the social-security field.'[28] This new perspective is immensely important. What we have tried to do in this chapter is precisely what was called for by the Financial Secretary to the Treasury. The picture which emerges from this information is that the amount lost in tax abuse is massive compared with the loss from social-security fraud. And yet the demand is for greater and greater control procedures to prevent benefit abuse and stiff resistance from some quarters to quite small measures to control the growing problem of tax evasion. However the campaign about the extent of benefit abuse does play an important part in reinforcing what we have tried to show in this book to be the completely erroneous view that the welfare state largely benefits the poor and is paid for by the rich. An unsuspecting reader of the British press could think that not only do the rich largely foot the welfare bill, but that much of what benefit is provided goes to 'scroungers', or, as they are sometimes more politely called, those without 'genuine' need. Again this anti-welfare campaign has helped to reinforce the view that welfare expenditure is unnecessarily high and that its resulting tax burden has helped drastically to narrow income differences in the post-war world.

References

1. *Report of the National Assistance Board, 1951*, Cmnd 8632, HMSO, 1952, p. 8.
2. *Report of the National Assistance Board, 1956*, Cmnd 181, HMSO, 1957, p. 15.
3. 'Characteristics of the Unemployed: Sample Survey June 1973', *DE Gazette*, March 1974, p. 212.
4. FRANK FIELD, 'Low Pay Under the Counter', *Low Pay Bulletin* No. 8, April 1976.
5. *Hansard*, 28 October 1975, Vol. 898, Cols. 355–6.
6. DENIS MARSDEN and EUAN DUFF, *Workless*, Penguin Books, 1975, p. 247.
7. ibid., p. 247.
8. RUTH LISTER, *As Man and Wife?*, Child Poverty Action Group, 1973.
9. *Report of the Committee on Abuse of Social Security Benefits*, Cmnd 5228, HMSO, 1973, p. 224 (italics in the original).

10. ibid., p. 51.

11. A. B. ATKINSON, *Unequal Shares*, Penguin Books, 1974 p. 120.

12. ibid., p. 10.

13. MICHAEL MEACHER, 'Labour's Achilles Heel', in P. Townsend and N. Bosanquet, eds., *Labour and Inequality*, Fabian Society, 1972, p. 195.

14. op. cit., p. 216.

15. *Hansard*, 12 November 1974, Vol. 881, Col. 275.

16. ANTHONY SUMPTIM, 'Overseas Settlements', *Law Society Gazette*, 3 November 1976.

17. *Report of the Commissioners' of Her Majesty's Inland Revenue*, Cmnd 6302, HMSO, 1975, Table 20.

18. ibid., p. 17.

19. ANTHONY CHRISTOPHER, 'Faces Unwashed', *Taxes*, August 1973, p. 400.

20. ANTHONY CHRISTOPHER, 'The New Revenue Powers', *Taxes*, May 1976, p. 210.

21. ANTHONY CHRISTOPHER, 'Tax Evasion and the Self Employed', *Taxes*, October 1974, p. 482.

22. FRANK FIELD, *What the Unemployment Figures Really Show*, Child Poverty Action Group, 1976.

23. MOLLY MEACHER, *Scrounging on the Welfare*, Arrow, 1974.

24. Letter to CPAG from DHSS.

25. *TUC Economic Review*, 1975, p. 97.

26. *Hansard*, 3 May 1976, Vol. 901, Col. 849.

27. *The Times*, 5 May 1976.

28. *The Times*, 14 May 1976.

9 Inequality and the Welfare State

The tax system is one of the corner-stones of Britain's welfare state. As one government minister recently expressed it: 'The tax man is the Robin Hood of our time, taking from those who can afford it the means whereby we can pay every worker the wage that really matters, the social wage.'[1] At the beginning of this book we went back to some of the basic principles underlying this system of taxation – an exercise which finance ministers have apparently failed to undertake for twenty years or more. These principles stated that the income tax should be progressive, that it should acknowledge differences in taxable capacity and that the poor should be exempt. Such principles have never been explicitly applied to the other elements of the tax system – national-insurance contributions, expenditure taxes or local-authority rates – except in a very half-hearted way. Nevertheless, there is a general belief that the tax system as a whole is progressive – that it takes from the rich to give to the poor. How realistic is this widely held view of British taxation? In previous chapters we have examined separately each of the main forms of taxation. Here we fit the pieces of the jig-saw together. First we consider each type of tax to see whether it conforms to the accepted principles of equity and progressiveness which we have described. Second, we examine the extent to which each tax increases or decreases the level of economic inequality. We then bring these fragmented pieces together to see what the overall picture looks like: to see how progressive the whole system is and to ask the question 'who pays the bills?'.

The second corner-stone of the welfare state is the range of benefits and services provided by the government out of taxation. It is generally assumed that these are enjoyed most by the poorer sections of the community, and that the combination of a tax

system which takes from the rich and social welfare provision
which gives to the poor is a powerful force towards the reduction
of economic and social inequalities. In the second half of this
chapter we will be looking more closely at the distribution of
public expenditure to ask the question 'who benefits?'.

Is Taxation Progressive?

In the preceding chapters, we have examined the administration
and effects of each type of tax in some detail, but before we bring
them together to look at the overall impact it is perhaps worth
summarizing our main findings. Income tax is both the most
important and the most progressive single form of taxation. But
in Chapters 2 and 3 we found that, with the increasing importance
of personal income tax in the years since the war, there have been
a number of developments which have seriously modified its
progressive nature. With the abolition of the reduced rates of tax
and the widening of the standard-rate band, income tax is now
basically proportional. The only exception to this is the higher-
rate tax structure which effects less than 2 per cent of the taxpaying population. All other income taxpayers, from the very
poor to the rich, pay at the same marginal rate, currently 35p in
the £. An element of progressiveness has been retained through
the system of personal allowances, which ensures that a smaller
proportion of the income of poorer households is treated as
taxable, but in recent years even this mild element of progression
has been undermined. Governments have allowed inflation to
erode the value of the personal allowances, with the result that
tax is now payable below the official poverty line. At the same
time there has been a proliferation of the many expenditure
reliefs which can be claimed to avoid the payment of taxation and
which benefit most high-income groups. These ensure that the
average rate of income tax remains constant over a very wide
range of incomes. As the TUC pointed out as long ago as 1968,
'the progressivity implicit in the different rates of tax is very
much reduced when account is taken of the allowances which
can be set off against it'.[2]

In Chapter 4, we looked at the financing of the insurance side of the welfare state. Most people treat the income tax and national-insurance contributions as a single tax. This is perhaps a realistic attitude, since the two types of tax – though intended for different purposes – are now collected together through the same PAYE machinery. In addition, national-insurance contributions are perhaps more important as a determinant of living standards for workpeople at the lower end of the income scale than income tax itself. On earnings of £30 a week, for instance, a typical (two-child) family pays virtually no income tax, but national-insurance contributions will take £1·73 from their pay packet.

Taken together, the regressive nature of national-insurance contributions offsets to a large extent the mildly progressive effect of income tax. As we saw in Chapter 4, despite the conversion of the social-security tax from a flat rate to a proportional basis, it remains regressive, breaching most of the accepted principles of equitable taxation. In the first place, it incorporates even less recognition of differential ability to pay than the income tax. Contributions at the full rate (currently 5¾ per cent) are payable on all earnings once they exceed £13 a week – less than one half the tax threshold for a one-child family. At the same time the contributions make no allowance for differing family circumstances. A family with four children has the same liability to national-insurance contributions as a bachelor with the same earnings. Finally the ceiling for national-insurance contributions, beyond which they become a flat-rate tax once more, ensures that they take proportionately less from the better-off household. On earnings up to the basic tax threshold (£31·40 for a two-child family in 1976–7) the marginal rate of tax is 5¾ per cent, jumping to 40¾ per cent once the threshold is crossed. It remains at this rate up to the earning ceiling for national-insurance contributions (£96 a week in 1976–7), at which point it *drops* to 35 per cent, rising to 40 per cent only beyond the surtax threshold. The employee contributions to the national-insurance scheme are therefore regressive, causing considerable hardship to the poor in work in order to finance the national-insurance benefits payable to the poor out of work (pensions, unemployment benefits, etc.).

This brings us to indirect taxes. These fall into two categories.

First there are those on final goods and services – the expenditure taxes and excise duties, VAT and domestic rates. In Chapters 5 to 7 we examined the increasing regressiveness of indirect taxes in recent years and found that this was due largely to the increasing burden of local-authority rates, which bear particularly heavily on low-income households. Local domestic rates are particularly regressive because they are assessed according to the value of property, and bear a very weak relationship with household income. This means that the burden falls disproportionately on low-income households. To mitigate this effect the government introduced a rate rebate scheme in 1966 (which was significantly improved in 1974). Nevertheless, low-income households who do receive rebates can still pay a higher proportion of their income in rates than households at the higher end of the income scale. At the same time there are a significant number of households with an income well below the average who do not qualify for a rebate at all. In such cases 10 per cent or more of the family income can be taken in rates. In terms of horizontal inequity as well, rates can be particularly regressive, though mitigated again by the effect of rebates. Larger families obviously require more housing space and are therefore called upon to contribute proportionately more to local revenue. As one commentator has argued, the rate burden operates for this reason as a negative family allowance.[3]

Amongst the expenditure taxes, that on tobacco is the most regressive of all. As we saw in Chapters 5 and 6, this tax, which has increased steadily over the years, now takes roughly twice the proportion from the income of low-income households as from richer families. The introduction of VAT into this country was engineered in such a way that the burden was marginally higher on high-income than on low-income groups. Nevertheless, the tax bears more heavily on low-income groups than would be the case if considerations of equity were taken fully into account.

The second type of indirect taxes are those on intermediate goods and services, including taxes on raw materials and labour. Local-authority rates on commercial and industrial property and the employers' contributions to the national-insurance fund fall into this group. As we have already seen, the employees' contributions bear more heavily on low-income groups than on the better-paid. But an element of fairness does seem to have been retained through the employers' contributions, commonly regarded as a direct benefit to their staff. While this belief lingers in the minds of the general public, however, it has since the late sixties been discarded in official accounting exercises. The employers' contributions to national insurance are now regarded as 'an indirect tax on intermediate goods and services' in the recognition that firms merely pass the contributions on through the price as an extra labour cost. Indeed, when the government announced an increase in the rate of the employers' contribution in July 1976, the Chancellor met criticisms that this would create a squeeze on profits by pointing out: 'It is open to employers who can afford to do so in their competitive situation to pass on this increase in wage costs in the form of prices.' He estimated that this would bring about an increase of about 1 per cent in the price level, and assured firms that 'the addition, like the existing contributions, will be an allowable cost for the purposes of the price code and corporation tax'.[4] So it is the consumer, and not the employer, who makes up the contributions to the national-insurance fund. The employers' national-insurance contributions may be more regressive than most indirect taxes. Inevitably, the tax will be concentrated on the price of goods produced by labour-intensive industries, many of which provide the goods most important in the budgets of low-income families.

Taxation and Inequality

Drawing the effects of each type of tax together we can see that the belief in the progressive tax system is built on shaky foundations. Income tax and surtax seem to be mildly, but only mildly, progressive in their effects on different income groups. Social-security contributions offset the progressiveness of direct taxes overall because they tend to bear more heavily on those with low incomes. Finally, any redistributive impact that remains in personal income taxation is offset by the effect of local-authority rates and expenditure taxes. This is not a new discovery. Examining the structure of taxation as it stood nearly fifteen years ago,

Merrett and Monk arrived at a surprising conclusion: 'The combined incidence of direct and indirect taxes is such that the overall distribution [of income] is little improved. The improvement that does occur is largely the result of progressive income taxes on the very highest income groups not being counterbalanced by regressive taxes as is the case in the lower income ranges.'[5] As we saw from Chapter 2, the progressive effects of income taxes have been reduced considerably in the years since that conclusion was reached.

Some taxes therefore reduce the degree of economic inequality, but others actually increase it. The relative impact of different types of taxes on the distribution of income has been estimated in an analysis carried out by Professor J. L. Nicholson. To begin with, he needed some measure of the degree of inequality and for this he used the 'Gini coefficient of vertical inequality' – perhaps the most commonly used measure in studies of income distribution. If the value of the coefficient is equal to zero, this suggests the unlikely situation of complete equality. If it is equal to one (or to 100 per cent) this describes the even more unlikely situation in which all income goes to one individual. The lower the value of the coefficient, the greater the equality of incomes.[6] Although the Gini coefficient is a relatively simple way of measuring the degree of inequality, it has a number of drawbacks. First, as A. B. Atkinson has pointed out, it incorporates an implicit value judgement about how equal incomes *should* be. Secondly, it makes no allowance for counterbalancing changes in different parts of the income distribution. For instance, over the past few years there has been a tendency for the share of income going to the very richest households, and that going to the poorest, to get smaller while the share going to those in the middle has increased.[7] But the impact of the worsening position of those at the bottom is cancelled out to some extent by the changes affecting those at the very top. The Gini coefficient will not be able to reflect this situation. Indeed, if the two changes balance out it may appear as if the distribution of incomes is unchanged.[8]

These deficiencies in the particular type of measure chosen will not necessarily affect our conclusions about the *relative* impact of different taxes on the income distribution, though we should bear them in mind when considering Nicholson's results, which are shown in Table 28. The table shows the progressive or regressive effects of each type of tax.

The detailed results of the analysis confirm our general conclusions. The only progressive taxes according to Nicholson's estimates were, as we might expect, income tax and surtax, duties on wines and purchase tax on motor vehicles. The reason for the progressiveness of these last two is of course that higher income-groups devote a proportionally larger amount of their total expenditure to these items. Of the wide range of regressive taxes which Nicholson listed, duties on tobacco were the most regressive, followed closely by duties on beer, local rates and national-insurance contributions paid both by employees and employers. Purchase tax, which has now been replaced by VAT, was found to be mildly regressive, while SET, also replaced by VAT, was roughly neutral in its redistributive effects. Nicholson concluded that 'total payments in all taxes combined have formed a remarkably constant proportion of original income among families of any given type at different levels of income . . . The progressive effect of some taxes is largely offset by the regressive effect of others and all taxes combined have very little net effect on the Gini coefficient of inequality', though he found that 'total taxes as a proportion of income show a moderate tendency to decline as the size of family increases. Thus, if horizontal [redistribution] were included, the net effect of all taxes might be mildly progressive.'[9]

In his evidence to the Royal Commission on Income Distribution, Nicholson updated the evidence on the extent to which each category of tax increases or decreases the degree of inequality. All direct taxes together (including in this case only income tax and surtax and employee national-insurance contributions) would together have reduced the degree of inequality by 2·23 percentage points in 1972. This is despite the fact that, as we see from Table 28, national-insurance contributions would have increased the value of the Gini coefficient to some extent. The analysis also confirmed the regressive effects of indirect taxes. Taken together, indirect taxes on final goods and services (such as local rates, VAT and duties on drink and tobacco) increased the degree of

TABLE 28. Effect of taxes on inequality, 1970

	Effect on 'vertical' inequality measured by change in Gini coefficient[1] *(percentage points)*
Progressive taxes	
Surtax	−0·27
Income tax	−2·66
Duties on wines	−0·03
Purchase tax on motor vehicles	−0·03
Regressive taxes	
Indirect taxation on intermediate products (rates)	+0·05
Employees' national insurance contributions	+0·13
Purchase tax on clothing and footwear	+0·03
Employers' national insurance contributions	+0·12
Duties on oil	+0·16
Local rates (net)	+0·23
Betting taxes	+0·02
Indirect taxation on intermediate products (oil)	+0·15
Indirect taxation on intermediate products (other)	+0·09
Duties on beer	+0·26
Purchase tax on foods	+0·08
Duties on tobacco	+0·83
Miscellaneous indirect taxes[2]	+0·11

NOTE: Certain taxes have been excluded, either because they are relatively neutral (e.g. SET) or because they show wide fluctuations from year to year (e.g. duties on spirits)

1. Weighted averages for six main types of family.
2. Mainly excise duties on matches and radio/TV and other (excluding driving) licences; also certain stamp duties, and fees paid to public authorities.

SOURCE: J. L. Nicholson, 'Distribution and Redistribution of Income in the UK', in D. Wedderburn (ed.), *Poverty, Inequality and Class Structure*, CUP, 1974, p. 80.

inequality. It is estimated that these alone pushed the Gini coefficient up by 1·43 percentage points. Indirect taxes on intermediate goods and services – rates on commercial property and employers' national-insurance contributions – further increased the value of the coefficient by 0·34 percentage points. Together the effect of all taxes was to reduce the degree of inequality by less than half of 1 per cent (0·46 per cent).[10] The belief in the progressive tax system is a myth.

Does the Welfare State Redistribute Income?

There is however a second element to the general belief that the intervention by the State in the determination of incomes is progressive. As well as levying taxes on different groups in the community, governments also distribute various benefits. These are either in the form of collectively provided services, such as defence, law and order, the national health service, education, social services, roads and so on, or in the form of benefits paid in cash to households. Each of these is financed out of taxation, printing money or borrowing, so while we are primarily concerned with the tax system, it is important to consider how such benefits are distributed. Even if taxes themselves are not progressive in effect, benefits financed out of the proceeds may be.

Since 1962, the Central Statistical Office (CSO) has carried out an analysis of the incidence of taxes and benefits on households, using information provided in the continuous *Family Expenditure Survey* (*FES*).[11] The *FES* provides information on the 'original income' of households before any taxes have been paid or benefits received. It also shows the amount of income paid in direct taxes and the amount received as cash benefits, such as family allowances, family income supplement, old age pensions, supplementary benefit and so on. From this information it is possible to estimate the distribution of 'disposable income' (after all direct taxes and cash benefits). Finally, the *FES* gives information on expenditure patterns from which it is possible to estimate the impact of indirect taxes as well as the amount paid in rates, car tax, motor vehicle licences, driving licences, TV licences and so on by each household. In addition to this, the CSO makes certain assumptions about the allocation of the main benefits in kind – education and the health service – to families of different size and composition. This gives an estimate of the distribution of final income – after all taxes (both direct and indirect) have been paid and after all benefits (cash and in kind) have been allocated. On the basis of these estimates, the CSO publishes its assessment of the total impact of taxes and benefits on households of different composition and income.

The Effect of Direct Taxes

Taking first the impact of direct taxes the CSO found that income tax and surtax tended to take a larger proportion of high than of low incomes, as we would expect from our earlier discussion, for all types of household. A two-child family (two adult and two chidren) falling into the income range £1,194 to £1,749 paid only 1·6 per cent of its income (including cash benefits) in tax. If it fell into the income range above £5,490, 18·2 per cent of that income would be taken as income tax and surtax. At the same time, the single person in the £1,194–1,749 income group would have paid 15 per cent in income tax – almost ten times the proportion paid by the two-child family with the same income. To some extent this overstates the vertical and horizontal progressiveness of average tax rates, because they are taken as a proportion of income *plus* cash benefits such as family allowances and family income supplement. For low-income and larger families these benefits will represent a larger addition to incomes, so that the lower proportion paid in tax by these households reflects the effects of cash benefits rather than of tax liabilities alone.[12]

National-insurance contributions level out to some extent the proportion of income taken in direct taxes. In this case, the impact appears progressive at the very lowest income ranges, taking an increasing proportion as income rises. However, this is solely because the lowest-income households contain fewer economically active members who are not subject to contributions at all. The proportion taken is highest for households with workers who are low-paid. Amongst households receiving incomes from work, the contributions fall as income rises. The two-child (two adult) family for instance pays almost 4 per cent in contributions if its income is between £1,194 and £1,749. With an income above £5,490, the contribution is 2·2 per cent. National-insurance contributions do not differentiate between the number of dependants, so the proportion taken in each income group remains almost constant no matter how many children there are in the family. In some cases larger families actually contribute proportionately more to the national-insurance fund than smaller households in the same income group.[13]

What is the overall redistributive effect of all direct taxes together? The result is a considerable narrowing in the overall progressive impact. The proportion taken in tax by the two-child family in the £1,194–£1,749 range trebles with the addition of national-insurance contributions (from 1·6 per cent to 5·5 per cent). That of the same type of family in the highest income range merely increases from 18·2 to 20·4 per cent.

The Effect of Indirect Taxes

Local-authority rates, even including the effect of rebates payable to low-income families, are highly regressive in terms of vertical inequality. We have seen in Chapter 7 that the single adult on the lowest band of income paid almost four times the proportion contributed by a single person in the highest group (7·3 per cent compared to 1·9 per cent). The poorest two-child families (falling into the income range £1,194 to £1,749) contributed 3·4 per cent of their income in local-authority rates, compared with the contribution of 2·1 per cent by the same type of family in the highest range. Rate rebates are related to the number of dependent children in the household, so that the horizontal inequity of local-government finance is reduced somewhat at the lowest income levels. This is counterbalanced by the greater needs of housing space (and therefore of rate liability) generated by larger families. The net effect is that the average proportion of income taken in rates is roughly constant for all types of families within each income group, though the variation within each household group can be considerable.[14]

Finally, taking all indirect taxes together, we find the inequity that we would expect. The single adult with an income of under £381 a year in 1974 paid 27·3 per cent of his disposable income in indirect taxes. If he had received more than £5,490 a year his indirect tax liability would have been in the region of 12·7 per cent. Two-child families in the range £1,194 to £1,749 paid slightly more than a quarter of their disposable income in indirect taxes, but only 14·3 per cent if they received an income of more than £5,490.[15]

Although the lower-income groups pay less income tax and surtax than those higher up the scale, the difference is made up in the extra national-insurance contributions and indirect taxes that they pay. The net result is a tax system which is basically proportional, and even regressive at the lowest income ranges.

Summarizing these results the Royal Commission on the Distribution of Income and Wealth concluded: 'the results of the CSO's work suggest that the progressive effect of direct taxation is largely offset by the regressive effect of indirect taxation. Thus the tax system has little effect on the overall shape of the distribution' of income. The Commission did however stress the importance of taking benefits into account. 'The combined effect of the tax system, the receipt of transfer payments and direct and indirect benefits in kind is a major redistributive one.'[16]

The CSO results showed that low-income families and those with more children receive more as benefits from the State (in cash and kind) than they pay in tax. For high-income households and those with fewer children the opposite is broadly true. These households pay more in tax than they receive in benefits, even if the amount of tax they pay is no greater proportionately than that contributed by low-income families. So the concept of 'net taxation' has been developed to accommodate traditional beliefs about the redistributive effects of the welfare state to take account of the effect both of taxes paid and benefits received. The 'net taxation' of high-income groups is indeed larger than that of low-income households, according to the official estimates.

Taxation, Benefits and Increasing Inequality

To illustrate the overall effect of taxes and benefits, the Royal Commission calculated the distribution of incomes in 1961–3 and in 1971–3 in terms of (a) original income; (b) net income (after direct tax and cash benefits); and (c) final income (after indirect taxes and the allocation of benefits in kind). Their results are shown in Table 29.

TABLE 29. Effect of taxes and benefits on distribution of income

Percentage shares of original, net and final income received by decile groups, 1961–3 and 1971–3

United Kingdom   Income unit: household

Decile group	Original income		Net income		Final income	
	1961–3	1971–3	1961–3	1971–3	1961–3	1971–3
	%	%	%	%	%	%
Top 10 per cent	27·4	26·9	23·6	23·5	23·5	23·4
11–20 per cent	15·7	16·8	15·1	15·5	15·2	15·5
21–30 per cent	13·0	13·9	13·0	12·9	12·8	12·9
31–40 per cent	11·5	11·8	11·1	11·0	11·1	11·1
41–50 per cent	9·3	10·0	9·1	9·7	9·8	9·6
51–60 per cent	8·0	8·4	8·2	8·4	8·5	8·3
61–70 per cent	7·0	6·6	7·3	7·0	7·2	6·9
71–80 per cent	5·4	4·2	6·0	5·6	5·9	5·5
81–90 per cent	2·4	1·3	4·2	4·0	4·2	4·2
91–100 per cent	0·2	0·1	2·4	2·6	1·8	2·6
Gini coefficient %	40·3	42·3	32·6	32·6	32·8	32·4

SOURCE: Royal Commission on the Distribution of Income and Wealth, *Initial Report on the Standing Reference*, Cmnd 6171, HMSO, July 1975, Table 24, p. 62.

Over the ten-year period, the inequality of original incomes worsened noticeably – a tendency reflected in an increase in the Gini coefficient from 40·3 per cent to 42·3 per cent. The share of original income going to the lowest 30 per cent of households fell by nearly one third, while higher-income groups improved their position somewhat. Nicholson has shown that most of this increase in inequality occurred after 1969.[17] Part of the increase was due to a statistical change in the treatment of employers' national-insurance contributions, but a large part of the real increase in inequality was due to the fact that the number of pensioner households and the number of unemployed increased considerably over the period. Partly too, the increase in inequality of original income may have been due to the effects of inflation, with different income groups managing to adjust their incomes to rising prices at different rates according to their strength in the labour market and the source of their income. This may itself have been exacerbated by the increasing bite of taxation. Those groups in a position to do so may have tried to offset the effects of falling net incomes by obtaining higher gross incomes.

The distribution of net incomes was considerably more equal in both years than that of original income alone, and apparently remained static over the period, with the Gini coefficient at 32·6 per cent. This was probably largely due to an improvement in the levels of benefit payable to those at the bottom, offset by a shift in the tax burden down the income scale. The maintenance of the Gini coefficient at the same level is, however, somewhat deceptive. Even after accounting for progressive direct taxes and cash benefits, the share of income received by the poorest 30 per cent fell slightly, from 12·6 per cent to 12·2 per cent. This was offset by a reduction in the share going to the top 40 per cent, while the middle-income groups gained ground. It is interesting to note that the reduction in the share of income going to the top 10 per cent over this period was mitigated to a large extent by the effect of taxes and benefits.

The portion of the table showing the distribution of final income suggests that, apart from an increase in the share of income going to the poorest 10 per cent (explained by the increased number of pensioners with a relatively high use of health provision), the distribution of final income changed very little over the period. It also shows that the allocation of indirect taxes and benefits in kind make little difference to the shape of the distribution. Low-income households are assumed to benefit more from the provision of benefits in kind, but they also pay a larger proportion of their income in indirect taxes. The two cancel out, leaving the distribution of final income little different from that of net income.

Nevertheless, the distribution of final income (after the payment of all taxes and the allocation of all benefits) was considerably more equal than the distribution of 'original incomes'. The CSO analysis therefore provides the statistical justification for the belief in the equalizing effects of the welfare state. Taxes do not redistribute income, but public expenditure does. Or does it? To answer this question we now examine in detail the official evidence presented on this issue. In four important respects we suggest that the CSO data overstate the effects of taxes and benefits in redistributing resources towards the poorest households. First, the sample of households on which it is based has a tendency to reflect imperfectly the distribution of incomes before taxes and benefits, since the highest and lowest income groups are under-represented and some forms of income are excluded altogether. Secondly, a large proportion of all taxes are left out of the analysis, which might be expected to show an even harsher tax burden on the poor. Thirdly, in the allocation of benefits, two thirds of public expenditure remains a mystery and the 'tax-allowance welfare state' is not allocated as public expenditure at all. Finally, certain benefits are allocated as if they were used equally by all families, yet the evidence suggests that in many cases a disproportionate amount of resources are absorbed by higher-income groups. We take each of these points in detail below.

The Distribution of 'Original' Incomes

The CSO readily admit that their analysis is subject to a number of drawbacks, one of which is that it is based on information collected in the Department of Employment's *Family Expenditure Surveys*. These surveys are primarily intended to provide information on expenditure patterns with which to construct the Retail Prices Index, but they contain a large amount of useful data on the size and type of incomes received by households of different composition. They also record the amount paid by these households in direct taxes and the cash benefits which they receive. From their recorded expenditure patterns it is possible to work out the indirect taxes paid, while estimates of the use made of education, health services etc. can be made on the basis of their age composition and size. About 7,000 households approached complete the questionnaire for the survey in full, but the rate of response amongst the very poorest families and high-income groups, smaller families, the self-employed and older households is lower.[18]

It is not surprising to learn that income is understated in the *FES*, since people would normally prefer the government not to know exactly what they receive. One might expect this to be most true in the case of non-monetary income (fringe benefits, rent-free accommodation, subsidized meals, etc.), the income of the self-employed and those incomes which tend to circumvent the normal channels leading to the tax man.[19] If different groups under-record their income to a different extent – and it seems probable that higher-income groups will have both the incentive and opportunity to do so – then our picture of the distribution of income, and consequently of the impact of taxes and benefits, is distorted still further. The effect of this is magnified by the exclusion of wealth and capital gains from the *Survey* altogether. In addition we know that certain items of expenditure, such as that on alcohol and tobacco, are seriously understated by most people. Since these are items which carry a heavy burden of taxation, results derived from the *FES* may lead us to belittle the true impact of these regressive expenditure taxes.[20]

The picture offered by the *FES* is therefore imcomplete in a number of respects. Because of this the CSO has to make a number of adjustments to the data before it begins its analysis and these, it acknowledges, are arbitrary. For instance, additional income is 'imputed' to certain households to represent income in kind such as that received by owner-occupiers and those in rent-free accommodation, as well as to those receiving free or subsidized meals, cheap fuel and so on. The CSO warns, however, that 'the coverage of fringe benefits is not comprehensive'.[21]

Company cars, low-interest mortgages and other 'perks' are

not fully taken into account. Yet we know that these additions to income are substantial for certain sections of the population and are increasing as an explicit means of avoiding both taxation and incomes policies. An inquiry carried out for the Royal Commission on the Distribution of Income and Wealth revealed that the average cost to their companies of fringe benefits given to those earning more than £10,000 a year was approximately £2,335 – equivalent to 23 per cent of the recipient's gross income. In the case of a manager on £24,000, the cost to his company of fringe benefits was as high as £6,909 or 29 per cent of gross income. For the most part these benefits are not subject to income tax. At the other end of the earnings spectrum, the cost of 'fringe benefits' amounted to a mere £56·20 per annum for the average manual worker in manufacturing industry.[22] This means that the true incomes of those at the lower end of the income scale are more accurately recorded in the analysis than are those of high-income groups.

The Invisible Tax Burden

Equally arbitrary is the decision as to which benefits and taxes should be included in the analysis, and it is this aspect of the CSO's method which has attracted most criticism. Allocated taxes, in 1974, represented only 51·5 per cent of total government receipts, while only 37 per cent of public expenditure was allocated to households as benefits. As Peacock and Shannon (the severest critics of the analysis) argue, no reliable conclusions can be drawn about the redistributive impact of government activity from an analysis which considers a little over one third of the expenditure which makes up the welfare state and a half of the government receipts which are collected to finance it.[23] The principle behind the choice of taxes and benefits, they infer, is the ease with which they can be evaluated and attributed to households. And since it is easier to allocate taxes than it is to decide who gains from public spending, the resulting picture portrays a very lopsided government budget. In 1974, for instance, the casual observer of the 'welfare budget' illustrated in the CSO study would be excused for believing that the government was operating a massive budget surplus, spending less than three quarters of the revenue it raised through taxes.

In effect, then, 'the CSO study implicitly evaluates the benefits from defence, administration, police, museums, libraries, parks, roads and so on at *zero*: in which case it is hard to understand why the populace are prepared to pay taxes for them'.[24] A more realistic approach, in Peacock and Shannon's view, would be to balance the social-service benefits which are allocated with taxes which are 'earmarked' to pay for them. A large part of the welfare budget, for instance, is financed out of national-insurance contributions; a certain proportion of local-authority rates might be identified as intended for specific local services, and those benefits financed out of general taxation could be assumed to absorb a proportional amount of tax revenue in relation to other central government services. This would provide a balanced 'social-welfare budget' against which the effects of changes in taxes or benefits on income distribution could be measured. Such a comparison, they argue, would be more useful than that at present drawn from the CSO analysis, which appears to compare an actual situation (final income after taxes and benefits) with a politically implausible one. The 'distribution of original incomes' described in the CSO studies as the starting point before the subtraction of taxes and addition of benefits is a world in which government activity is absent; a world, therefore, in which original incomes themselves would be very different (the salaries of public employees for instance), and a world in which economic behaviour would be unrecognizable. Peacock and Shannon view a comparison between such a world and the 'distribution of final incomes' as less than helpful in evaluating the impact of the welfare state.

Setting aside for the moment these important conceptual criticisms, we need to consider how the conclusions about the redistributionary effects of taxation and public expenditure would be altered if we could fill in the gaps in the CSO picture. First we need to look at the taxes and benefits which are excluded altogether. We then question some of the basic assumptions on which the CSO allocates the rewards of public spending to different income groups.

The main types of taxes excluded from the CSO's calculations are corporation tax, taxes on capital, national-insurance contributions paid by public employers and some expenditure taxes which it was not possible to allocate to households. Together these represented about 20 per cent of government finance in 1974, the remaining 30 per cent being raised mainly through borrowing and other receipts such as interest on loans, rents, dividends and trading surplus. In the choice of those taxes as the ones to be excluded Peacock and Shannon are again critical, detecting 'a curious, old-fashioned Marxist tinge' in the CSO approach. 'If taxes on wealth and profits are borne by rentiers and capitalists – unproductive members of society – they are of no consequence in any calculation of society's welfare.'[25] As neither profits nor wealth are themselves fully included in the income distribution on which the analysis is based, the complaint that the taxes on these items are left out of the reckoning is somewhat unjustified. As Semple and Boreham explain, 'to include capital gains tax and corporation tax in the analysis would call for a change in the definition of household income'.[26] And if this broader definition of income were adopted, it would most likely reveal a much greater degree of inequality than appears at present. If capital gains and capital gains tax had been included in the analysis, for instance, the degree of inequality recorded would have been higher than that recorded at present, while the degree of redistribution accomplished through the tax system would have registered as even less, because of the relatively low rate at which the tax has always been set.[27]

The exclusion of corporation tax also has implications for the CSO conclusions about the effects of direct taxes, even though not all profits are included. We have already noted the evidence that companies tend to pass corporation tax on to the consumer through the price. Under these circumstances, the tax should perhaps be treated as another form of indirect tax on intermediate products. If they were included, it might therefore lessen still further the apparent progressive effects of 'direct' taxation. By comparison, the allocation of direct taxes on personal incomes presents few problems – most households being aware of and willing to disclose how much they actually pay (as opposed to how much they should pay). But expenditure taxes present much greater difficulties. We noted above the problems associated with alcohol, tobacco and confectionery, which carry a high burden of tax but tend to be under-recorded in the *FES*. Similarly, durable goods, which are also subject to high rates of tax, are not normally paid for all at once, and the tax on these items has to be spread over longer periods, which inevitably creates problems of estimation.

The CSO conclude from their investigation that the tax system as a whole is at best proportional. This conclusion is based on an analysis of only part of all tax revenue. The incidence of other taxes is not known, but it would be reasonable to suggest that the CSO conclusions might be affected if the missing pieces could be fitted into the picture. On balance it seems probable that the finance of public expenditure would appear to bear even more heavily on low-income groups than appears from the present analysis. But the problems of accurately allocating taxes between households and income groups pale into insignificance when we consider the difficulties involved in deciding who gains from public expenditure.

The Missing Welfare State

There are four main types of public spending which it is impossible at present to allocate to households as benefits: that on defence and administration; roads, research and investment grants; environmental and protective services; and capital expenditure on the social services. We can only make an intuitive guess as to the effect that including these benefits would have, although the authors of the 1974 article on the incidence of taxes and benefits do point out that 'it might be possible to allocate some of the relevant spending on police and fire services to those types of households making the greatest demands on property protection services'.[28] By definition, we might expect this to push the advantage of public expenditure towards higher-income groups. The same intuitive reasoning may also be applied to spending on environmental facilities such as parks, libraries and so on, which tend not to be highly concentrated in the deprived areas of the country.

Clearly, our conclusions about the effectiveness of the tax man 'as Robin Hood' are very sensitive to the way in which the majority of public expenditure is distributed between households. One third of public expenditure which can be allocated to households *may* benefit most the poorest households and the largest families (conclusions which we will question in due course) but two thirds of this expenditure remains a mystery. Nicholson and Britton have attempted to reallocate these missing elements according to two hypothetical assumptions (either that all households receive an equal cash benefit from the remaining expenditure or that they benefit in proportion to their final income before the distribution of the remaining items). Their conclusions were that 'measures of the extent of redistribution, or of the overall progressivity of the system, are bound to be sensitive to the treatment of the residual'.[29] Jane Peretz, also of the CSO, has attempted to find out just how important the missing expenditures are to the conclusions that public spending redistributes income. Using arbitrary assumptions about the use made by households of employment services and industrial training, of roads and public transport, improvement grants and option mortgages, water services and refuse disposal, recreation and other local facilities, legal aid, libraries and arts provisions, and of the personal social services, she was able to give an assessment of how the CSO conclusions might change with the inclusion of the missing expenditure. This exercise led Mrs Peretz to the conclusion that: 'The general effect of including these additional categories has probably been to reduce somewhat the degree of redistribution to poorer households which is implied. This is because these categories of expenditure are mostly on services etc. used by the whole population or, in some cases, used more by the better-off . . . the net effect of having better information about the users of the various services could be to make a further reduction in the degree of redistribution implied.'[30]

So far, then, the official investigations have suggested that the tax system itself is not a source of redistribution, but that the benefits which those taxes finance do benefit poorer households most, leading to an overall progressive effect of the social-welfare budget. But this conclusion about the redistributive impact of public expenditure is based on very shaky foundations indeed, derived from a consideration of a small proportion of all government spending. As yet there is no way of allocating the missing expenditure in any satisfactory way, but it is clear that even on very arbitrary assumptions the effectiveness of the welfare state as a redistributive mechanism is considerably less than we originally expected. Finally, let us consider the assumptions used by the CSO in allocating that proportion of public spending which they do distribute to particular households.

Who Gains from the Social Services?

Transfer payments in cash – family allowances, supplementary benefits, pensions and so on – are attributed to households as they are recorded in the *Family Expenditure Survey*. Cash payments such as family allowances provide a proportionately high benefit to low-income households because of their flat-rate nature. Means-tested benefits (supplementary benefit, family income supplement, etc.) are aggressively progressive at the very lowest income levels, simply because they are withdrawn as income rises. National-insurance benefits (pensions, unemployment benefits and so on) as well as supplementary benefits are payable to households who, by definition, have very low or negligible 'original income', since these provide the main source of income. Here we can see the absurdity of the comparison between the distribution of 'original income' and that of 'final income' (after the welfare state has been at work), which was pointed out by Peacock and Shannon. Pensioners and the unemployed are treated as having almost no original income until they have cashed their Giro cheque at the Post Office. These are then compared with the original income of wage-earners and salary-earners defined not as their income before the receipt of the pay packet but after. The distribution of original incomes against which we are measuring the redistributive impact of the welfare state is one in which a distinction is drawn between the *source* of income as well as its *level*.

The CSO analysis therefore shows cash benefits to be dramatically progressive. But one side of the equation is excluded at this point. In Chapter 3 we argued that tax allowances provide a form of welfare provision for households which is analogous to that of cash benefits. 'These tax reliefs,' the CSO acknowledges, 'tend to have more effect on tax paid as a proportion of income by the better-off households because these households usually pay out proportionately more of their incomes in mortgage interest and insurance premiums, and have more taxable income against which to set these reliefs.'[31] The impact of such 'fiscal benefits' is therefore to offset the progressive effects of cash benefits. But this is not reflected as a separate stage of the analysis. The allowances are taken into account, but only covertly through the amounts of tax actually paid by households.

Although the distribution of income before and after the payment of cash benefits is displayed, we are not allowed even a glimpse of the true effects of tax allowances on the level of inequality. Not one of the CSO tables present actual tax paid as compared with tax liability if the allowances and reliefs had not existed. Their purpose as a specific form of social-welfare provision is therefore disguised. It should be borne in mind, however, that if allowances had been distributed in this way, the conclusions about the progressive nature of cash benefits would be very different.

Once cash benefits and taxes have been added to and subtracted from household incomes, the CSO turns to the allocation of 'benefits in kind', the distribution of expenditure on such services as education, the health services and so on. Two types of problem emerge here which should cause us to be cautious about the conclusions drawn from the analysis. One is the question of how the benefits assumed to be received by households are to be valued. The second problem is to decide how such expenditure should be distributed between households to decide which groups benefit most.

The CSO's answer to the first question (on the evaluation of benefits) is to value the services at their cost of provision. To estimate the distribution of education expenditure, for instance, the *FES* provides information on the type of school or other institution attended and the Department of Education and Science supplies an estimate of the annual cost per child attending each type of educational establishment. Peacock and Shannon have argued that a more realistic approach would be to value the services at market prices, that is the cost of buying the service if it were not provided by the State. But education provides the only example in which a healthy private market exists alongside the State system, and the approach could not be applied to other services. Even in the education sector, they admit, the comparison would be very 'hazardous'. Adjustments would have to be made for differences in the amount and quality of the two types of service, while the price of private services may depend largely on the level of State provision itself.[32] But Peacock and Shannon do raise the very real problem of subjective valuation of the services provided – a problem which the CSO analysts acknowledge: 'The sums give some general indication of the current cost of the resources used by each type of household, but they may bear little relation to the value which the household concerned would put upon these services.'[33]

This brings us to the second major problem encountered in an attempt to allocate the benefits of public expenditure. In deciding the distribution of benefits in kind, the *FES* gives no indication of the actual use made of the services. It is therefore necessary to estimate the probable use of benefits in kind according to the size and age composition of the household. Pensioner households and those with young children are known to make greater use of the health services, while families with school-age children will reap most benefit from the existence of State education. But while it is theoretically possible to make assumptions about the use of such services by different *types* of household, allocating these benefits to different income groups is inevitably more precarious.

The CSO's conclusion is that public expenditure redistributes income in favour of poorer households. A very large proportion of this expenditure is in the form of benefits in kind such as the NHS and State education as well as the provision of local-authority housing. As a last stage of our examination we will consider the assumptions on which the CSO optimism is based when taking account of these three major items of expenditure.

Education expenditure is distributed to families with school-age children on the assumption that the benefit is equal to the average cost of keeping a child at each of the various educational establishments. Even on this assumption, the analysis shows that education expenditure is regressive in its distribution of resources: 'there is a tendency for better-off parents to be older and consequently to have older children: that is to have fewer children under school age and more children in secondary school than less well-off households with the same number of children. For this reason they will tend to benefit more from the education service.'[34] Information collected in the *General Household Survey* showed that this differential use of educational facilities extended to schooling both below and above secondary-school age: 'Pre-school education in nursery schools was more widespread among children whose fathers were in professional, managerial or intermediate non-manual occupations than among those whose fathers were in manual or junior non-manual jobs, and a similar but much more marked difference prevailed in relation to attendance at day nurseries and play groups.' At the same time, the *Survey* found that nearly three in four children from professional homes stayed on at school beyond 14, while only one in four of those from skilled and semi-skilled manual backgrounds did so. Amongst the children of unskilled manual workers, only one in five received schooling beyond the age of 14.[35] The evidence of a relationship between education and social class suggests not only that the children of higher socio-economic groups received more schooling (in terms of pre-school and further education) but that the benefits derived from that education varied considerably. Levels of educational achievement tend to be consistently lower for children of lower socio-economic groups, as are the chances of going on to further education. This is not due to differential ability. One major study showed that 34 per cent of middle-class children in one intelligence rating went on to full-time higher education, while only 15 per cent of those from manual working-class homes with the same measured intelligence did so. Similarly, children from higher socio-economic groups tended to receive education generally considered to be of a higher standard: 38 per cent of all school children came from the homes of white-collar workers, but these children accounted for 59 per cent of all grammar-school pupils.[36]

As we noted above, the CSO's 'cost of provision' method of valuing benefits ignores the subjective aspects of social-welfare provision. In the field of education expenditure, the importance of this omission is brought into its sharpest relief. As the National Child Development Study explained: 'By the time children start school, they have acquired an orientation to the world embracing norms and attitudes which affect their response to school. Many working-class children will find these norms and attitudes are in significant respects different from those adopted by the school; they will tend to be judged by standards which are alien to their previous experience.'[37]

The subjective factors which lead to differential benefits from expenditure on education exert their influence in two ways. First, middle-class children clearly gain more per unit of education expenditure than their working-class counterparts simply because they are attuned to the norms and values on which that education is based. Secondly, although the CSO analysis treats education predominantly as a consumption good, it is important to remember its importance as an investment good. The greater use made of education expenditure by middle-class children today will be reflected in their higher earnings in later years. The official analysis, as Peacock and Shannon have warned, merely excludes the capital element of expenditure from the calculations and assumes that current expenditure yields benefit only in the year in which it takes place.[38]

What about expenditure on the health service? The CSO allocates this benefit in kind according to the age and sex of the members of each household. Once more, it is the composition of the household which is taken into account rather than its income. Any vertical redistribution through such expenditure is therefore assumed to be a function of the differing composition of households by income. The *General Household Survey* again throws light on the realism of this assumption, showing, for instance, that adult semi-skilled and unskilled people use the general practitioner service to a much greater extent than higher socio-economic groups. Part of the reason for this is that workers from these groups would be more likely to require medical certificates if absent from work, while their working environment would make greater demands on their physical fitness. But while it was true that amongst those of working age the lower socio-economic groups made greater use of the GP service, this was not true in respect of children and the elderly – the two categories of household member allocated most benefit from the NHS in the CSO analysis. The *GHS* further warned that 'these conclusions do not take relative morbidity levels into account ... when standardized for age, the semi-skilled and unskilled (particularly the latter) had very much higher than expected rates of chronic and acute sickness, while the professional and managerial groups had much lower rates than expected.'[39] When this factor was taken into account, it was found that in proportion to reported chronic sickness the semi-skilled and unskilled in fact made *less* use of the GP services than other groups did. And even when they did use GPs, there is evidence that the quality of the service they received was generally poorer. The Scottish Home and Health Department reported in 1973 that the average consultation with a patient from Social Class 1 was approximately one and a half times as long as that with Class 5 patients.[40]

In his evidence to the Royal Commission on the Health Service, Julian Le Grand attempted to estimate the cost to the NHS per person reporting ill in each socio-economic group. He found that, although professionals, employers and managers represented 13·9 per cent of those reporting ill, they absorbed 17·5 per cent of NHS expenditure. On the other hand, semi-skilled and unskilled manual workers accounted for 31·9 per cent of those reporting illness, but received only 27·5 per cent of expenditure. That meant that the top two socio-economic groups received over 45 per cent more expenditure per person reporting ill than those in the lowest two groups. Part of this was due to the different age structures of the two groups, but, even after this had been allowed for, the professionals, managers and employers received almost 35 per cent more expenditure per person reporting ill than those from semi-skilled and manual backgrounds. Although, as Dr Le Grand warns, these figures are only rough estimates and cannot be taken as exact, they show a strong bias in the distribution of health service resources. He suggested a number of factors which might be at work to explain these discrepancies. In the first place, differential access to the health service may still exert a strong influence, both in terms of the better facilities available in middle-class localities and the higher costs faced by lower income groups in terms of travel and earnings lost while seeking medical attention. Secondly, the fact that the NHS is still predominantly staffed by members of the middle class may act as a deterrent to the potential working-class patient. Finally, lower socio-economic groups may be more 'tolerant' of ill-health.[41] Dr David Owen, while Minister of State for Health, acknowledged the consistency of the bias revealed by such evidence and admitted that the simple facts 'that the percentages of children who had never attended a dentist or who had not been immunized were always higher for those in the lower social groups are enough to cause any government to wonder whether resources are being correctly directed'.[42]

Such problems of the actual allocation of resources are ignored in the CSO assumptions. The advantage conferred on households of the various benefits in kind is assumed to vary according to need. But variations in need bear no known relationship to variations in the actual use made by different income groups of State services, or indeed the quality of benefit obtained.[43]

Finally, we turn to the distribution of public expenditure on housing. Our first and most fundamental criticism here must be that a distinction is drawn in the CSO analysis (as in other public accounting exercises) between two types of housing subsidy. Both are financed from public revenue, yet only one – that benefiting most the poorer households – is allocated in the CSO calculations. As we argued in Chapter 3 the tax relief awarded on mortgage interest is one of the largest forms of fiscal benefit which at present exist. The purpose of the benefit is to help households to meet their housing costs in the same way as rent allowances, rebates and local-authority housing subsidies. In 1975–6, mortgage-interest tax relief cost the Exchequer an estimated £950 million – approximately 40 per cent of the cost of all housing subsidies (including the tax relief itself).[44] We know also that it is the better-off households who reap the most benefit from this tax subsidy. This is true not only because the subsidy is itself regressive – increasing with income – but because it is on the whole the better-off members of the community who represent the bulk of the home buyers. Turning again to the *General Household Survey*, we find that 58·7 per cent of professionals (socio-economic group 1) were buying their house with a mortgage, while only 6·3 per cent of the unskilled manual workers (group 6) were doing so.[45]

The imperfections of the housing market in Britain wreak havoc with any attempts to assess the distributive effects of housing expenditure, and we should be well aware of the importance of this when considering housing subsidies as part of the welfare state. The mortgage interest relief is only one part of this problem – equally formidable difficulties arise in trying to assess the impact of the subsidies actually considered in the CSO analysis. These consist mainly of subsidies to local-authority tenants (including rent rebates) and rent allowances to private tenants.

The value of the benefit received by council tenants is assumed to be the difference between local authorities' current-account expenditure and the rents actually paid (less rebates). It is then allocated to individual dwellings in relation to their rateable value. One problem that arises here, noted by Webb and Sieve, is that households do not actually benefit from their share in the current-account expenditure less the contribution they make to that account through their rents. Rather the benefit to those in local-authority accommodation in terms of relative living standards is the rent they pay compared with the rent they would have to pay in the private rented sector. The subsidy to local-authority tenants, measured in this way, is actually higher than that recorded in the CSO calculations. 'If all citizens could rent council houses,' Webb and Sieve point out, 'the subsidy would merely constitute an addition to incomes. This is very far from the case; the number of people wishing to rent greatly exceeds the accommodation available. People are selected according to housing need and residential qualifications ... Council housing is not always allocated in practice to the poorest families.'[46] Frank Field, using *GHS* and *FES* data, has underlined the importance of the distinction between those who benefit from council housing and the very lowest income groups. 'Unless a poor family is able to gain a local authority tenancy (where the overlap between poverty and bad housing is usually broken) they will have to depend on the inferior private sector . . . By and large it is the poorest who occupy the worst housing.'[47]

The CSO's investigation suggests that housing subsidies generally benefit poorer households. However, as even the official report acknowledges, 'the implicit subsidies received by those getting mortgage relief' is excluded.[48] As we have seen, a large proportion of all housing expenditure (excluding capital expenditure) is represented by this benefit through the tax system to higher-income groups. Being particularly regressive in its impact, this part of the 'housing budget' probably offsets to a large extent any redistributive effect of local-authority subsidies. But even here, the CSO calculations present something of a misleading picture. Local-authority tenants receive a much larger subsidy (in terms of its effects on their standard of living) than the CSO's method of calculation would suggest. This might shift the balance of advantage back towards those in the lower half of the income distribution, but certainly not to the very poorest households, since on the whole local-authority tenants are not exclusively concentrated amongst this group.

Conclusion

The belief in an egalitarian welfare state financed through progressive taxation does not therefore stand up to careful examination. On the one hand the overall effect of British taxation is at best roughly proportional and is probably regressive at the lowest income levels. Income tax is mildly progressive, but its effect is offset by the regressive impact of national-insurance contributions, expenditure taxes and local rates. Some taxes therefore reduce the degree of economic inequality but others actually increase it. The net result is to leave the distribution of incomes very little changed.

If the contribution of all groups in society to the public revenue is roughly proportional, it does appear to a casual reader of the official evidence that the vestiges of income redistribution by the State remain in the sharing of public expenditure. Hence, the CSO analysis tells us that: 'sums of allocated benefits, which are in effect part of the "social wage" which can be allocated in this exercise to households of particular types, are largest *per capita* for retired households and for households with children. The amounts are highest for those with lowest original incomes.'[49]

This optimistic conclusion is based on a partial view of the landscape of taxes and benefits: only half of all government receipts are considered, and only one third of what these receipts are spent on. On the tax side, the inclusion of the missing elements would probably reveal an even more regressive system of public finance than the present incomplete picture suggests. It is officially acknowledged that, if we are hoping for a levelling of economic inequalities, we should not look to the tax system. The responsibility for redistribution is placed firmly on the shoulders of public expenditure, which is considered 'unambiguously progressive'. When we look more closely at the analysis, however, we find that such a conclusion cannot confidently be drawn from the evidence which is at present available. First, most public spending is left out of the reckoning, yet there is evidence that if it were included the distribution of benefits might look very different. Second, the assumptions on which social-service benefits are allocated to households is very tenuous. The services are generally valued at the cost of provision and are allocated to households according to their eligibility and composition rather than their actual use. As a result, the CSO 'probably allocates benefits more in accordance with the broad intentions of social policy than with the reality of social service utilization'.[50] At present it is not possible to allocate all benefits precisely according to their use by households, although there is a wealth of evidence indicating which groups make greatest use of public services. By selecting examples from such evidence, we can see that the assumption in the official analysis that poorer households make greatest use of public services is open to doubt. In fact in many cases it appears that the greatest benefit is derived by the better-off.

The official analysis of the CSO offers an attempt to shore up the belief in the redistributive impact of the tax and benefit 'welfare state'. Such a belief cannot be supported by the evidence. We need to focus our attention on the impact of taxation in

Britain and on the measures which are necessary to bring about a fairer distribution of the tax burden.

References

1. BARBARA CASTLE, *Financial Times*, 8 July 1975, quoted by C. Trinder, 'Inflation and the Social Wage', in P. Willmott (ed.), *Sharing Inflation?*, Temple Smith, 1976.
2. TUC, *Economic Review, 1968*, p. 79, para. 255.
3. D. PIACHAUD, 'Poverty and Taxation', in B. Crick and D. Robson (eds.), *Taxation Policy*, Penguin Books, 1973.
4. *Hansard*, 22 July 1976, Vol. 915, Cols. 2017/8 and 2021.
5. A. J. MERRETT and D. A. G. MONK, 'The Structure of UK Taxation, 1962/63', *Bulletin of the Oxford University Institute of Economics and Statistics*, August 1966, reprinted in their *Inflation, Taxation and Executive Remuneration*, Hallam Press, 1967.
6. For a detailed discussion of this and other measures of inequality see the Royal Commission on the Distribution of Income and Wealth, *Initial Report on the Standing Reference*, Cmnd 6171, HMSO, July 1975, Chapter 3.
7. ibid., p. 62.
8. See A. B. ATKINSON, 'On the Measurement of Inequality', *Journal of Economic Theory*, Vol. 2, 1970, reprinted in Atkinson (ed.), *Wealth, Income and Inequality*, Penguin Books, 1973.
9. J. L. NICHOLSON, 'The Distribution and Redistribution of Income in the United Kingdom', in D. Wedderburn (ed.), *Poverty, Inequality and Class Structure*, Cambridge University Press, 1974, p. 81.
10. Royal Commission on the Distribution of Income and Wealth, op. cit., Table 25, p. 64. The figures are not strictly comparable with Table 28 since they are based on ten main family types (excluding pensioners and households with more than two adults). The estimates in Table 28 are based on six main family types.
11. The articles which describe the analysis are published each year in Central Statistical Office, *Economic Trends*. The article on which we draw in this chapter is M. NISSEL and J. PERETZ, 'Effects of Taxes and Benefits on Household Income 1974', *Economic Trends*, No. 268, HMSO, February 1976.
12. ibid., Table B, p. 82.
13. ibid., Table C, p. 82.
14. ibid., Table E, p. 83.

15. ibid., Table F, p. 84.
16. Royal Commission on the Distribution of Income and Wealth, op. cit., p. 68, para. 172.
17. NICHOLSON (in Wedderburn), op. cit.
18. W. F. F. KEMSLEY, 'Family Expenditure Survey: A Study of Differential Response Based on a Comparison of the 1971 Sample with the Census', *Statistical News*, No. 31, HMSO, November 1975.
19. See R. M. TITMUSS, *Income Distribution and Social Change*, Allen & Unwin, 1962.
20. See M. S. LEVITT, 'The Redistributive Effects of Taxation in the Report of the Royal Commission', *Economic Journal*, September 1976.
21. CSO, op. cit., p. 89.
22. A. SINFIELD, 'Benefits Beyond the Fringe', *Low Pay Bulletin* No. 9, Low Pay Unit, June 1976.
23. A. PEACOCK and R. SHANNON, 'The Welfare State and the Redistribution of Income', *Westminster Bank Review*, August 1968.
24. ibid., p. 44.
25. ibid., p. 38.
26. M. SEMPLE and A. J. BOREHAM, 'Future Work of the Government Statistical Service', in A. B. ATKINSON (ed.), *The Personal Distribution of Incomes*, Royal Economic Society, Allen & Unwin, 1976, ch. 9.
27. NICHOLSON (in Wedderburn), op. cit., p. 84.
28. CSO, op. cit., p. 88.
29. J. L. NICHOLSON and A. J. C. BRITTON, 'The Redistribution of Income', in A. B. Atkinson (ed.), *The Personal Distribution of Incomes*, op. cit., ch. 10.
30. J. PERETZ, 'Beneficiaries of Public Expenditure', in V. MORRIS (ed.), *Distributional Effects of Public Expenditure on Social Policy*, Routledge & Kegan Paul, 1977.
31. CSO, op. cit., p. 82.
32. PEACOCK and SHANNON, op. cit., p. 40.
33. CSO, op. cit., p. 82.
34. ibid., p. 87.
35. Office of Population Censuses and Surveys, *General Household Survey*, 1972, HMSO, 1975, p. 155.
36. For a review of the evidence see F. FIELD, *Unequal Britain: A Report on the Cycle of Inequality*, Arrow, 1974.
37. R. DAVIE, N. BUTLER, and H. GOLDSTEIN, *From Birth to Severn*, Longmans, 1972, p. 28, quoted in Field, op. cit.
38. PEACOCK and SHANNON, op. cit., p. 41.

39. *General Household Survey*, 1972, op. cit., p. 212.
40. Scottish Home and Health Department, *Time Study of Consultations in General Practice*, Scottish Health Service Studies, No. 27, 1973, quoted by J. LE GRAND, 'The Distribution of Public Expenditure on the National Health Service', Evidence to the Royal Commission on the Health Service, University of Sussex, Mimeo, June 1976, p. 18.
41. ibid., pp. 13–14.
42. DR DAVID OWEN, 'Inequalities in Health Provision and Care', John Alfred Law's Memorial Lecture Series, Merthyr Tydfil, 14 May 1976.
43. A. L. WEBB and J. E. B. SIEVE, *Income Redistribution and the Welfare State*, Occasional Papers on Social Administration, No. 41, Bell, 1971, p. 63.
44. CHRIS HOLMES, 'Housing Expenditure: How it Breaks Down', *Roof*, Shelter, May 1976. See also CHRIS TRINDER, 'Housing Expenditure: Who Benefits Most?' in the same issue.
45. *General Household Survey*, op. cit., p. 32.
46. WEBB and SIEVE, op. cit., p. 50.
47. FIELD, op. cit., p. 53.
48. CSO, op. cit., p. 86.
49. ibid., p. 87.
50. WEBB and SIEVE, op. cit., p. 73.

10 Tax Comparisons with Europe

Britain's poor economic performance since the Second World War, the emigration of professionals and the general 'British malaise' have all been attributed at one time or another to what is felt to be the unduly heavy burden of taxation borne by the British people in general, and in particular the managerial classes. In this chapter we put this belief under the microscope and compare the rates of direct taxation, including social-security contributions, for different income groups with our EEC partners.'

Direct Taxation

One of the reasons for Britain's sensitivity about her taxation is perhaps the relative lack of guile with which it is collected. People are more resentful about paying income taxes than they are about paying their social-security contributions, though they are less likely to benefit from the latter than the former. Despite this somewhat illogical but very real preference, the British people pay an unduly high proportion of their income in income taxes and an unusually small proportion in the form of social-security contributions, as illustrated in Tables 30 and 31. For example, altogether in Britain income tax accounts for about 40 per cent of revenue from taxation, compared with 18·2 per cent in France. When we compare social-security contributions we find almost the reverse position. In France 41·4 per cent of revenue from all taxes comes from this source, compared with 16·1 per cent in this country.

The limited weight of VAT as a source of revenue is similarly politically unpopular, though desirable to supporters of a progressive overall tax system. Receipts from VAT in the UK represent only 19·5 per cent of receipts from taxes on income and wealth. This figure contrasts with 41 per cent in Germany, 80·1 per cent in Italy and fully 121·4 per cent in France.[1]

Britain relies particularly heavily on excise duties upon specific items such as beer and tobacco, as we saw in Chapters 5 and 6,

TABLE 30. Direct taxes, social-security contributions and indirect taxes as percentages of revenue from taxes[1] and social-security contributions in 1971

	Direct taxes	Social-security contributions	Total direct taxes and social-security contributions	Indirect taxes
Belgium	32·4	29·9	62·3	37·7
Denmark[2]	46·6	5·1	51·7	48·3
France	18·2	41·4	59·6	40·4
Germany	30·8	32·0	62·8	37·2
Irish Republic[3]	30·4	9·2	39·6	60·4
Italy	21·4	38·9	60·3	39·7
Luxembourg[3]	39·7	33·4	73·1	26·9
Netherlands	35·3	37·5	72·8	27·1
United Kingdom:				
1971	40·8	14·5	55·3	44·7
1972	39·2	16·1	55·3	44·7

NOTES:
1. Revenue from taxes comprises taxes on income and taxes on expenditure received by central government and local authorities.
2. Figures relate to 1969.
3. Figures relate to 1970.
ORIGINAL SOURCES: *EEC National Accounts*, 1961–71; *UN Yearbook of National Accounts Statistics*, 1971; figures for the United Kingdom are from *Preliminary Estimates of National Income and Balance of Payments 1967–72*, adjusted to international definitions.
SECONDARY SOURCE: *Hansard*, 2 May 1973, Vol. 855, Cols. 325–6.

despite the fact that consumers are considerably more conscious, and therefore less tolerant, of specific duties than they are of a more general tax such as VAT (or purchase tax, which preceded it). The greater awareness of excise duties reflects in part the much higher percentage of value which excise duties tend to represent (64 per cent in the case of tobacco, for example, in contrast with a basic VAT rate of 8 per cent).

Britain, then, appears to have a system of direct and indirect taxes designed to convey to the taxpayer as clearly as possible that a considerable proportion of his income is taken from him

TABLE 31. Personal direct taxation as proportion of total revenue

	%
Denmark	48·0
UK	32·1
Germany	28·1
Netherlands	27·9
Belgium	27·4
Luxembourg	26·6
Ireland	22·8
Italy	12·7
France	11·1

NOTE: In this table, personal direct taxation includes both national and local taxes on earned and investment income and on capital gains; it is shown as a percentage of total central and local government revenue from taxation and social-security contributions.

SOURCE: *Revenue Statistics of OECD Member Countries 1965–72*, Table 13, reproduced in *Hansard*, 12 March 1975, Written Answers, Col. 166.

by the Exchequer. Other European states appear to be more skilful at concealing the fact that they take a still higher proportion of the nation's wealth in taxes (Table 32).

As far as the overall effect is concerned Britain cannot claim to be heavily taxed, but the second allegation often made against the British tax system is that it penalizes unduly the middle- and upper-income groups.

Only an analysis of the equalizing impact of total taxes in each of the nine EEC member states would test the truth of this allegation. However, the most recent official publication of an international comparison of the equalizing effects of taxes proves to be grossly unsatisfactory on a number of counts.[2] Firstly, the analysis includes only five of the nine EEC countries (France, Germany, Italy, the Netherlands and the UK) and the data for Italy is unusable because only the post-tax distribution of income is given. Secondly, the data is out of date, referring to 1970 in the case of France, 1973 in the case of Germany and the UK and 1967 in the case of the Netherlands. In Germany in particular, significant tax changes have occurred since 1973, so that an analysis based upon the earlier data is unsatisfactory.

TABLE 32. The proportion of GNP collected in taxes and social-security contributions in 1973

	%
Norway	54·8
Denmark	51·4
Sweden	49·4
Netherlands	49·2
Austria	42·8
West Germany	42·2
France	41·0
Belgium	40·1
Britain	37·7
Italy	32·3

SOURCE: *Labour Weekly*, 9 January 1976.

In view of the absence of any comprehensive official information on the equalizing impact of the EEC tax systems or information which would permit a full analysis of the equalizing impact of the total tax system in each of the nine member states, we shall compare in this chapter the relative burden of personal income taxes in the nine EEC countries (on the basis of the Inland Revenue summaries of each of the EEC tax systems) together with the redistributive effects of cash family allowances. It will be important to bear in mind Britain's greater dependence upon direct taxation than most of her neighbours'. Taxpayers in Britain at every level of income can expect to pay a higher proportion of their income in personal income taxes (though the analysis does not show the much smaller percentage of income in Britain paid in VAT and social-security contributions). What we are concerned to illustrate in this chapter is the relative burden of direct personal income taxes at *different* levels of income.

The main limitation of the analysis is our inability, owing to the lack of the relevant data, to combine the redistributive effects of *all* taxes in each of the member countries. The second but less significant limitation is our inability (again owing to the lack of information) to include all the tax allowances in our analysis. This point will be returned to in a later section of this chapter.

Three simplifying assumptions have been made for the purposes of the analysis: firstly, that all income is earned income; secondly, that full employment prevails in each of the countries covered; and thirdly, that each household has only one income earner.

Treatment of Local Taxes

A complete analysis of EEC tax systems and their redistributive effects would include comparisons of local tax systems in the nine countries. Although the data available do not permit us to include local taxes in our calculations of the tax burden at different levels of income except in the case of Denmark, where local taxes can constitute more than half the tax burden at lower levels of income and well over a third at higher income levels, we outline below the essential features of each of the local tax systems of the nine EEC member states.

Both income and property taxes apply at local level in Belgium and Denmark. The local income taxes are levied at rates fixed by each local authority and thus vary from one area to another. In Denmark the communal (or local) income-tax rates range from 11 to 20·6 per cent, the highest rate being applied in Copenhagen. To these taxes are added the County Income Tax which also varies (from 4·6 to 7·7 per cent), though no County Income Tax applies in Copenhagen and Frederiksberg, which bear particularly heavy communal taxes.

The Belgian local property taxes on actual or imputed income from real property are akin to British rates, while Danish local authorities assess properties for local tax purposes on the basis of their capital values (the method recommended by the Layfield Committee for adoption in Britain).

In Italy local taxes apply primarily to business income with exemption of all employment income and some forms of investment income. In the six remaining EEC states property taxes provide the main source of local-authority revenue. The tax rates vary with the local authority in each of the six countries (France, Germany, Ireland, Luxembourg, Netherlands and the UK) and assessment is based either on market value of properties (in Germany and Luxembourg) or upon the rental value (as in France, Ireland, the Netherlands and the UK). Additionally, revenue is obtained as a proportion of business income in Germany and Luxembourg.[3]

In view of the peculiarly heavy burden of local taxes in Denmark, these have been incorporated into our analysis. It should therefore be borne in mind that the relatively high rates of taxation in Denmark do include this 'extra' element.

TABLE 33. Average earnings within the EEC in 1975

	£
UK	2,777
Belgium	3,697
Denmark	5,278
France	2,018
Germany	3,859
Ireland	2,362
Italy	2,220
Luxembourg	4,753
Netherlands	3,484

SOURCES: ILO, *Year Book of Labour Statistics* (average hourly earnings in manufacturing industry); *Hansard*, 24 February 1976, Col. 188 (average weekly hours of work per manual worker); *Trade and Industry*, 27 February 1976, p. 598 (wage indices); *Financial Statistics*, No. 164, December 1975, p. 122, Tables 103 (exchange rates, January 1975).

Our analysis of the differential income-tax burdens within the EEC is based upon four income groups; (1) households with incomes at two thirds of average earnings, (2) those with average earnings, (3) those with incomes at twice average earnings, and (4) those with incomes at five times average earnings. The average earnings data and its sources are summarized in Table 33.

A Comparison of Tax Thresholds within the EEC

When assessing the level of income at which taxpayers become subject to a positive rate of tax in each of the nine states, we have taken two household types for illustrative purposes – the single-person household and married couples with four children. One of our objectives is to illustrate clearly the differential treatment of households with and without dependants – hence the choice of large rather than small family households. In order to compare the impact upon the taxpayer of very different tax structures, it has been necessary to translate the tax allowances of each country into a form similar to the British tax allowances. For example, in Belgium the tax payable on the first 300,000 fr. of income (plus 35,000 fr. for each dependent child after the third) is reduced by 50 per cent for families with four children. This deduction has been made from the taxes payable on the first slices of income, taxable at the lowest rates of tax, in order to provide a tax threshold and marginal rate of tax comparable with those of the UK. The only tax allowances taken into account are those for the expenses of acquiring income, the earned income allowance and allowances for dependants. In addition some systems (in France, Luxembourg and Germany for example) include provision for a slice of income to be subject to a zero rate of tax, thus lifting the tax threshold above the level of income implied by the total of allowances.

Table 34 gives details of the tax thresholds as a proportion of average earnings in each country. In the UK for example a single taxpayer will begin to pay a positive rate of tax when his income reaches 24 per cent of average earnings. In France, where a relatively smaller proportion of total revenue is levied in direct personal income taxes, a single taxpayer will pay no income tax until his income reaches 57 per cent of average earnings. As will be seen from Table 34, single taxpayers in only two EEC countries are subject to a lower tax threshold than single taxpayers in the UK. In Denmark, the single person's tax threshold is at 12·8 per cent of average earnings and in Luxembourg 18 per cent. In the case of married couples with four children the UK tax threshold at 68 per cent of average earnings is above that in Luxembourg, Germany, Belgium, Denmark and the Netherlands, but substantially below the thresholds in France, where people begin to pay tax when their income reaches 146 per cent of average earnings, and Ireland, where the threshold is at 78 per cent. In Denmark and Germany the tax thresholds for families appear unduly unfavourable, partly because of the recent abolition of child tax allowances and their replacement by tax-free family allowances in respect of each child. A very different picture emerges when full account is taken of cash family allowances (Table 35).

Variable Tax Thresholds

In both Belgium and Luxembourg the tax threshold varies with the level of income. In Belgium the expenses allowance is calculated as a percentage of income and in Luxembourg families with four children, for example, are entitled to child allowances of 4 per cent of income plus £355. The tax threshold in both these two countries increases directly with income and cannot readily be compared with the tax threshold of the UK, where we have allowances of a single value irrespective of income. For illustrative purposes the tax thresholds at average earnings are given in Table 34 for Luxembourg and Belgium, though it should be borne in mind that these thresholds are still lower than the 44 and 55 per cent of average earnings suggested in the case of households with below-average earnings.

A Nil Tax Threshold

The new Italian tax system introduced on 1 January 1974 applies the schedule of tax rates to every lira of income, thus providing no tax threshold. Personal allowances are then credited against the final tax bill. In order to compare the burden of this system of taxation at different levels of income with the tax burden in

TABLE 34. Tax thresholds and marginal rates of personal income tax in the nine EEC member states

	Tax threshold as proportion of average earnings		Marginal rate of tax at ⅔ average earnings		Marginal rate of tax at average earnings		Marginal rate of tax at 2× average earnings		Marginal rate of tax at 5× average earnings	
	Single %	Married 4 children %	Single %	Married 4 children %	Single %	Married 4 children %	Single %	Married 4 children %	Single %	Married 4 children %
UK	24	68	35	0	35	35	40	35	70	65
Belgium	29	55	10	10	30	10	40	37·5	47·5	47·5
Denmark[1]	12·8	25·7	30	30	47·5	47·5	60·2	60·2	60·2	60·2
Germany[2]	27	41	22	22	30	22	?	?	?	?
Ireland	24	78	26	0	35	26	35	35	70	65
Italy	—[3]	—[3]	13	13	16	16	25	25	35	35
Luxembourg	18	44	33	24	48	30	57	52	57	57
Netherlands	25	50	25	20	31	25	49	49	66	66
France	57	146	15	0	20	0	40	10	50	25
Average	27·1	63·5	23·2	13·2	32·4	23·4	43·2	37·7	56·9	53·1

NOTES:
1. In Denmark family allowances are paid but no child tax allowances, and the tax threshold and marginal rates of tax therefore appear unduly unfavourable to families in Denmark. (In 1975 the tax-free family allowance in Denmark was approximately 130 Dkr per child, equivalent to a tax allowance of £990 per year for four children.
SOURCE: Danish Government Information Dept.
2. The full tax schedule for West Germany is not available and several calculations have therefore not been possible. With the exception of Italian tax credits, all the tax schedules have been interpreted in such a way as to render them comparable with the UK system of tax allowances. The impact of the taxes has not however been affected.
3. Italy has no tax threshold. Every lira of income is taxed and tax credits are then deducted from the total tax bill. In calculating the marginal rates of tax, the credits have been set against tax payable at the lowest rates of tax until all the credits are exhausted.
SOURCE: Board of Inland Revenue, Overseas Tax Developments, Issues 1 to 9, 1975.

TABLE 35. Cash family allowances in the nine EEC member
countries in 1975 for families with four children

	Net family allowances as % of average earnings	*Tax threshold as % of average earnings, including the tax allowance equivalent of family allowances for families at ⅔ average earnings*	
		£	*%*
Denmark[1]	8·9	4,885	92·5
Luxembourg	13·1	6,631	139·5
Ireland	8·5	2,612	110·6
UK[3]	5·5	2,328	83·8
Netherlands	20·1	4,525	129·8
France[2,4]	33·0	8,372	414·8
Italy	10·6	1,467	66·1
Belgium[1,4]	30·1	4,885	132·1
Germany	20·1	5,105	132·3

NOTES:
1. The Danish and Belgian family allowances for 1975 have been taken
at the mid point between the allowances for 1974 and those for 1976 (the
1975 data are not available).
2. The family allowance data for Luxembourg and France applies to 1974.
The results are less favourable for these two countries than they would be
if it had been possible to use the 1975 data.
3. The UK child tax allowances will be phased out over a three-year period
beginning in 1977. As from April 1977 family allowances will be tax free
and, in the first year, will be valued at £1 for the first child and £1.50 for
each subsequent child. The annual value of the tax-free child benefit for
a four-child family will be £286 in 1977, somewhat higher than the allowances in both Ireland and Italy though well below those in the remaining
six EEC countries.
4. The Belgian and French tax allowance equivalents of the family allowances are given at income levels of twice average earnings since no tax is
payable at average earnings.
SOURCE: Board of Inland Revenue, *Overseas Tax Developments*, Issues
1 to 9, 1975.

the remaining eight EEC countries, the Italian tax credits have been set against the tax payable on the first slice of income. The result has been to reduce the effective tax rate on the first £1,314 of income to 5·8 per cent in the case of a single person and 1·5 per cent in the case of a married couple with four children.

British taxpayers are not only subject to unusually high marginal rates of tax at the highest levels of income but also at income levels well below average, and it is in the case of families at the lowest levels of income that the divergence between the allowances and tax rates in the UK and our European neighbours is most marked. The marginal rate of tax of a taxpayer with a wife and four dependent children and an income at 68 per cent of average earnings is *more than double* the average for the EEC as a whole at comparable levels of income. On incomes five times average earnings the UK marginal rate is more in line with that of our neighbours at 65 per cent (Table 34, Column 10), and this is still more true of the middle-income range. Marginal rates of tax are of relevance primarily to work incentives, and on the assumption that money is a particularly potent incentive for unskilled workers, for whom work provides little or no inherent satisfaction, it can be argued that the British system of taxation encourages absenteeism, short periods of unemployment and an undesirable degree of job mobility amongst the unskilled. The impact of national-insurance contributions and the progressive loss of means-tested benefits as incomes rise blunt still further the monetary work incentive of the lower-paid (an issue developed in Chapter 3).

Before examining the comparative average tax rates of the nine EEC states we need to outline the fundamental differences in the tax structures of the UK and those of France, Luxembourg, Germany and Italy.

Tax Structures in the EEC

Under the family part system the basic allowances for the expenses of acquiring income and for employment income are deducted from gross income. The taxable income is then

divided into family parts in accordance with the family responsibilities of the taxpayer, as follows:

Family responsibilities	Family parts
Unmarried, divorced or widowed with no dependent children	1
Married. No dependent children	2
Unmarried or divorced with one dependent child	2
Married or widowed with one dependent child	$2\frac{1}{2}$
Each further dependent child	$\frac{1}{2}$

A married couple with four children would thus divide their taxable income into four family parts ($2\frac{1}{2}$ parts for the married
couple and one dependent child plus half a part for each of the
three additional children). Tax is then deducted from one family
part in accordance with the tax schedule. The tax bill is finally
multiplied by four to arrive at the total tax payable. The result is
that allowances for dependants increase as income rises even
more substantially than they do in the UK. At very low incomes
of two thirds average incomes no tax is paid by a family with
four children. The tax advantage over the single person at this
evel of income is a mere £364. At incomes five times higher than
average earnings, however, the single taxpayer pays £1,572·5
more in tax than a married man with four children. This situation arises because the slice of income subject to *each* successive
rate of tax, including a zero rate, is four times greater for the taxpayer with four children than it is for the single man. Families
with several children become subject to the higher rates of tax,
therefore, only if they have very high incomes indeed.

Luxembourg operates a similar family part system to the
French one, but only for families in specified categories, those
with incomes below £4,367 and two dependent children. The
income limit is somewhat higher for families with one child and
lower for families with three children. The system does not apply
at all to families with four or more children or to families with
incomes above the specified limits. For the excluded families a
system of allowances similar to the UK child tax allowances
applies, the only difference being that for families with incomes

between about £5,000 and £10,000 these are comprised of a percentage of income plus an allowance in cash terms for each child, so that the benefit of the child allowance varies directly with income (increasing as income increases and vice versa). Only on incomes in excess of £9,924 is the child tax allowance given at a flat rate regardless of income.

Germany operates a system of income-splitting whereby the tax charged is twice the amount which would be due on half the joint taxable income of husband and wife. This method is undoubtedly of benefit to couples where one partner earns very much more than the other, as in most households with dependent children. The main difference between the family part system and that operated in Germany is that no tax allowance or family part applies to children. Instead, a generous tax-free child endowment is paid on a monthly basis amounting to a total of £774 per year for a four-child family (Table 35). This sum contrasts with the UK family allowance of £234 per year which is taxed and clawed back, and together with child tax allowances is worth only £480 per year to the taxpayer with a wife and four children.

It has not been possible to incorporate the German tax rates fully into Tables 34 and 38 because the full German tax schedule is not available. From the information to hand we can deduce that the application of the income-splitting system and the generous child endowment scheme ensure that German families with four children pay no *net* positive tax up to an income of £5,105 per year and only 22 per cent on incomes up to £9,765. These figures are arrived at by crediting the child endowment against the taxes payable on the first slice of income to arrive at the *real* loss from income after taxes and the child endowment have been taken into account.

The Italian system, as already noted, does not provide for any tax threshold. Nevertheless the tax schedule includes fully twelve lower-rate tax bands below the UK basic rate of 35 per cent. It is the very low rates of tax on incomes at or below average which influence the average rates of tax paid. Little impact on the overall tax bill is made by the tax credits, which amount to a total of £113, including a fixed credit of £24, earned-income credit of £24, a wife's credit of £24, and an expenses credit of £8 and £33 for four children, the latter sum applying only to families with incomes below £2,627.

Reduced Rate Bands

In defence of Britain's relatively high basic rate of 35 per cent and the absence of any lower rates, the Inland Revenue have argued

TABLE 36. EEC tax rates below the UK basic rate (percentages)

Belgium	20	30						
Italy	10	13	16	19	22	25		
	27	29	31	32	33	34		
Luxembourg	18	20	22	24	26	28	30	33
Netherlands	20	25	31					
France	5	10	15	20	25	30		
Germany	22	30·8						
Ireland	26							
Denmark	14·4	28·8						
	(these Danish figures are national tax rates and are augmented to 30% and 47·5% by the communal and County Tax rates)							

SOURCE: *Overseas Tax Developments 1975*, Issues 1–9.

vigorously that any lower-rate bands are administratively indefensible and would result in a serious revenue loss. The rates of income tax operated by our EEC partners are shown in Table 36. The UK is alone in operating a national tax system with so little allowance for the low-income earner.

Average Tax Burdens at Different Levels of Income

When considering the average tax rates paid in the nine EEC countries it is important, as mentioned earlier, to bear in mind that these do not take account of the tax allowances given in most of the countries concerned in respect of mortgage interest, life-assurance premiums and national-insurance contributions for example. Table 37 provides a summary of the information available concerning most of the main allowances and it will be seen that allowance is made for mortgage interest in each of the nine countries, and for national-insurance contributions in all but Denmark and the UK (in both the latter countries national-insurance contributions are of relatively limited significance).

In terms of the proportion of income paid in income taxes, the UK has one of the *least* progressive direct-tax structures for single people of the nine EEC countries. The relative position of married couples with four children in the UK and elsewhere is somewhat less clear-cut. The fact that no tax is payable on incomes at two thirds of average earnings is misleading in that the tax threshold is only 2 per cent above this level of income in the UK. More significant is the relative burden of taxation upon families with incomes *between* two thirds of average earnings and average earnings. In the UK wealthy families (incomes five times average earnings) who pay 3·8 times more of their incomes in direct taxes than families at average earnings. On the same basis, in Belgium the rich pay seven times more; in France more then eight times more; in Ireland seven and a half times more; and in Italy and the Netherlands four times more. Only in Denmark and Luxembourg are direct taxes less redistributive among large families than they are in the UK. However, in all these countries the burden of direct taxes on the rich is very much less marked than it appears, when all tax allowances are taken into account. We know in the UK for example that the *actual* percentage of income paid in income taxes in 1975 by families with four children and average earnings was approximately 9 per cent, whereas at twice average earnings the percentage paid was some 16 per cent.[4] The UK thus has one of the least progressive direct tax-systems in Europe and the degree of progression is considerably smaller if all tax allowances are taken into account.

The generosity of our EEC neighbours to low-income families compared to the UK is still more marked when cash family allowances are taken into account. The tax allowance equivalents of family allowances have been incorporated into Table 38, thus giving us the notional average tax rates in each EEC state

TABLE 37. Expenses allowed as a deduction against income for the purposes of income tax

	Belgium	Denmark	France	Germany	Ireland	Italy	Luxembourg	Netherlands	UK
Contributions for old age pensions	✓	×	✓	✓	a proportion only	✓	✓	✓	×
Contributions for sickness insurance	✓	×	✓	✓	a proportion only	✓	✓		×
Contributions for unemployment insurance	✓	×	✓	✓	a proportion only	✓	✓	✓	×
Deduction from wages and salaries used for the purchase of shares for an employee[1]			✓	✓					
Cost of travel to and from work	✓	✓	✓	limited amount	×	×	limited amount	limited amount	×

	Interest on a loan used by an individual to purchase shares in the company employing the taxpayer[2]	Mortgage interest
	√	√
	√	√
	×	√
	√ though limited to income derived from the shares	√
	√ limit of £2,000 per annum	√
	√	√
	√	√
	√	√

NOTES:

1. In France deductions from employees' wages and salaries, together with similar amounts contributed by the company on the employees' behalf, for the purchase of shares issued solely for subscription by the employees are, subject to certain limits, exempt from income tax.

A similar concession is provided in Germany with the advantage that the limits upon the deductions vary according to the employees' circumstances.

2. In the UK a particularly regressive and specific tax concession is allowed on interest payable on a loan used by the individual to acquire ordinary shares of a close trading or estate company in which he has *an interest of 5% or more, and for which he works full time in a management capacity*. In other member states more general provisions govern interest payments and cover interest for the particular purpose indicated.

SOURCES: *Hansard*, 6 August 1970, Vol. 916, Cols. 1064–6, and Inland Revenue summaries of EEC tax systems.

at the four different income levels after receipt of family allowances and payment of direct taxes. Whereas families at the lowest level of income in the UK benefit from the net effect of family allowances and direct taxes to the extent of 8·2 per cent of income, those elsewhere in the EEC benefit to a considerably greater extent (with the sole exception of families in Denmark).

Of some significance is the widespread adoption of tax-free family allowance systems in Europe. Five of the nine member states provide cash allowances free of tax, and four of these apply to every dependent child, including the first. In 1975 only France and the UK limited the cash allowances to the second and subsequent children, though in France a cash supplementary allowance was paid to families with only one wage-earner and this supplement is paid in respect of every child, including the first. In every other respect the French child allowances are amongst the most generous within the EEC. The French family part system ensures a relatively high tax threshold for families while the tax-free cash allowance of £665 per annum (and more in the case of children from ten years) provides a wage supplement which is of particular benefit to low-income families.

Although our analysis has been based upon 1975 data it is important to mention the reforms of the UK referred to in the notes to Table 35 which will begin to come into effect in April 1977 when the family allowance will become tax free at a value of £1 per week for the first child and £1.50 for each subsequent child. Child tax allowances for children under 11 will be withdrawn, and those for older children reduced, over a period of three years (1977–9) and it is assumed that the tax-free child benefit will be increased accordingly. The net effect of these changes in 1977 will be to increase the annual family allowance for a four-child family from £152 net of tax to £286 tax free. At the same time child tax allowances will be reduced by the amount of clawback and tax which would have been paid on the child benefit if the structure had not been reformed. The UK allowances will in 1977 be above the 1975 levels in both Ireland and Italy though well below the allowances in the remaining EEC countries (even in 1975!).

In contrast to the consistent lack of generosity to families in

TABLE 38. Notional average rates of tax at various income levels, treating cash family allowances as negative rates of tax

| Income level | Two-parent families with four dependent children 1975 | | | | | | | | |
	UK	Belgium	Denmark	France	Germany	Ireland	Italy	Luxembourg	Netherlands
$\frac{2}{3}$ average earnings	+8·2	+43·1	5·3	+49·4	+22·1	+12·7	+13·9	+11·7	+25·1
average earnings	5·5	+26·1	14·1	+33·0	+7·1	+3·5	+4·6	0·9	+9·1
2× average earnings	21·3	+4·0	33·8	+15·5		13·8	7·7	27·4	14·0
5× average earnings	40·9	23	49·3	1·4		35·3	21·9	40·4	42·0

NOTES: All the data for the above table relates to 1975 with the exception of the family allowance data for France and Luxembourg, which relates to 1974.

Where the net effect of average direct taxes and cash family allowances is an addition to income, this has been indicated with a +.

the UK, Luxembourg and the Netherlands seem unsure about the need to encourage or, on the other hand, to discourage large families.

Whereas in both these states the child tax allowances decline with the size of family, the cash allowances *increase* with the number of dependent children. The effect in Luxembourg of restricting the application of the family part system to those with less than four dependent children is to allow a higher tax threshold for a three-child family (at £3,297) than for a four-child family (at £2,058). The tax incentive to limit family size to three children in Luxembourg is only partially offset by the increased cash allowances for the fourth child. The Netherlands make a less sharp distinction between 'acceptably small' and 'unduly large' families. The tax allowances for children are merely successively reduced for second and subsequent children, so that the tax allowance for the third child, for example, is approximately one third as generous as that for the first; and the allowance for the fifth and sixth children are little more than one tenth the value of the allowance for the first.

In contrast, Italy and Belgium treat large families more favourably than small ones for tax purposes. In Italy, tax credits for children are so small – £7 per year for the first child rising to £22 for the fifth – that the effect is minimal. Furthermore, no tax credits are given for children if the taxpayer's total income exceeds £2,628, with the result that families with high incomes pay only 1 per cent less of their income in direct taxes than do single taxpayers.[5]

The Belgian tax credit system is considerably more generous to families with three or more children and particularly to those with incomes at or above the maximum income for which the allowances are permitted. A four-child family, for example, will be credited with 50 per cent of tax due on their initial £4,421 of income. The advantage of the percentage tax deduction system is of maximum value to taxpayers with at least £4,421 of income. Tax allowances in Belgium are thus approximately proportional to income, leaving the redistributive function to the very high tax-free allowances (of 30·1 per cent of average earnings for a four-child family). At first glance the Italian system appears more equitable, with tax credits limited to low-income households. However, in terms of the vertical redistribution of income, it is the level of cash family allowances which is of greater significance and it is in this respect that the Italian system falls well behind the Belgian one.

The net effect of combining a progressive schedule of marginal tax rates with a system of tax allowances is to reduce the degree of progression in the direct tax system as a whole. This is particularly true of the family part and percentage allowance systems. Only cash family allowances go some way towards meeting the needs of low-income families and it is disturbing to note that it is this most redistributive element in the family support system which is maintained at such an unusually low level in the UK. Whereas the average annual net family allowance for a four-child family within the EEC is £548, the UK provides only £234 for a four-child family with an income below the tax threshold and £152 for families with an income of 68 per cent of average earnings or above.

Conclusion

Contrary to the well-established view in this country, the UK population cannot claim to be heavily taxed. We pay a smaller proportion of our GNP in taxes and social-security contributions to the Exchequer than any other EEC member state with the sole exception of Italy. A significant psychological difference however between the UK tax system and those of the majority of our neighbours is the relatively heavy burden of the much resented income tax in this country and the unusually small social-security contributions which, despite their similarity of function and impact, are more acceptable to the taxpayer. The balance of UK revenue derived from excise duties and the VAT also increases the taxpayer's awareness of the degree of taxation and thus his resentment of it.

Despite the limitations of our analysis of the marginal and average income tax rates in the nine EEC countries, it has been possible to illustrate the degree to which the UK penalizes both high-income households and, to a still greater degree, those with average and below-average earnings. Taking into account only the basic allowances, UK families with incomes of five times average earnings pay 3·8 times more of their income in income taxes than those at average earnings; but in Belgium the rich pay seven times more; in France eight times more; in Ireland seven and a half times more and in Italy and the Netherlands, four times more. If all tax allowances including those for mortgage interest and life-assurance premiums were taken into account, these results would be modified but would, we believe, leave the *relative* redistributive effect in the nine states unchanged.

The heavy burden of direct taxes on low-income households in the UK is accounted for by our unduly low tax threshold applying to single taxpayers; and the unusually high basic rate of tax which applies to families when their incomes reach just over two thirds of average earnings (in the case of a four-child family) and at 24 per cent of average earnings in the case of single taxpayers.

The tax structures within the EEC vary considerably, with important consequences for their redistributive effects. The family part system operated in France and Luxembourg provides particularly generous allowances for dependants, with the value of the allowances increasing sharply with the level of income. The flat-rate allowance system of the UK on the other hand favours families to a much smaller extent, though again the value of the tax allowances increases with income. The Italian system of tax credits with a finely graded schedule of progressive marginal tax rates could have a profoundly redistributive effect upon net income. The child credits apply only to families with incomes below a specified limit and are not of any greater value to households at the maximum allowed level of income than to those with lower incomes. However, the credit levels are extremely low (a total child credit of £33 per year for four children, for example) so that very little is achieved through the tax system.

More effective than tax allowances as a method of income support for families are cash family allowances provided in every country within the EEC. It is here that the UK performance is at its worst in relation to our EEC neighbours (even after the 1977 reform). The net annual value of family allowances for a four-child family in this country in 1975 was £234 per year (and approximately one third of this was clawed back from child allowances). In marked contrast, the net annual value of family allowances for a four-child family in France was £665; in Germany £774 and in Belgium £1,111·8p, for example. The UK was amongst the four EEC states where family allowances continued to be taxable; and only in France and the UK were family allowances restricted to the second and subsequent children. Britain's poor record will be only marginally affected when the family-allowance system is phased into a tax-free child-benefit scheme over a three-year period beginning in April 1977. The reform will bring the structure of our system of family support more into line with our EEC neighbours, but the levels of allowance at £1 for the first child and £1·50 for the rest in 1977 (or £286 tax free per year) will remain well below the EEC average and abysmally low even in relation to the 1975 allowances in France, Germany and Belgium.

References

1. *Hansard*, 6 August 1976, Vol. 916, Col. 1061.
2. OECD, *Studies in Resource Allocation, Public Expenditure and Income Maintenance Programmes*, July 1976.
3. *Hansard*, 6 August 1976, Vol. 916, Cols. 1062–3.
4. *Economic Trends*, February 1976, p. 82, Table B.
5. Board of Inland Revenue, *OTD*, Issue No. 9, 1974.

11   Taxation in the Eighties:
The Emerging Debate

In this book we have tried to build up a picture of Britain's system of taxation in the 1970s. We have returned to the foundations of the system to uncover the basic principles on which it is built and have then examined each part of the superstructure as it has developed to see how faithfully those principles have been pursued. In addition, we have tried to place taxation in its true context as we see it, side by side with the parallel system of social security. Our purpose has been to challenge one of the most deep-rooted beliefs about the welfare state in Britain, that the tax system takes from the rich to finance the benefits payable to the poor through the social services. In this final chapter we draw together our findings and offer proposals for a radical restructuring of the British tax system.

Taxation – Principles and Objectives

We began our study with an exercise in 'fiscal excavation', trying to uncover and identify the fundamental principles of taxation in Britain – principles which three hundred years of expansion and piecemeal reform have discarded and obscured. Such a beginning was essential to equip us with the criteria against which to judge the tax system as it stands today and to guide us along the necessary lines for reform. Chapter 1 therefore outlined a brief history of taxation in this country and the debate which accompanied its development. From early beginnings which saw anything but flat-rate or proportional taxation as dangerously radical, the principle of progressive taxation emerged in the nineteenth and early twentieth century. By the first quarter of this century the principle was firmly established, based on the belief that only those with incomes above subsistence should contribute to public revenue and that the burden of taxation should be distributed in such a way as to achieve equality of sacrifice between taxpayers. These two principles – that the poor should be exempted from the income tax and that higher-income groups should contribute proportionately more to government funds – have remained at the heart of beliefs about the British tax system.

With the increasing demands of public revenue, however, the principle that the poor should remain exempt was discarded. One of the practical considerations which had always reinforced that principle was that collection of taxes from the great mass of working people at the lower end of the income scale was administratively difficult and financially unrewarding. The small sums to be collected from each taxpayer were insufficient to cover the cost of collection. The establishment of the Pay As You Earn system of tax collection in 1944 overcame many of these administrative problems. It was now both simple and administratively lucrative for governments to extend the tax net to many manual and clerical workers who had previously been exempt, and the wartime demands for public expenditure made such an extension necessary. The system of income tax which emerged after the war was therefore very much broader based than that which preceded it.

The Shifting Burden of Direct Taxation

Despite this extension of the income tax to the majority of wage-earners the principle that the poor should be exempt was still upheld. But as we saw in Chapter 2, post-war developments in direct taxation brought about an erosion both of the principle of exempting the poor and that of progressivity. These changes fell into two categories. First there were the effects of inflation on an unchanging tax system, which involved the devaluation of the basic allowances through which the principles of equity were to be achieved. As a result the tax threshold – the point at which income tax begins to be paid – fell for a two-child family from a level equivalent to above-average earnings to well below half the average wage. In terms of the extra revenue raised, the effects of inflation were most advantageous to governments. It was now possible to collect increasing amounts in income tax (through the greater numbers of families being pulled into the tax system and those becoming subject to higher rates) without overt changes in the structure of tax rates and allowances which might have been unpopular. But as the government is prepared to admit, raising revenue through inflation and 'fiscal drag' in this way carried with it substantial redistributive consequences. The greatest impact was felt by those at the lower end of the income scale for whom an increase in money wages to keep pace with inflation meant a very large jump in marginal tax rates. At the same time the larger allowances which could be claimed by families with children were also eroded, so that the principle of horizontal equity (that such families should contribute proportionately less to public revenue) lost much of its practical impact.

These apparently automatic changes in the incidence of direct taxation were reinforced by deliberate policy adjustments during the late post-war period. The most important of these was the withdrawal of the reduced rates of tax which had ensured a progressive graduation of tax rates between wage-earners and salary-earners at different levels of income. These two developments together – the falling tax threshold brought about by inflation and the abolition of the reduced rate bands of tax – involved a substantial increase in the burden of taxation falling on low wage-earners. Not only did families begin to pay tax at a lower level of real income but they began to pay it at a higher marginal rate.

While changes in taxation policy were shifting the incidence of income tax further towards the lower-income groups, the treatment of those higher up the income scale was considerably less harsh. In contrast to the increasing rate at which ordinary workpeople began to pay tax, marginal rates of surtax remained unchanged throughout the post-war period. During that period, however, other changes were taking place to lower the tax burden of the rich through the extension of allowances and reliefs to which they had previously been ineligible.

Our analysis of post-war developments in the income tax revealed an underlying pattern of political preferences which manifested itself as a higher tax burden on the rich under Labour governments, a reduction in their burden under Conservative, together with a reduction in everyone's burden when an election was imminent. Despite these political ebbs and flows, however, the consistent trend was for an increase in the tax liabilities of the lowest-income groups counterbalanced by a general reduction, over time, in those of the better-off. This movement of the tax base downwards is the inevitable result of the decision by governments of both persuasions to raise increased revenue covertly through inflation rather than by changes in rates and allowances which would necessarily have reflected the principles of equity which we have already outlined.

The Income Tax in the Late Seventies

Chapter 3 set out to describe the income tax which these developments since the war had created. The first principle that the poor should be exempt had been sacrificed to political expediency and the need for extra revenue. The tax threshold is now lower than the official poverty line defined either as the supplementary-benefits level (the 'safety net' level below which no family without an income from employment should fall) and the eligibility levels for family income supplement.

The consequences of this situation run deeper than the betrayal of traditional principles and have their effects on the actual living standards of many low-income families. Tax has become an engine of poverty in Britain. A taxation policy which has developed without guidance from general principles now finds itself in conflict with the aims of social policy. As a result, many low wage-earners, especially those with families, would be better off unemployed and dependent on supplementary benefit, inadequate though the standard of living afforded by SB is. At the same time, we have the absurdity of one government agency making cash payments to families because their income is considered inadequate, while another takes an equal or greater amount back as income tax. Finally, the entanglement of taxes, which no longer recognize the official criteria of poverty, and means-tested benefits, which do, has created the situation of the poverty trap. An increase in money income may leave families worse off than if they had never received it. The result is that low-income families face higher marginal rates of tax than the very richest households – something of an anomaly in a supposedly progressive system of income tax.

This brings us to an assessment of the income tax today in the light of the progressive principles which we have identified. The post-war changes which we described in Chapter 2 effectively converted the structure of tax rates into a proportional one through the abolition of reduced rates and the widening of the standard rate band. In effect, therefore, the great majority of taxpayers are subject to the same marginal rate of tax (currently 35 per cent). The only progression is applied to those paying at higher rates, which account for less than 2 per cent of all income-tax payers. In fact the true situation, when we take into account compulsory national-insurance contributions, is even worse than this. The marginal rate of tax faced by those at the lower end of the wage-earning scale is nearly 41 per cent, compared with only 35 per cent for those earning more than about £6,000 a year.

The only instrument of progression that remains are the tax allowances, which are intended to ensure that the proportion of income which is taxable rises as income rises. Looking at the system of allowances, however, we have found that they perform this function poorly. Tax allowances increase in value as income rises because they exempt not the bottom slice of income but that at the top. The allowances will therefore be worth more the higher is the highest marginal rate of tax paid by the household. And of course increases in the allowances are of no value to the very poorest households who pay no tax.

There is an added dimension to the regressive effects of tax allowances. With the withering of the real value of the basic personal allowances brought about by inflation since the war, there has been a new growth of other expenditure allowances and reliefs which are of greatest benefit to the better-off households. Two prominent examples of this are the mortgage interest relief and that for life-assurance premiums. The development and expansion of such reliefs, which cost the exchequer several thousand million pounds each year in lost revenue, reflect the same inconsistency that we identified in other aspects of taxation policy.

A taxpayer can claim against tax for his mortgage repayments, but not for his rent; he can claim his payments into voluntary life assurance or superannuation schemes, but not for the contributions which he has to pay into the National Insurance Fund; he can claim for his fees to a professional body, but not his subscriptions to a trade union, and so on.

The proliferation of such reliefs and allowances has led us to argue the existence of two parallel welfare states in Britain – one for the poor, administered through the social-security system, and one for the rich, which operates through the income tax. Tax allowances represent a form of social welfare provision no less than the cash payments available to low-income households. Both are intended to provide support for households with their family, housing or other recognized commitments. But in terms of generosity and administration, the two welfare states are incomparable. The petty rules, the inadequacy of payments and the humiliation of clients which characterize the social-security system are absent in the administration of tax allowances. And as we showed in Chapter 8 inspection and enforcement of the social-security system is much more rigorous than that of the Inland Revenue.

Tax and Social-Security Abuse

Our assessment of the degree of economic inequality is profoundly affected by the extent to which different types of income – fringe benefits, part-time earnings, tips, expense accounts etc. – go undisclosed and unregistered in the official sources.[1] Chapter 8 attempted to throw further light onto the question of which groups benefit most from such additional forms of income and therefore whether the distribution of income is more or less equal than the published data suggests. We found that the extent of social-security abuse was so small as to have no significant effect on the estimates of income going to low-income families. Nor is it possible on any published data to change the trends in the distribution of income by taking into account the amount of income earned by such groups but not declared to the authorities. A whole battery of measures are employed to limit the number of wrongful claims for social-security benefit. These 'control procedures' effectively limited known abuse of all social-security benefits to a fraction over £2 million in the financial year 1974–5.

While we do not have even unofficial estimates of the extent to which the poor, including those in work, are involved in the cash economy, such estimates do exist on the extent of tax abuse. These estimates suggest that the official data on the distribution of income severely understate the command over resources enjoyed by some higher-income groups. One expert from the Inland Revenue Staff Federation has estimated that up to £500 million is lost annually from self-employed persons who understate their income for tax purposes. On top of this we have seen that death duties – which were the main form of tax on capital – were effectively a voluntary tax. In 1975, the year in which death duties were replaced by the capital transfer tax, we estimated that for each £1 paid in duties another £3 was avoided. In that year, the yield from death duties should have been £1·6 billion. In fact, only £412 million reached the Inland Revenue.

Tax evasion is therefore considerable and it should be borne in mind that the conclusions which we draw from this study – for instance on the shifting burden of income tax in Chapter 2 – are based on the nominal liabilities of different groups, taking no account of the fact that much of this liability may be sidestepped through tax evasion or avoidance. If we were able to take this into account, the increasing relative contribution of low-income groups would appear substantially greater. Abuse of the second welfare state (of tax allowances) is far greater than that of the first. Yet tolerance of such abuse against the social-security system is much lower than that of tax evasion. This is partly due to the belief that it is the wealthy who pay the costs of social-security provision while lower-income groups merely reap the benefit.

Who Pays for the Welfare State?

To throw further light on the commonly held belief that the welfare state is largely financed by the rich for the benefit of the poor we considered in Chapter 4 the social-security tax. Here we attempted to show that this was yet another integral part of the mythology which has grown up since the Second World War concerning the burden of taxation. Apart from the first Old Age Pensions Act, each successive welfare reform has been accompanied by measures which ensured that the working class have by and large paid for it. Indeed, we noted that Neville Chamberlain went on record as describing the ideal welfare reform as that for which the working class paid the whole cost.

The principle of flat-rate national-insurance contributions was enshrined in the Beveridge reforms, which largely came into effect in 1948. However, Beveridge envisaged that a considerable part of the national-insurance scheme should be financed from the Exchequer, that is from progressive taxation. We have seen how this crucial premise on which the reforms were built was quickly demolished. Moreover, the introduction of graduated benefits and contributions by the Conservative government in 1961 increased the regressive way in which social-security benefits were financed. Although the Exchequer was by then paying a much reduced contribution to match part of the flat-rate taxes imposed on both employees and employers (the latter of which was passed on in increased prices to the consumer) no such matching contribution was forthcoming in respect of graduated contributions.

Major reforms in social-security contributions came into effect in 1975. Although these have lessened somewhat the regressive nature of what has always been a social-security tax, the ceiling on graduated contributions ensures that the percentage of income taken from the higher-paid groups as a contribution to the welfare state falls as income rises. In some very important respects therefore, the financing of the welfare state has played its part in increasing the tax burden of lower-income groups.

Our first four chapters were concerned with the administration and effects of the direct tax system. No less important in terms of the distribution of the tax burden are the main forms of indirect taxation – the expenditure taxes and local-authority rates to which we addressed ourselves in Chapters 5, 6 and 7.

Expenditure Taxes

The British Exchequer gains £5,240 million a year from excise duties, the vast majority of which is paid by consumers of tobacco, alcoholic drinks and hydro-carbon oils. The second major element in our expenditure taxes is VAT, which replaced purchase tax and SET in 1973 in preparation for Britain's entry into the Common Market (providing approximately £3,455 for the Exchequer in 1975–6). The most regressive of all these taxes is that on tobacco, which accounts for a proportion of low incomes twice that of incomes above £5,490 a year. The introduction of VAT on the other hand was so engineered that the burden is marginally greater (at 3.3 per cent) on high incomes than it is on the lower-paid (at 2·3 per cent), at least for the time being. In Chapter 6 we also noted the increasing regressiveness of indirect taxes as a whole in recent years and found an explanation in the increasing burden of local rates, which bear particularly heavily on low-income households, and the increase in the tobacco tax over time.

The changeover from purchase tax to VAT resulted in an almost uniform increase in the tax burden throughout the income scale of approximately 1 per cent of income. Our concern, however, has been to analyse the effects upon the distribution of income of the second stage of the harmonization process as the structure and rates of excise duties and the VAT are brought into line within the EEC. At present excise duties are approximately twice as high in this country on the items affected as they are in other EEC member states. Harmonization of excise duties can be expected to result in a substantial reduction in the tax on tobacco and beer and a somewhat smaller reduction in revenues from spirits, wines and hydro-carbon oils. The subsequent harmonization of the VAT rates to within a range of 3 to 4 per cent throughout the EEC would probably involve the imposition of a lower rate of the tax on food and fuel in Britain (at perhaps 5 per cent) and an increase in the basic rate from 8 per cent to at least 12 per cent initially, together with an extension of the tax to a much wider range of goods and services.

The net effect of all these changes would be to increase marginally the regressiveness of the British tax system. Of equal importance would be the shift in the burden of expenditure taxes from items widely recognized to be deleterious to health to items such as food, fuel and clothing. Having relinquished the purchase tax, which had the full potential of VAT without the administrative disadvantages, for the sake of harmonizing our tax structure with that of our European neighbours, it appears that Britain will have to forgo the pattern of expenditure taxes which we believe to be preferable.

Local Taxation and the Distribution of Incomes

In recent years the rating system has come under considerable scrutiny and has been found wanting in at least two important respects. In the first place there is the lack of buoyancy of the system, which is of some consequence in the current inflationary times. Local authorities find their costs rising sharply and their income remaining largely unchanged in the absence of specific and unpopular increases in the level of rates. However, for the purposes of this book the most serious criticism of the rating system is its regressive impact upon the British tax system.

Despite the introduction of a rate rebate scheme for low-income households in 1966–7 and significant improvements to the original scheme in 1974, it remains true today that nearly one third of the households eligible for financial help with their rates do not claim a rebate; secondly, low-income households who do receive rebates can still pay a higher proportion of their income in rates than households at the higher end of the income scale; and thirdly, a substantial number of households with incomes well below average earnings do not qualify for a rebate and pay 10 per cent or more of their income in rates.

In an attempt to reverse the recent trends, the Layfield Committee recommended the introduction of a local income tax to replace a substantial proportion of current government grants. The three main weaknesses of the proposals are: that it is incompatible with the need for government control over the growth of local-authority spending; that the proposal could, if implemented, give rise to a serious unevenness in the provision of vital services by local authorities in different parts of the country; and that the proposal would not affect the existing rating system. For these three reasons we reject the Layfield Committee's proposal in favour of a reorganization of local-authority finance involving the abolition of domestic rates and their replacement by a local income tax of 4½p in the pound, which would provide an independent source of income for the major spending authorities; our proposal envisages that non-domestic rates would be retained as a source of income for the smaller authorities; and the role of government grants would be to cover the cost of providing minimum standards of all the main local-authority services – minimum standards which should be nationally determined but the level of grants for which should be related to the needs of each local authority and the ability of its population to pay. Local authorities would be responsible for the provision of additional services over and above the minimum standards and would have available the local income-tax revenue with which to provide these services in accordance with local demand and preferences. In this way the responsibilities of both government and local authorities could be clearly defined and the responsibility for both spending and revenue would lie with the appropriate authority.

Inequality and the Welfare State

Having considered each of the elements of the tax system separately we attempted in Chapter 9 to assess the overall effect on the distribution of income. Looking at the complete picture we asked the question 'Do taxes redistribute income from the rich to the poor?' Our answer, anticipated in each of the previous chapters and contrary to generally accepted beliefs, was 'no'. In fact, drawing on official evidence, we found that a number of taxes, including the national-insurance contributions, expenditure taxes and local-authority rates considered above, actually increased the degree of economic inequality. This regressive effect was only partially offset by the mildly progressive impact of income tax and surtax. The overall result was that all taxes combined were roughly proportional across income groups, even taking a slightly larger proportion of the incomes of the very poorest households. The evidence also presented surprising results concerning the belief that economic inequality has been steadily reduced in Britain in recent years, largely under the influence of a progressive tax system. In fact, economic inequality has worsened somewhat over the years and this trend has been only partially mitigated by the effects of taxation.

Even this conclusion, which is drawn from official estimates of the incidence of taxes is open to doubt. This data excludes certain important elements of income and only one half of all sources of government receipts are included. Other forms of taxation, such as that on companies, would if included increase the regressive impact of all taxes. The official analysis does, however, tell us that while taxes are not progressive, the public expenditure which they finance is. Again we doubt the validity of this assertion. Slightly less than two thirds of all public spending is left out of the reckoning and there is strong evidence to suggest that if it were included the redistributive effects which are apparent from a partial analysis would largely disappear. At the same time, the assumptions on which the included expenditure is allocated are in many respects unrealistic. Benefits in kind, such as education and the health service, are attributed to households according to apparent need, that is in relation to the size and composition of the family. If one looks closely at the evidence, however, it becomes clear that if allocation were made according to use (rather than need) then the benefit to higher-income groups would appear even greater than that conferred by the welfare state on the poor. Finally, while the official analysis emphasizes the effect of cash benefits on lower-income groups, the parallel benefits payable to high-income groups through the tax system are ignored completely.

The need for fundamental change is evident. Taxation in Britain does not conform to the principles of equity and fairness to which most people subscribe. In addition we saw in Chapter 10 that, although the overall burden of taxation in Britain is lower than that amongst our EEC partners, its distribution is very different. Taking into account the basic allowances only, UK families with incomes five times average earnings pay 3·8 times more of their income in income tax than those at average earnings, compared with seven times more in Belgium, eight times more in France, seven and a half times more in Ireland and four times more in Italy and the Netherlands. At the same time, the tax threshold in Britain is unusually low and the rate at which tax begins to be paid unusually high. It is against this background that we outline our own proposals for a radical change.

The Income Tax – a Proposal

When we began work on this book, we were aware of a number of inequities which existed within the tax system, although we did not appreciate their full extent. As such we already had a number of proposed reforms in mind and had stated them in other places.[2] These included the reintroduction of reduced rates of tax, substantial raising of the tax threshold, and ensuring that allowances could be claimed only at the standard rate. Such changes would have made a substantial difference to the equity of the tax system, certainly in its treatment of the poor, with whom we are primarily concerned. But these constituted minor adjustments compared with the changes required to restore the system of taxation to the principles on which most people believe it should be based. Any change in the tax structure today must at the very least correct the damage caused by thirty years of erosion by inflation, piecemeal concessions to one group or another and the short-term whims of governments. Because we have come so far along that road, the return journey will be expensive. It is estimated that to do no more than raise the tax threshold to the official poverty line would cost £1,230 million.[3] To introduce a reduced rate of tax of 20 per cent on the first £500 of taxable income would cost another £1,650 million.[4] The cost of reforms even as minor as these limits severely any room for manoeuvre if we try to rebuild on the ruins which confront us. Our only alternative is a root and branch reform of the entire tax system. We are not the first to realize the need for such fundamental reform. *The Economist*, for example, has proposed the abolition of the present 'multi-rate, multi-allowance system' and its replacement with a flat-rate tax of between 15p and 17½p in the pound on all incomes of all kinds from all sources.[5] With the savings which would accrue under such a system from a reduction in avoidance and evasion, administration and, above all, the costs of allowances, it is estimated that the change would mean an actual increase in revenue. While we share the belief embodied in this and other proposals for radical change[6] that only major reform will correct the many problems manifested in the income-tax system, we are concerned that such change should bring about a fairer distribution of the tax burden.

Throughout this book we have reasserted the underlying principles of income tax. We do not apologize for repeating them here, since they have been too easily forgotten by policy-makers over the years. Equity demands that two criteria be fulfilled. The first is that the poor should not pay tax at all; the second that the proportion of income paid in tax should rise as income rises. It is only under these circumstances that the tax burden and the sacrifice it imposes can be fairly distributed. In the past, the first principle was met by the adoption of an exemption limit whereby the recipients of income below a certain level were excluded altogether from the tax-paying population. The second principle was implemented through a progressive graduation of marginal tax rates. As the tax system has developed, however, the two roles – of exempting the poor and of ensuring a progressive graduation of effective tax rates – have been given to the system of tax allowances. This change marked a fundamental shift in the interpretation of the basic principles of taxation. An exemption limit excludes certain households from the tax system, but those who do qualify to pay income tax (on the grounds that their income is above an acceptable minimum level) pay tax on each pound they earn. The operation of the tax allowances is rather different. Although they fulfil the same purpose of excluding certain households altogether, they do this by treating a certain proportion of the income of all households as exempt from tax. No matter how high a household's income, a fixed amount of that income is treated as non-taxable. As a result, the allowances also have the effect of graduating the effective rates of tax paid by different income groups.

While this appears to have the advantage of using one mechanism to fulfil two roles, the system has considerable drawbacks as the Royal Commission on the Taxation of Profits and Income pointed out in 1954 (see Chapter 3). The problem is that allowances confer a benefit on all households, and their value increases as we move up the income scale. This means that any increase in the level of the allowances intended to exempt the very poorest households is extremely expensive. For example, of the £1,230 million cost of raising the tax threshold to the level of the official poverty line, only a fraction would be absorbed in taking those at the bottom of the income scale out of tax. A disproportionate amount of the cost would be allocated to the richest taxpayers, who would gain most from such a measure. Because of this problem the Commission reported 'that the practice of looking to the personal allowances and earned income relief to provide effective exemptions has had the effect of distorting the tax structure at the lower end of the scale, in that the starting point of liability is lower than it could reasonably be expected to be if the needs of subsistence are borne in mind. Yet an artificial depression of the starting point is always to be expected if exemption can only be achieved by increasing the figure of the personal allowances. For the circumstances that make it right to raise the starting point are not by any means the same as those that justify any general reduction of taxation.'[7]

The corner-stone of any fundamental reform of personal income tax must be the separation once more of these two roles: a specific exemption limit is needed to exclude the poor from the tax system rather than using allowances for this purpose; the graduation of effective tax rates would then be achieved by the use of marginal tax rates which rise in even and progressive steps. We therefore propose that the personal allowances in their current form be replaced by a specific exemption limit. Incomes below this level will be excluded from tax altogether, but those who earn more than the limit will be assessed for tax on each pound that they earn. This will not of course apply to the child tax allowances which we assume will be replaced as planned with the child benefit (although there will be a need to ensure that the benefit is set at an adequate level). The main allowances to be replaced will be the single and married persons' allowances.

The problem with a specific exemption expressed as a maximum level of income beyond which an individual becomes a taxpayer is that it carries with it a dramatically high marginal tax rate as incomes move above the exemption limit. The first increment of income above the exemption would bring the recipient into liability for tax on the whole of his income. One means of mitigating this problem would be to limit the cash amount payable in tax to a specified ceiling, the procedure employed when such an exemption applied in Britain. This would not, however, overcome completely the danger of creating a poverty trap at the exemption threshold. The alternative which we propose is the adoption of a 'vanishing exemption' which diminishes in value as income rises without being withdrawn abruptly at a crossover point. The principle would be the same as that with which rent and rate rebates are administered, the exemption being reduced by a set proportion of the difference between income and the specified level of eligibility.

Such a system would ensure a smooth withdrawal of the exemption as income rises without creating high increases in marginal tax rates at any point. For instance, income up to a maximum of £1,000 might qualify for a 100 per cent exemption. On incomes above this level, however, the value of the exemption could be reduced by one third of the difference between gross income and the maximum exemption of £1,000. At £2,000 therefore, the exemption would be £666·66; at £3,000 it would be £333·33; and at £4,000 it would have been withdrawn completely.

An exemption of this type could not, of course, fulfil the functions at present carried out by the allowances in graduating effective tax rates. The responsibility for ensuring a progressive structure of effective tax rates would then fall to the marginal rate structure itself. The current proportional structure of marginal rates would be replaced, under our proposed scheme, by tax at a rate of perhaps 10 per cent on the first £1,000 of taxable income (which in the case of those receiving more than £4,000 would coincide with gross income) rising in steps of 10 per cent on each additional £1,000, subject to a maximum of perhaps 75 per cent. Table 39 illustrates the effect of this change on the structure of effective tax rates.

For the single person on the average wage these proposals would make little difference to tax liability if introduced at the rates suggested. Assuming an average income of £4,000, the amount of tax payable would be £1,000, or 25 per cent of gross income. This would compare with a tax liability of £1,142·75 (or

28½ per cent) under the present circumstances. Although a wage-earner with this level of income would be entitled to no exemption whatever, the rate of tax at which he pays on each pound of his income starts at a relatively low level of 10 per cent, rising in steps of 10 per cent up to 40 per cent on his last thousand. For a person on half the average wage (say £2,000) the change would mean a very substantial reduction in the amount of tax paid, from almost £800 at present to £150. On an income twice the average (£8,000) tax liability would increase from £2,782·25 (35 per cent)

TABLE 39. Tax liability now and under the proposed reform

Gross income	Exemption	Under proposed system		Under present system	
£	£	£	%	£	%
1,000	—	—	—	92·75	9·3
1,500	833·3	66·67	4·4	267·75	17·9
2,000	666·7	166·7	8·3	442·75	22·1
2,500	500	300	12·0	617·75	24·7
3,000	333·3	500	16·6	792·75	26·4
3,500	166·7	733·3	21·0	967·75	27·7
4,000	—	1,000	25·0	1,142·75	28·6
8,000	—	3,550	44·4	2,782·5	34·8
10,000	—	5,050	57·0	3,909	39·1
20,000	—	12,550	62·8	10,948·75	54·7

to £3,550 (44 per cent). On £10,000 the change would represent an increase from a tax bill of £3,909 (39 per cent) to £5,050 (50 per cent).

The change would therefore involve a redistribution of the tax burden up the income scale, although it should be remembered that this would do no more than restore relative tax liabilities closer to the situation which used to exist. The figures we use are merely illustrative, based on the assumption that the single person on the average wage should be no worse off. Our purpose here is to argue the principle. Actual rates of tax and levels of exemption could be varied to achieve the desired distribution of the tax burden. Of course, reducing the tax liabilities of below-average income receivers would involve a substantial loss of revenue. This would be counterbalanced by the fact that allowances for those receiving more than about £1,750 would be smaller than those at present granted, and would be withdrawn altogether from those receiving more than £4,000. If it is not possible to introduce this reform at nil cost, the scheme should be implemented initially on the basis that a married couple on average earnings should not be made worse off, rather than a single person, as in our illustrations.

The personal allowances in their present form would therefore disappear. The single and married person's allowances would be replaced (along with allowances for other non-child dependants which it is considered necessary to recognize) by exemption limits, while the child tax allowances are replaced by child benefits payable in cash. It would be necessary to 'index' the value of both the exemptions and the benefits to ensure against erosion and distortion through inflation.

The problem remains of the various expenditure reliefs and allowances. As we have argued in Chapter 3, these have no place in an equitable tax system. It may be that society wishes to encourage certain forms of spending and saving, but to try and achieve this through the tax system can lead only to distortions and inequities. It would therefore be necessary to phase out these allowances. We recognize that households have contractual commitments undertaken on the basis of the tax relief which can be claimed and that to withdraw such allowances overnight would cause considerable hardship, particularly to those at the lower end of the income scale. We therefore propose that cash limits be imposed on the amount of revenue to be forgone through such allowances. For example the total annual amount allowable for mortgage interest might be fixed at £1 billion. The concession would thereby be gradually withdrawn over time as the value of the limits were reduced by inflation. At the same time, however, it would be necessary to ensure that the diminishing value of the allowances were fairly distributed. One step in this direction would be to restrict all such allowances to their standard-rate value.

This gradual withdrawal of the expenditure reliefs would pave the way for the second stage of reform. As the amount of revenue committed to such allowances declined it should be possible to implement actual reductions in the amount of tax paid by households. Government subsidies for certain types of expenditure could be replaced by an increase in the disposable income of households to spend as they choose.

National-insurance contributions are now collected from employees by the Inland Revenue along with the income tax through the system of P A Y E. As we argued in Chapter 4, the contributions effectively represent a social-security tax which bears particularly heavily on the lower-paid. We do not accept the need for a separate levy collected in a regressive way. The national-insurance contributions should be merged with the income tax to be collected in a progressive way. The ceiling on the contributions would of course be abolished.

We do not pretend that such radical changes in the tax system would be simple. We have only sketched in the bare outlines of a more equitable system, although there would remain many anomalies and inequities to be overcome. Other elements of the tax and social-security systems would have to be brought into line. In addition, there would remain the problem of abuse.

Even under a radically reformed income-tax system there would still be a need to prevent both tax evasion and avoidance. We suggest that three reforms will be necessary. The first, the Revenue's policy of allowing tax evaders to remain anonymous if they co-operate with inquiries into back duty, should end. Anthony Christopher of the Inland Revenue Staff Federation has pointed out that this may require a change in the law, and that if 'wilful deceit' is inadequately defined then much sharper language must be found. 'When Lord Sandys (formerly Duncan Sandys) decides not to keep £140,000 compensation for resigning as a consultant, when two Lonrho directors pay up to £350,000 and £200,000 respectively for houses purchased with company money, when Sir Denis Lowson gives back £5 million, I am even more of the opinion that the Revenue back-duty gains from "cooperation" are far outweighed by the deterrent effect of the expectation of publicity if under-assessment is confirmed.'[8] Secondly, there is an urgent need for both the legal and accountancy professions to put their own house in order in respect of helping clients to avoid paying tax. As Anthony Christopher has noted, at one end of the scale profitable tax-avoidance work is over-coming all pretence to truly ethical standards. At the other, turning a blind eye to evaders is not far removed from collusion.[9] The Revenue should outline in a discussion document the growth in the tax-avoidance industry and then detail the kind of practices, with case examples, where the legal and accountancy professions have been behaving in an unsocial way. The government should make it clear that unless the professions respond constructively to this initiative by the Revenue they will seek a public inquiry into this aspect of their work with a view to imposing new rules of conduct.

Thirdly, there is an urgent need to try and combat the growth in the cash economy. As long ago as 1955 the Royal Commission on the Taxation of Profits and Income called for the placing of a statutory responsibility on every trader to keep records of his transactions. It has been suggested that one way of enacting this recommendation is for the government to establish a register for the self-employed.[10] All the self-employed should be required to register their status with the Department of Employment. In return the Department would issue work certificates to each registered self-employed person. Furthermore the Department could make use of the National Giro system, which at the moment is neither overworked nor the great success originally forecast. Each self-employed person would be given a Giro account number and this would be entered on their certificates. Those who then use the services of a self-employed person would be able to ask for the certificate, and in so doing check whether the self-employed person had registered himself. After the work was completed payment would be made into the self-employed person's Giro account. The honest self-employed would have nothing to fear from this reform. Indeed there would be substantial gains. Apart from having their accounts kept for them by the National Giro, those self-employed who register themselves as such with the DE, and whose monies were paid into the Giro account, could also be eligible for unemployment benefit. At present the self-employed are penalized. Although they pay £2·41 (men) and £2·10 (women) a week in national-insurance contributions plus 8 per cent on profits and gains between £1,600 and £3,600 per annum, they are not allowed to draw unemployment benefit. With the changeover we are suggesting, together with their willingness to register for work at the Department of Employment, those self-employed who find themselves out of work could for the first time claim unemployment pay.

The Emerging Debate

We believe that during the remaining years of this century one of the big debates on home issues will be concerned with the question of relativities. Increasingly people will move away from the position of referring to the rewards of those nearest to them in the pecking order to one in which comparisons are made across class boundaries.[11] This emerging debate will centre on attempts by people to express what they believe to be the proper relation between the highest-paid and lowest-paid members of the working community. Within this framework individual groups of workers will attempt to justify their position or changes in their rank order. Already certain groups of workers have shown the very real bargaining power they bring to this discussion.

We have seen from Chapter 9 that the tax system has had very little impact on the redistribution of income in the late post-war period. At best, it has managed to offset part of the inegalitarian trends which have emerged in the most recent years. A large part of this failure is due to the inadequacy of taxation in its present form. But we would be naïve to expect the tax system to overcome all of the extreme inequalities which at present exist. The national debate on differentials will need to continue side by side with the debate on how best to reform the tax system. We have proposed a maximum marginal rate of tax on earned income of 75 per cent, which is substantially below the highest existing rate. It should be borne in mind that we suggest this change against a background of changes which should take place in the distribution of income before tax.

Perhaps the most we can demand from a progressive tax system is that it distributes the burden of taxation fairly between different groups. To try to use taxation as a veneer on an inegalitarian society such as ours can only have disappointing results. The deep-rooted inequalities which exist underneath would soon reassert themselves through avoidance and evasion. Tax reform must go hand in hand with social and economic changes designed to achieve a fairer distribution of national resources. Taxation cannot compensate for an unequal society.

References

1. W. G. RUNCIMAN, 'Occupational Class and the Assessment of Economic Inequalities in Britain', in D. Wedderburn (ed.), *Poverty, Inequality and Class Structure*, Cambridge University Press.
2. See for instance F. FIELD, *The New Corporate Interest*, CPAG, 1976.
3. *Hansard*, 11 May 1976, Vol. 911, Col. 127.
4. *Hansard*, 13 May 1976, Vol. 911, Cols. 220/1.
5. 'How to Cut Income Tax to 15%', *The Economist*, 24 April 1976.
6. For instance the Conservative government proposals for a tax-credit scheme and the proposal for an expenditure-based tax put forward by John Pardoe, MP, at the Liberal Party Conference, October 1976.
7. Royal Commission on the Taxation of Profits and Income, *Second Report*, Cmnd 9105, HMSO, 1954, para. 160, p. 49.
8. ANTHONY CHRISTOPHER, 'Faces to Wash', *Taxes*, August 1973.
9. ibid.
10. F. FIELD, 'Fiddlers on the Roof', *Guardian*, 26 January 1976.
11. For a view of this issue see W. G. RUNCIMAN, *Relative Deprivation and Social Justice*, Routledge & Kegan Paul, and W. W. DANIELS, *The PEP Survey on Inflation*, Broadsheet No. 553. Political and Economic Planning, 1975, which updates the Runciman thesis and shows that this process has not yet begun.

Index

More about Penguins and Pelicans